Ruth Golan

The Consciousness Bearers

Ruth Golan
The Consciousness Bearers

Senior Editors & Producers: Contento De Semrik

Translated from Hebrew:
Ruth Golan, Jonathon Martin, Mona Zupnik

Editor: Sherrill Layton
Design: Ivan Bogod | Contento De Semrik
Cover Design: Benjie Herskowitz

Copyright © 2013 by Contento De Semrik
and Ruth Golan

All rights reserved. No part of this book may be translated, reproduced, stored in a retrieval system or transmitted, in any form or by any means, electronic, photocopying, recording or otherwise, without prior permission in writing from the author and publisher.

ISBN: 978-965-550-223-7

International sole distributor:
Contento De Semrik
22 Isserles, 67014 Tel-Aviv, Israel
Semrik10@gmail.com
www.Semrik.com

Ruth Golan

The Consciousness Bearers

When Psychoanalysis Encounters the Evolution of Spirit

Contento De Semrik

Table of Contents

Preface | *What's a psychoanalyst doing in the spiritual field?* | 7

PART I
Eppur si muove! — nevertheless, it does move! | 21
About narrow-mindedness and the Real | 39
What lies behind identification? | 51
The woman's silence | 67

PART II
Psycho-Evolution | 85
What is evolution? | 93
The integrative model—Psycho-evolution | 147
In the vicinity of Andrew Cohen | 225

PART III CINEMA
What does the woman want? | 261
On Love and Perversion | 308
Beyond boundaries—The evolution of consciousness from a cinematic point of view | 345
The Mother's Language, the Father's Language, Parasitic Language and Erotic Language | 413

Bibliography | 423

preface
What's a psychoanalyst doing in the spiritual field?

"...He is a mortal vehicle of a (possibly) immortal substance—like the inheritor of an entailed property, who is only the temporary holder of an estate which survives him" Freud, S. (1914) *On Narcissism: An Introduction*, p.78.

For the main part of my spiritual life as an adult I have moved along two paths. Along one path I explored the mind and psychic causality from the perspective of psychoanalysis. The other path is that of the spiritual seeker after transcendental truth, truth that touches upon the reason and the purpose for our being here in the world.

On the cusp between childhood and adolescence I read two books that influenced and continue to influence me all along the way. Freud's *The Interpretation of Dreams* and Ouspensky's *The Psychology of the Possible Evolution of Man*—based on the teachings of Gurdjieff.

Throughout the years I moved along the two parallel paths. For many years I engaged in the practice of Lacan's unique and radical interpretation of Freudian psychoanalysis. I explored and wrote about combining the psychoanalytic dialogue with the dialogue of contemporary culture. I also wrote poetry.

This book is about the move to a more spiritual direction, which came about as a result of the meeting of the two paths. The meeting resulted from, among other things, discomfort and disappointment arising from my perception over time in the results of psychoanalysis, particularly in relation to the failure to transcend pathological narcissism that I encountered among both analysts and the analyzed.

This sense of unease led me to seek out and discover anew the developmental process of the spirit in the individual and in the universe as a whole. The universe responded to my call and brought about a fateful meeting with spiritual teacher and philosopher Andrew Cohen, who developed a teaching that he calls "Evolutionary Enlightenment." Since the start of the millennium I have been his student and associate on the path.

I do not mean to say that the determinations of psychoanalysis in regard to the human spirit are mistaken. I mean that they are limiting if not viewed in a broader context and when they are not integrated in the spiritual dimension.

This book is based principally on the teachings of three individuals—Sigmund Freud, Jacques Lacan and Andrew Cohen—and on the opportunity that opened up for me to look anew upon the significance of life and our role in the world.

The Consciousness Bearers

Meaning of the title The Consciousness Bearers

In Primo Levi's last published book *The Drowned and the Saved*, a first-hand account of the holocaust both wonderful and terrible, he wrote that Nazis used to say to Jews "...but even if someone were to survive, the world will not believe him...we will destroy the evidence together with you" *(Levi, 1988, p.11)*.

Many years after the holocaust this is how it became, survivors were dubbed *Geheimnisträger*—Bearers of the Secret.

When considering a title for this book this term occurred to me and I realized that this book seeks to be the response of Life and Eros to the death drive, because not only are we all Bearers of the Secret—we are also the Bearers of Consciousness. Like a shepherd bearing a yoke of water for his flock. To where? Why and for what? This book attempts to find ways of approaching these fundamental questions.

When I approach the task of writing about the path (Tau) in psychoanalysis and the place of the evolution of the consciousness of the cosmos, I do it with awe and reverence. I dare to put into words a question that all my thinking life and deeds have been centered around. This work is the beginning of a kind of concluding act that provides me with new realizations and illuminations. These illuminations have implications for me—they fill my heart with both pleasure and terror.

From time to time I am obliged to stop writing and go out into nature to observe, for example—a couple of lizards making love on the branch of an olive tree. Can this be described as "making love?" Do they have a world, Heidegger asks. Or is this merely imagery within my language and culture-saturated gaze?

The answer does not spring forth just from the realm of theoretical consideration but rather from deed—from praxis, from clinical observation, from the act of teaching, from personal and collective experience. All of these I will endeavor to serve up in this book as a composite.

If we look at psychoanalysis from the aspect of the evolution of consciousness, we can see Freud's discoveries, as well as Lacan's journey through his reading of those discoveries—and the development that occurred in both their theories—not only as new theoretical understanding but as a developmental journey, initially Freud's and then Lacan's—in regard to knowledge of man and the world. Jung expressed it in one of his letters: "Altogether, your theory has already brought us the very greatest increase in knowledge and opened up a new era with endless perspectives" *(Freud-Jung, 1988, p.11)*.

This isn't just about the development of different perspectives but also a qualitative development in consciousness in relation to knowledge. Doubtless these things have already been uttered and written by important and leading philosophers and individuals. Nevertheless, I burn to speak out about these matters as I understand them, in the way that they are actually imprinted upon my body, my psyche and my spirit.

§ Introduction

Psychoanalysis was created in the period when traditional religion was in decline while the value of cultivating the individual and his-her "freedoms," needs, desires and passions was on the rise. Ulrich Beck referred to the phenomenon as "individualization."

The philosopher Carl Popper felt that our evolution from closed to open society was the deepest change that humanity had ever come through (Popper 1977). And we are still struggling with the desire to relinquish our individual identity, which itself was achieved through struggle, in favor of the harmony of the collective. We were formed through natural selection in such a way as not to know the truth but rather to subjugate it to group loyalty. Tribalism, since it developed naturally, does not require explanation but individualism, so rare and always found in collision with family and culture—does.

The modern self only began to develop in the eighteenth century. The process of individualization only began at that late stage.[1] The eighteenth century led to a new way of comprehending the self which stemmed not only from social attitudes and imitating given cultural mores, rather mainly from individual identity formed by the individual him-herself. This new ideal depended on cultivation of a multi-faceted individuality, expressed in philosophy, literature, theatre, music and visual art.

---

1   This concept is not referring to Jung's concept of individuation but to the process of consolidation of the separate self.

Obviously psychoanalysis played a dominant role in that dramatic cultural change due to the way in which it revealed the depth and complexity of the human spirit, as well as the abundance contained in reflexive thought. The individual self was gradually replacing God.

Freud, who announced that he was atheist, actually brought God in (through a side entrance) by basing his teachings on the oedipal triangle. With this triangle he gave the symbolic father, or rather the function representing the father, the place that Lacan later referred to as "the Other"—the function that establishes the law, the prohibition and limitation of pleasure.[2] However, since Freud's, and even Lacan's (who died in 1980) time, fundamental changes in culture and society have continued to occur. Today, we are encountering the results of the death of God—the collapse of all the ideology and values, the ending of all prohibitions and limitations in relation to enjoyment.[3]

Nowadays we are witnessing the Other being divested of all its authority. We are witnessing the rise of discomfiture and confusion that results from the lifting of prohibition—as we all are aware—prohibition is the initial stimulus of desire.

---

[2] Jung was much engaged with the influences of various religious and mystical aspects on the human psyche and its development, but, in my opinion his teachings are biased towards occultism and mysticism. For a comprehensive discussion on the differences between Freud, Lacan, and Jung see Binyamini, 2009, pp.155-199 (in Hebrew).

[3] A translation of the French word *jouissance* which delineates pleasure mixed with pain. Enjoyment is beyond the pleasure principle and is connected to repetition and to the Real.

When there is no prohibition or limitation and man may do as he pleases, from whence will arise the passion for innovation? The result of the process is a decline into endless consumerism (including spiritual consumerism), as well as cultivation of pathological narcissism.

Another consequence is the rising tendency towards dogmatic religiosity, the emergence of oppressive archetypes, either real or imagined, or deity in the form of the totalitarianism of market forces and ratings, the imperative to strive for enjoyment. Is it possible to think of some other alternative? Can psychoanalysis find new ways of contending with these changes?

Lacan, who foresaw what was to come about, saw (as Jacques-Alain Miller conceived it) the future of psychoanalysis as turning into a religion, however outrageous that may sound. "The fact that Lacan transformed the analytic cure into analytical experience makes it possible to compare the experience of psychoanalysis with that of religion. Of course, nowadays the relevant religion of the 21st century (when not fundamentalist) is centered on religiosity, experience and cure rather than dogma and ceremony" (Miller, 2007).

In this book I want to offer a different direction, a different context—in which all these changes are part of a developmental, evolutionary process that began with the cosmos coming into being. Evolution is a relatively modern concept, propounded by Darwin around one hundred and fifty years ago. Now that it is generally accepted in the Western world, it isn't challenging for us to consider evolution in material/biological terms. It's harder for us to look at it in terms of an intentional developmental process that has interiority—the non-manifest spiritual realm—as well as an exteriority—the material, biological realm. It's yet more challenging to attempt to view these realms in a non-dual context, the implications of which are that considering them as separate systems is a fundamentally flawed approach. The universe is evolving both materially and spiritually and human beings, having developed the capacity of self-reflexive thought, are expressing the most advanced level of evolution that the universe has yet attained. We, Humanity—are the bearers of consciousness.

In attempting to express this perspective—in which the attainments of psychoanalysis can be seen as attainments of the evolutionary process, I use a schematic model that I developed, which portrays the psychological dimensions and the spiritual dimension of human consciousness in a singular context. It seems to be paradoxical—for hundreds of years there have been attempts to disassociate the two or cancel out one or the other—even though they each inseparably, encompass one another.

Psychoanalysis is the most comprehensive and profound teaching for exploring the psyche as it is. Evolutionary Enlightenment explores the psyche in the context of its potential to become.

Regarding context

The terms *context* or *perspective* refer to where we position ourselves and the way in which we define our experiences—emotional, psychological, philosophical and ethical. Context changes throughout history and has determined how we conceive our lives and their significance. My perspective in writing this book is that humanity is the product of almost fourteen billion years of evolution—material and in consciousness—to the point of beginning to become aware of itself. The universe and the humanity which it has produced ascend through various levels of development in consciousness. A lower level of development is reflected in a shallower, limited, less inclusive context/perspective. As consciousness and culture develop, our perspective broadens and deepens and becomes more inclusive. At a low level of development we are *egocentric*—we don't really see beyond ourselves and the world exists solely to reflect back to us. As human consciousness has developed it broadened to the level of the *ethnocentric*—our sense of self including the family, clan, tribe (so many of the problems and conflicts occupying humanity are still based on this low level of consciousness); *mythocentric*—our sense of self identified with a commonly held religious tradition transcending blood, cultural or geographical factors; *nation-centric*—our sense of self identified with a commonly held sense/institution of nationhood. Today *global-centric* consciousness is becoming increasingly evident, in which our sense of self is first and foremost as a citizen of the world. Beyond the global-centric begins to emerge the *cosmo-centric*—when our sense of self is identified with the evolutionary process of the universe in its entirety. This level of consciousness however, is in a very early stage of emergence.

Structure

This book comprises three sections.

The first section is devoted to articles that appeared in various journals. They relate to a transitory period—one during which I began to comprehend the spiritual context of life, which led me to scrutinize psychoanalysis from a new angle.

The second section sets out the integrative model I developed to present the insights into the human psyche gained by psychoanalysis, within the broader context of the evolutionary process. The model also presents Evolutionary Enlightenment's vision for human development on the level of the individual and in a collective context.

The third section covers three series of lectures I delivered at the Tel Aviv Cinematheque in which I used cinema as a means of describing and demonstrating various aspects of psychoanalysis and the evolution of consciousness. In editing these, I have tried to retain the original structure. I would really recommend seeing the featured movies—both before and after reading about them. The lectures focus on three subjects: "What does a woman want?" "Upon love and perversion," and "The development of consciousness, as mirrored in cinema." The films chosen reflect my personal tastes and the suitability of each as a tool to demonstrate the subject of the lecture. Where appropriate I have sometimes included content that appeared in other sources, including content that appeared earlier in the book, as well as excerpts from my previous book *Loving Psychoanalysis* (Golan, 2006).

Concluding the lecture series is an article about Nurit Aviv's excellent film *From Language to Language*. This book, too, attempts to move from language to language—from the language of psychoanalysis to the language of spirituality—to encompass the important insights of the one within the eternity of the other.

Also in this book I use different typefaces to help differentiate between the two literary styles found within it—the academic and the freely associative.

The teachings and quotes of Andrew Cohen are used freely in this book without specific references. They are drawn from hundreds of hours of his lectures and workshops that I attended or heard, as well as from his editorials in his magazine *EnlightenNext* (formerly *What is Enlightenment?*).

A Note of Thanks

Firstly to Andrew Cohen, who literally opened up the world for me. It is my sincere hope that this book successfully imbues the insights and understanding that I have received from his teaching, my personal experience of transformation as a result of being his student and the wondrous privilege of being one of his associates on the path to enlighten consciousness in the world.

I would also like to thank my friends and colleagues in both the fields of psychoanalysis and spirituality—companions over many years with whom I have shared my initial ponderings and from whom I have learnt so much of significance and depth; Amir Freimann and Shlomo Lieber, who perused my writings and commented on various aspects (and sometimes inaccuracies). Rivka Warshawsky, Ruth and Avi Rybnicki, Liora Goder, Alex Liban, Beni Gleitman, Gavriel Dahan—psychoanalysts.

Jonathon Martin, Igal Moria, Yael Cherniak and the members of the Israel group of Evolutionary Enlightenment practitioners.

Special thanks to my friend and colleague Mona Zupnik, who came to my rescue when I most needed it.

Thanks, too, to literary editor Uri Weisfelner and the editors of Contento de Semrik Publishing for their faithful support.

part I

Eppur si muove! — nevertheless, it does move!

This short essay gives an initial outline of a broader research project. The project was conducted in order to re-examine some of the conclusions reached from viewing psychoanalysis not as a form of scientific, philosophical, or even psychological research, but as research that includes the researching subject—meaning that psychoanalytic research is inseparable from clinical work.

The purpose of such research is not merely to gather information or knowledge, but to reveal elements relating to truth and cause in a way that will influence and bring about change, and transformation.

This concept is valid in relation to both praxis and, in a different way, learning. Transformation is movement of the psyche—in a specific direction.

With the opening of the Clinical Section in Paris in 1977, Lacan established the couch as the clinic. He said that we have to "clinicize"—to lay the patient down. He meant that the term "clinic" should lead us to reconsider our own clinical work: the treatment we give, our transition from the position of analysand to that of analyst, and the way we relate to transference. Lacan used the opportunity to assert that "Clinical psychoanalysis must consist not only of analytic examination but also examination of the analysts" (Lacan, 1977b).

I feel that it is too easy for us to forget what Lacan really meant by allowing ourselves to be satisfied merely by the more interesting intellectual and theoretical elements of psychoanalysis.

Sometimes even testimonies regarding the Pass process[4] seem to be no more than a creative way of expressing analytic insights, devoid of real effects. This is both stimulating and worrying. A glance at working relationships within the analytic institution, for example, can leave one wondering in regard to the effect that psychoanalysis has on the analysts themselves.

At this point, I tend to believe that we fail to apply our professional ethics in our personal lives. As soon as we get up off the analyst's armchair, we stop being ready to listen freely and openly, to cast off our tendency towards narcissism and to contemplate in a way that is free of ego.[5]

---

4 The Pass is the process invented by Lacan in which the analysant testifies to the theoretical conclusions he derived from his own analysis.
5 The concept of the ego is used in psychoanalysis as the organizing structure of the psyche. Both in psychoanalysis and in spiritual teachings the ego is considered as an agency who is fixated in the narcissistic perception of the

The Consciousness Bearers

There is a difference between curiosity about psychoanalytic knowledge and studying it, because we have a sense that our fate depends on there being new breakthroughs in the field. When questions do start to be asked, genuine answers are generally found, but the real answers can seem too big for us to deal with because they require transition from the known to the unknown and a change in our ethical position. That is why we tend to bury the answers in a sheath of knowledge—"Interesting, I'd like to look into that." That is how we make sure that we will always be students. This course of action involves a lot of enjoyment, identification with psychoanalysis as an ideal, and identification with the ideals of psychoanalysis.

The critical question relates to the motive behind the research—or the desire that empowers the research. The individual that approaches psychoanalysis in order to know also wants to know about himself and his place in the world. I call such knowledge "living" or "erotic" knowledge—the opposite of the knowledge of universities. Whether or not a person admits it, there is a sense of dissatisfaction with what already exists, a hunger for deeper experience of being.

So psychoanalysis is really a kind of psychic motion. Or, more precisely, psychoanalysis deals with the conflict

---

self and the world. In this book I use the word "I" to mark the psychoanalytic concept (this is in fact the word that Freud uses—*Das Ich*), and the word "ego," to mark the narcissistic self.

between the dynamics of progress, regression, going round in circles, or being stuck in one place—a dynamic of internal and external events, of drives and representations, occurring within the framework of time.

§ The libido

Such dynamics are based on Freud's concept of libido. Lacan's initial definition of libido aided him in constructing the "mirror stage," the stage at which the ego becomes fixated. Miller used Lacan's scheme to illustrate the imaginary connection that runs between a and a',[6] with the libido in a circular motion, representing complete connection at the level of enjoyment—the level of libidinal drive. His definition is based on Freud's essay "On Narcissism" (Freud, 1914c). The connection at the imaginary level interferes most foully with the inter-subjective connection, blocking it, making it fixed and repetitive (Miller, 1995–96).

The axis upon which the libido registers obstructs the subject's symbolic connection with the Other, even to the point of disconnecting it. Enjoyment cuts off the genuine connection with the Other. As Miller put it, in psychoanalysis one has to overcome the libidinal connection in order to facilitate a genuine connection with the Other. When treatment is steered in the right way, enjoyment ultimately

---

6   ego and other

gives way, allowing for the motion itself to be transformed.

Lacan distinguished between two opposing types of libido:
1. Libido in a repetitive cycle from the ego to the world outside, in narcissistic terms—libido that can be transferred.
2. That which he termed "The libido of phallic auto-eroticism"—fixated, stagnant libido.

"The imaginary function is what Freud formulated to govern the investment of the object as a narcissistic object" *(Miller, 1995-96)*.

The permanent element of this circulation is phallic. In distinguishing between the two opposing forms—transitory and fixated—Lacan established the basis of what he later called the model of *enjoyment*.

In *The Four Fundamental Concepts of Psychoanalysis*, Lacan wrote:

"Everything that Freud spells out about the partial drives shows us the movement that I outlined for you on the blackboard last time, that circular movement of the thrust that emerges through the erogenous rim only to return to it as its target, after having encircled something I call the objet a. I suggest—and punctilious examination of this whole text is a test of the truth of what I propose—that it is in this way that the subject attains what is, strictly speaking, the dimension of the capital Other.

I suggest that there is a radical distinction between loving oneself through the other—which, in the narcissistic field of the object, allows no transcendence to the object included—and the circularity of the drive, in which the heterogeneity of the movement out and back shows a gap in its interval" *(Lacan, 1964, p. 194).*

Lacan located the libido of Freud in that gap created by the periodicity of the drive. In Lacan's XIth seminar (1964), he saw libido not as energy but as an organ, the substance of the Real[7]: biological life, unlimited by life or death. The libido represents life as something that cannot be annihilated, the pure drive of life—beyond the genealogical chain of sexual procreation. The libido, therefore, is a result of the separation between biological sexuality and human sexuality—as dictated by the symbolic order.

When Lacan began to teach, he thought that it would suffice to contend that it is not the signifier that attracts the libido but the image, the reflection. In time, he discarded this explanation because he discovered that the signifier itself is saturated with libido. He noted the material dimension of language and then distinguished the split subject as a non-libidinal effect of the signifier—a dead subject, an effect of signifiers—from *objet á* as a loaded effect of the

---

7   The Real is one of the three orders through which Lacan described the structure of the psyche. The other two are the Imaginary and the Symbolic. The Real is different than reality. It is what is excluded from the symbolic net language and culture. It is what one bumps into, about which one cannot say anything, only talk around it. The Real is the traumatic.

signifier. The signifier therefore has both a fatal effect in regard to the subject and a life-giving effect—enjoyment.

In this context, objet á is the symptom.

§ Fixation—the ego

The remarkable similarity between Buddhist teachings and the way Freud and Lacan establish the ego as an object was, for me, a novel and exciting revelation. According to both views, the object is formed out of the building blocks of identifications and is structured as a shield or screen to protect from unmediated encounters with the bodily or worldly Real.

The ego serves as a defense mechanism in the face of the dynamic uncertainty of the subject of the unconscious, its inherent otherness, and the sense of the uncanny that accompanies such encounters. Because of the imaginary fixation on the ego as our identity (Eastern wisdom refers to such fixation as "attachment"), the ego resists movement or change in desire. In analytic practice, the ego is considered to be a source of resistance and fixation. Reinforcing it merely serves to increase resistance. The attachment of the ego is the personal, imaginary perspective, which puts a stop to motion.

By undermining the attachment to the ego, psychoanalysis tries to restore the movement of desire, of its dialectic, to open up a free space in which the subject can dwell and move more freely through life's contingencies.

For Lacan as for Freud, the ego is not a subject but an object, constructed out of fixated identifications. It is but a structure formed by identification with the specular image of the "mirror stage." This is the place where the subject becomes alienated from itself, becoming its fellow men. In a structural sense, such alienation is similar to paranoia. Therefore, the ego is an imaginary product, the locus of resistance.

Thus, Lacan was very much against the idea that psychoanalysis should reinforce the ego. Since the ego is the seat of our illusions, reinforcing it only serves to facilitate further alienation and fixation of the subject.

The ego therefore constitutes the principal source of resistance to analysis. Since it is essentially fixed in the imaginary realm, it resists all subjective growth and change and also the dialectic motion of desire. By undermining the fixation of the ego, analysis attempts to restore the dialectic of desire and to usher in the subject's being.

Where does Lacan locate the ego in the make-up of the psyche? In the XXth Seminar (1972-3), Lacan distinguished between the two bodies that psychoanalysis relates to. One is the body defined by language—what is said about it and the way it is treated and touched. It is a sexual body in a process of birth and death. The other is the organism—that conglomeration of flesh imbued with inextinguishable life.

In this sense, language constitutes a kind of parasite on the organism, constructing as it does the symbolic body. We have two bodies—one mounted on the other and two languages—one mounted on the other. Language is mounted on the *lalangue*[8]. The process of recognition or the revelation of this is a reverse process: from the body to the organism. There is language and there is lalangue. However, I believe that the kind of speech that comes from the ego that Lacan refers to as "blah-blah" constitutes a third type of speech. This third form of speech is the talk of self-importance and knowledge that bestows false authority—it acts as a screen that covers the living, pulsating knowledge in the Real, which is connected with the unknown (Lacan, 1972-3).

Perhaps for Lacan the ego was a hybrid creature, connecting the organism—the body per se—with the symbolic body, or connecting the speaking being [*parlêtre*] with the subject when it is based on the pleasure principle.

I contend that in place of the non-existent sexual connection, we tend to construct an imaginary sexual link with our own ego, which becomes one of the principal obstacles

---

[8] This is the name Lacan gave to the tonic language, a language that is constructed from meaningless syllables like baby talk or like sounds that a couple can exchange while making love.

to analysis. We are trapped in phallic enjoyment in regard to our own self-image—our thoughts, moods, ideas, and so forth. They seem to us highly unique and important, whereas they are, in effect, the cause of our suffering. We find such suffering so very hard to give up because it constructs our "identity."

Time after time we come across clear examples of this phenomenon in our clinical work. However, apart from it being critical to psychoanalytic training, how will the analyst, when captivated by his own ego, be able to apply, for example, free-floating attention? (free of self-image, identifications, the known).

§ Horizontal and vertical movement

In psychoanalytic terms there are two forms of motion: there is repetitive cyclic motion, the motion of drive around the object causing enjoyment, and there is also the developing form of vertical motion.

Thus, the subject can go from fixation and compulsive repetitiveness to acting from free choice.

Ken Wilber (2001), an influential contemporary thinker and expert on Eastern and Western knowledge, distinguishes between the two functions offered by religion, but the distinction he makes can also apply to various fields in our culture—particularly psychoanalysis.

The Consciousness Bearers

Wilber distinguishes between horizontal and vertical movement. He refers to horizontal movement as "translation"—motion that generates meanings, deepening understanding, stories, interest, and interpretation. Horizontal motion only serves to reaffirm and reinforce the I. It cannot bring about a change in our level of awareness. It cannot liberate us from the ego.

There is also vertical movement—the movement of radical transformation and liberation. This kind of movement is characteristic of a tiny fraction of the population. Instead of reinforcing the fixated ego, it has the potential to destroy it. It is about emptiness rather than fullness, as well as revolution. Wilber refers to it as "transformation." Vertical motion puts the very process of translation in doubt, shatters it. With translation, the I finds new ways of thinking about the world. Transformation means changing the world rather than translating it.

The process of translation gives legitimacy to the I and its beliefs. Without translation there would be social chaos. Individuals who cannot translate with a reasonable level of integrity and precision—who are unable to construct a world of significance—fall into psychosis. The world ceases to be understood, and the boundaries between the world and the I begin to disintegrate. This is not a breakthrough—this is a crisis, disaster rather than transcendence.

While translation has a vital function, there is a point at

which it can no longer console and no new paradigms or myths can allay the sense of distress. The only way out is transformation—individually and collectively.

§ From the personal to the particular via the universal

Psychoanalytic treatment is a bit like starting out on a journey and having to visit various places on the way—starting from the personal, passing through the universal, and arriving at the unique, the particular.

At the initial session with a new patient, my first question is "What brings you here?" or "Why are you here?"

During the last session following nine years of treatment, one of my patients asked me, with tears in her eyes, "What have you brought me up for?" Her question came as a surprise for me, like a retrospective interpretation, shedding light on the entire nine-year process. It had a hair-raising effect, akin to her asking (like Jesus on the cross): "My God, My God, why hast thou forsaken me?" Was *that* what I had been doing in her analysis? Bringing her up?

In his essay "The Subversion of the Subject and the Dialectic of Desire in the Freudian Unconscious," Lacan said, referring to his investigation of the unconscious, "to the point at which it gives a reply that is not some sort of ravishment or takedown, but is rather a 'saying why'" (1966a, p. 283). He refers to the cause.

I believe that the route along which analysis flows, runs between the three questions, "What?" "What for?" and "Why?"

Patients respond to the first question in personal terms—their personal complaint, the story of their life, their own personal pain and anxiety. Treatment revolves around repetitive elements of their tale. From the repetition arise the symptom, the complex, and a structural diagnosis. The universal nature of his suffering—the structural character (i.e., neurotic, psychotic, perverse, etc.)—comes as an unpleasant surprise for the subject. The chaos of the signifiers is reduced to a kind of formula. The personal has to be taken through the universal prism, which changes the position of the subjects and their narcissistic investment in "being special." That is the first step. The next is the recognition of the *enjoyment* that is bound up with the subjects' suffering and adhesion to their symptom.

The subjects assume responsibility for their position regarding sexuation—their sexual preference—man or woman (beyond biology and sex) and that special combination of verbal enjoyment. These are the particular aspects of their subjectivity.

Only through adopting the position of "I don't know but I want to know" can they "pass through" and grow from the personal to the particular.

In this respect, drive belongs to the realm of universality. Drive is the movement around the fallen object, freedom from any object that can be perceived. Lacan defined the essence of the drive as the trace of the Act. Once it used to encircle our bodies, sealing off our empty erogenous orifices, just as the breast blocked our mouths and voices blocked our ears. Such partial organs are part of the totality of the *lamella*, that part of the libido that is desexualized—immortal, inextinguishable life.

Sexualization introduces death—the trace of an Act rather than the Act itself. The movement of drive, the enjoyment and satisfaction involved, are the movements of an automaton. They belong to the realm of cyclic, horizontal motion, and are not evolutionary.

Not so desire, which can never be satisfied. It has a metonymic possibility—replacing one object with another. There is also a dialectic faculty in Hegelian terms: generating a new metaphor when it engages [tyché] with the Real.

The gist of philosophy, including Eastern philosophy, has dealt with horizontal movement rather than with evolution. Even in referring to movement—"Everything flows" or "All is one"—it is the whole, the absolute, which is being referred to. In psychoanalysis, the phallic dimension constitutes a part of this totality. Like the movement of a pendulum—creation and extinction—there is and then there is not. The libido, too, has been characterized by the movement of here/there, life/death, Fort/Da[9]. Even in the Borromean context, which refers to four dimensions—symbolic, imaginary, Real, and the object that connects them—the connection is still cyclic: pincer grasped by pincer, dimension gripped by dimension; a chain of signifiers. In the past, vertical motion was the realm of the religions, but they, too, failed to refer to the evolution of consciousness, focusing instead on the development of morality.

Although in the realms of science—quantum physics—the border between matter and consciousness has been rent asunder, to the best of my knowledge the subject of research is not evolution—the new. There is a field, and there are things that affect that field.

Psychoanalytic practice, however, deals with evolution—personal, universal, and particular. This occurs through praxis rather than theory. Analysis cannot be discussed without discussing evolution—recognition of repetition, the fall of the ideal, giving up enjoyment, and so on.

The next step is to stop trying to become: to recognize the fact of partiality of the various passions and their limitations and to break free of them—that is, liberation.

The various scientific theories regarding the expansion

---

9 Those are the words used by Freud's grandson while playing with a reel in a day that his mother was away, throwing it away and bringing it back. See Freud's article "Beyond the Pleasure Principle" 1920, p.100.

and contraction of the universe also have an evolutionary element. This element exists in the anomalous, in the "not everything." Transition is the subject here—from the phallic to the feminine, giving up *enjoyment*, inventing knowledge, identification with the sinthome[10].

What does psychoanalysis exist for if not to prevent repetition? To liberate from fixation, to create a space for desire to move in, to improve the representation of drive with new metaphors? To fell the ideal? To leave identification behind?

Lacan also referred to the Pass as a possibility for evolution of knowledge through transmission.

§ The movement and training of the analyst

In referring to the training of psychoanalysts, Miller (2002) talked about "formation"—training—and what lies beyond training— "transformation."

The question of training becomes more refined when the objective is not only to accumulate knowledge but that certain subjective conditions should emerge: transformation of the subject's being, or training for wisdom, like in Zen—that is, subjective transformation without transmitting any specialist knowledge.

---

10 Synthome—a structure which is created at the end of analysis with which the subject can identify. It is constructed from a combination between the word "*symptôme*" (symptom) and the word "*saint homme*" (holy man).

Training requires that the psyche mutate. Genuine training transmits spirit and a path and is realized when the individual develops a new character. In real training we are always ready for surprises and the unknown—in the same way that interpretation works as an Act that leads to change in psychoanalysis. Study is not training. Miller's concept, in the wake of Lacan, says that proper training always starts after study. It includes within it "ignoring what one already knows" (Miller, 2002). Its aim is perfection.

In training—as in therapy—subjective transformation is what is sought after.

About narrow-mindedness and the Real

Spinoza

"... [I]t is made finite through its cause, which is necessarily God. Further, if it is finite through its cause, this must be so either because its cause could not give more, or because it would not give more. That he should not have been able to give more would contradict his omnipotence; that he should not have been willing to give more, when he could well do so, savours of ill-will [narrow mindedness], which is nowise in God, who is all goodness and perfection" (Spinoza, 1660, pp. 51–52).

I interpret this statement by Spinoza as meaning that the literal meaning of narrow-mindedness is vision of limited perspective. While man is afflicted by narrow vision, the vision of the Divine is absolute, and therefore the divine abundance is of an absolute nature.

Freud

In his essay "Remembering, Repeating and Working-Through" (1914g), Freud referred to treatment by analysis as broadening one's view: "and now we can see that in drawing attention to the compulsion to repeat we have acquired no new fact but only a more comprehensive view" (p. 151). Through analysis Freud sought to broaden one's point of view and reduce the limitations of one's perspective.

Holarchy

From an evolutionary perspective, there is direction in the way life on earth is developing and there is natural hierarchy in the world, which Arthur Koestler referred to as "holarchy." Reality is comprised of a whole/fragments or "holons." Holons are simultaneously complete in themselves and components of a greater whole. Everything is a holon of something else. Reality is comprised of neither things nor processes, but of holons, and is infinite.

Holons appear in holarchy, or natural hierarchy—an order of ever-increasing perfection: from particles to atoms to cells to organisms; from letters to words to sentences to paragraphs. What constitutes a whole on one plane becomes a fragment in relation to a higher plane. The lower does not include the higher, but the higher does include the lower. Evolution tends towards increasing complexity, further differentiation/integration, further organization/construction, increasing relative autonomy, and more and more *telos* (purpose).

Each evolutionary level transcends, yet includes, its subordinate level. Each new level is innovative, as metaphor is to language (Wilber, 2000).

In his book *The Fragile Absolute* (2000), Slavoj Žižek shows us that psychoanalysis functions in the intermediate zone of the contrast between factual "objective" knowledge and "subjective" truth.

Psychoanalysis exposes deceit uttered under the guise of truth (such as by obsessive personalities whose statements, while precise, actually deny their desire). It also exposes the speakers of truth under the guise of deceit (the hysterical process, or slips of the tongue that reveal the subject's desire) (Žižek, 2000).

The value of such truth is not what is important in psychoanalysis. What is important is the manner in which the transition between truth and deceit reveals the desires of the patient.

When a female patient contends that her father sexually abused her, the important factor is not the abuse as such; rather, it is its role in her symbolic economy and the manner in which the event was subjectified. It is not the event itself that is important but the way in which it is related to and the ability to register it in the make-up of the psyche, conscious or unconscious. Lacan interpreted thus what Freud called "the reality of the psyche."

If the evolutionary holarchic model is applied, we will be able to state that what is deceit on one plane becomes truth on another plane, while the transition between the planes reveals the desire. Desire for what?—for further expansion of consciousness or broadening of perspective. When there is no transition, if things get stuck, desire gets jammed—a symptom into which enjoyment is drained.

§ The experience

After many long years of psychoanalysis, that female patient has reached the point of certainty—she circumnavigates and surrounds the rock of the Real, that which cannot be described, which cannot be healed. She will have to bear that wound all her life; all that is left to do is "identify with the symptom," adjust oneself more comfortably to the symptom, and accept it.

She considers the Pass as an option, instead of which she opts for a spiritual workshop in India. After a week of meditation, contemplation, silence, and detachment from all that is known, the teacher speaks of the Real—in his own terms. "Get real!" he says, using "American" terminology. What comes to her mind is "Coca Cola—the real thing," and she chuckles derisively.

Then, seemingly from nowhere, the barrier—the Real—pops up from the very depths of her being. Doubt assails her—could this really be the Real? At that very moment of the question arising, the Real melts away and it is as if it had never been present. The world turns upside down. There is a sense of wonder and blissful dizziness, and an almost unbearable ease. That same dark god that had controlled her, to whom she had sacrificed so much, around which her whole life had revolved, has crumbled away in front of her like a cheap illusion. For her it was a leap in consciousness that made the Real imaginary. So where is the "real" Real hiding? If we see the evolution of consciousness in spiral form, the only Real that there is the Absolute, or full, perspective—unlimited all-encompassing vision. Every other Real can only be relative.

Two years later, the effects of the experience have taken root, stabilized, and her perspective continues to broaden.

§ The flower

Hegel

Hegel distinguished between dialectics as a science (knowledge)—the "synchronous" motion within the world of complete knowledge—and dialectics as a journey (truth), which is the movement towards it. The analogy is taken from the realm of flora—the journey of the tree from bud to fruit:

"...[I]n the same way when the fruit comes, the blossom may be explained to be a false form of the plant's existence, for the fruit appears as its true nature in place of the blossom. But the ceaseless activity of their own inherent nature makes them at the same time moments of an organic unity, where they not merely do not contradict one another, but where one is as necessary as the other; and this equal necessity of all moments constitutes alone and thereby the life of the whole" (Hegel, 1807, p. 68).

Hegel speaks of evolutionary leaps while comparing them to the birth of a child or to building a new world:

"It [the spirit] is indeed never at rest, but carried along the stream of progress ever onward. But it is here as in the case of the birth of a child; after a long period of nutrition in silence, the continuity of the gradual growth in size, of quantitative change, is suddenly cut short by the first breath drawn—there is a break in the process, a qualitative change—and the child is born. In like manner the spirit of the time, growing slowly and quietly ripe for the new form it is to assume, disintegrates one fragment after another of the structure of its previous world.

"That it is tottering to its fall is indicated only by symptoms here and there. Frivolity and again ennui, which are spreading in the established order of things, the undefined foreboding of something unknown—all these betoken that there is something else approaching. This gradual crumbling to pieces, which did not alter the general look and aspect of the whole, is interrupted by the sunrise, which, in a flash and at a single stroke, brings to view the form and structure of the new world" (Hegel, 1807, p. 75).

Thus dialectics stem from the fact that there is tension (contradictions) within the system of concepts. This tension cannot be relieved at the level of our current conceptual system. In order to solve it, new ideas have to be generated, but these also have to preserve some of the logic of the preceding stage that generated the tension.

Lévinas
In the aforesaid context, it is interesting to note the apparently opposite position that Lévinas took. To Lévinas, evolution occurs in retrospect—from absolute to relative. Opposite the analogy of the blossom that develops into fruit, we can bring Lévinas's reference to a Talmudic problem in the Shabbat tractate (page 88, 71–72), as it explains the verse from the Song of Songs: "As the apple tree among the trees of the wood, so is my beloved among the sons ..." (Song of Songs, 2:3). This passage from the tractate tells of Rabbi Hama who asked Rabbi Hanina why in this verse the Israelites are compared to an apple. Rabbi Hanina answers that, as is the case with the apple whose fruit precedes its leaves, so the Israelites preceded doing to hearing (Lévinas, 1968).

The fruit precedes the leaves and the flowers. The Torah is received prior to any inquiry, outside of gradual development. The epilogue precedes the story—"We will do and we will hear." The Torah in this sense is the Real.

The "yes" in "we will do" does not mean volunteering for doing per se, it does not envelop a wonderful "praxis" that precedes thought, while the blindness, even if it is the blindness of a trusting individual, is bound to bring about disaster. On the contrary: this "yes" is about sobriety without hesitation, without a guiding hypothesis, without a clue, without cognitive examination. It is about an evolutionary leap.

Lacan

In the XXth seminar, Lacan said: "...the ego [moi] can also be a flower of rhetoric, which grows in the pot of the pleasure principle that Freud calls Lustprinzip, and that I define as that which is satisfied by blah-blah" (Lacan, 1975a, p. 56). We know that the ego mediates between the subject and reality. We know that the reality that the ego mediates is actually made of the pleasure principle, which it represents. In this seminar, Lacan focused on symbolic language as a parasite of primal *lalangue*, the language of *enjoyment*. However, it seems that when he spoke of the ego's "blah-blah," he meant a third form of speech—speech as self-importance and empty "authoritative" knowledge, as a false mask that covers the living knowledge that pulsates within the Real—that stems from the unknown and is exposed more and more in the course of evolution.

§ Trauma and opportunity

Žižek

In *The Fragile Absolute* (2000), Žižek referred to the connection between the structure and its own event. On the one hand, the event is the impossible Real of a structure, of its synchronous symbolic order, the violent gesture that generated it. Synchronous structural order is a kind of defensive formation against the event that establishes it. On the other hand, one could contend the opposite: the status of the event itself (the mythic narrative of the primordial, violent establishing gesture) is phantasmic. This is phantasmic construction that is intended to relate to what cannot be related to (the sources of order) through concealing the Real of the structural antagonism (lack of possibility) that prevents synchronous structural order from achieving balance.

The Act as Real is an authentic Act, located between time and eternity. Žižek quotes Kant and Schelling regarding the Act. They see it as the point at which eternity intervenes in the process of time, the point at which the temporal causal chain is disturbed. Something appears, generated from emptiness (the revelation). Something that cannot be explained occurs as a result of the preceding chain. On the other hand, the Act is simultaneously the moment at which time rises from eternity. This voids the balance—this is the paradox of the eternal gesture that simultaneously realizes eternity while opening up the realm of the temporal/historic.

Eternity is not above time, in the simple sense of existing beyond time. Eternity is the name given to the event or the cut that supports and operates the temporal dimension as a sequence of failed attempts to capture it.

Psychoanalysis refers to this Act as "trauma." Trauma is eternal and cannot find form either in time or in history. It is the point of eternity around which time revolves. This is an event that is only accessible in time through the multiplication of its traces. Eternity and time are not mutually exclusive, in the simple sense of the word. There is no time without eternity. Temporality is maintained by our failure to grasp/symbolize/historicize the eternal trauma. If trauma enters the temporal/historic, the dimension of time itself will collapse into the eternal now, devoid of time. Eternity is that which is excluded—the exception that enables historical reality to preserve its consistency.

Psychoanalysis includes within it acceptance and admission that all of our verbal exchange formations are eternally haunted by "a leftover that cannot be divided." It is a ghost of traumatic remnant that resists confession—that is, integration with a symbolic world: it cannot be liberated, completed, or allowed to rest. This relates implicitly to the traumatic core that continues as an obscene remnant of a living-dead that keeps the world of verbal exchange "alive." Without the addition of this ghost, there is no life. Therefore, the ultimate objective of psychoanalysis is not the attainment of peace through confessing trauma but, rather, acceptance that our life also has an irreparable core of trauma. There is something in us that cannot find release—ever.

§ Evolutionary opportunity

Like Freud, Žižek (2000) halts in the face of trauma. By his description, it appears that the trauma does not enable an evolutionary releasing process. However, later in the book he wrote:

"Judaism stands for the paradox of Universalism which maintains its universal dimension precisely by its "passionate attachment" to the stain of particularity that serves as its unacknowledged foundation. Judaism thus not only belies the common-sense notion that the price to be paid for access to universality is to renounce one's particularity; it also demonstrates how the stain of unacknowledged particularity of the gesture that generates the Universal is the ultimate resource of the Universal's vitality..." (Žižek, 2000, p. 99).

What did he mean when he spoke of Judaism? Was he unwittingly speaking of the same Act that Lévinas was also referring to, whose significance becomes apparent only in retrospect, an Act connected with revelation and that leads to redemption—because trauma is simultaneously a threatening fixation that leads to anxiety while also offering the opportunity to awaken—*tyché*—the opportunity to take an evolutionary leap?

Something has occurred—an event that can be neither suppressed nor forgotten. Something has to be done—before and in place of recognition.

From a holarchic and evolutionary perspective, trauma is the opportunity to approach that place of broader perspective. When truth rises to a higher plane, what might be experienced by us as real in the context of the psyche can become imaginary.
GET REAL!

What lies behind identification?

In Dan Brown's thriller *The Da Vinci Code,* the plot is entwined with the myth of the search for the Holy Grail but in the spirit of the time, the grail in his book is not an object but a woman or sacred femininity. Perhaps it is The Woman. The map that leads to her is encoded within a container conceived by Leonardo Da Vinci in the form of a torus composed of rings engraved with letters. The container can only be opened by twisting the rings according to a specific code.

In one of Lacan's later seminars—"One Knew That It Was a Mistaken Moon on the Wings of Love (L'insu)" (Lacan, 16/11/1976)—he presents us with the trait of identification with an engraved torus composed of three such rings.

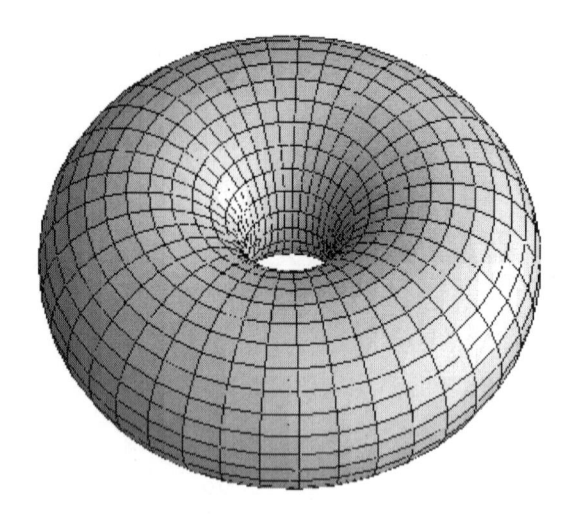

The three rings represent the three ways of identification outlined by Freud in "Group Psychology and the Analysis of the Ego" (Freud, 1921). Lacan contends that the three ways of identification are differing facets of the same mechanism. I contend that Lacan and Freud perhaps did not take into account the possibility of additional rings, rings not connected with the ways of identification rather with their perspective, which continues to broaden, as well as the evolutionary potential that lies within them.

To explain my contention:

What does Freud say to us regarding identification? Identification is a substitute for both sexuality and murderousness. It is a mechanism that is neither sexual nor aggressive, a mechanism essentially for dealing with the drive. Lacan defines identification as transformation of the subject that occurs when the subject adopts an image (Lacan, 1966, p.2), recognizes his/herself in a particular image and appropriates that image as his/herself. It begins with the "mirror stage." Lacan differentiates between imaginary identification and symbolic identification. Imaginary identification is the mechanism by means of which the ego is formed at the mirror stage. This is the way the ego is established by identifying with something exterior to it, or even opposed to it (Freud, 1921, p.22). Such identification involves both aggression and alienation. The self establishes the initial identification and gives birth to the ideal self.

Freud uses the term Identification in the two contexts—the metonymic, in which one image is substituted for another; and identification of the self with someone or something. When he first started teaching, he viewed identification as being principally connected with historic symptoms; the phenomenon of unconscious mimicry or mental contagion—i.e., incorporation.

In *The Interpretation of Dreams,* Freud spoke of the identification and the unconscious sharing a particular component common to both of them—phantasm[11]. The idea of *incorporation* having emerged between 1912-1915 in his essays "Totem and Taboo" and "Mourning and Melancholy." Here, the subject identifies orally with the lost object (Freud, 1912-13). In the 1914 article "On Narcissism" he details the dialectic that links selection of the narcissistic object with identification, while the subject is established along the lines of the model of early objects

---

11 In this book, the term *phantasm* refers to unconscious fantasy.

such as the parents (Freud, 1914). In other words, Freud develops and sophisticates the concept of identification, to the point it becomes an action by means of which the subject is established. Both the ego and the super ego, when they are differentiated from the id, are constructed through identification. Identification is a mechanism that replaces libidinal cathexis. These are the effects of Oedipus upon construction of the subject, when both the father and the mother are simultaneously objects of love and objects of competition. Perhaps such double values in relation to the object are a pre-condition for any identification.

In the seventh chapter of *Group Psychology and the Analysis of the Ego* (Freud, 1921), Freud struggles with this abstract concept and with the connection between identification and love of the object. In identification, he sees the initial form of emotional connection with the object, as well as what regressively replaces the choosing of the object that the subject is obliged to desert.

In this chapter he differentiates between identification and love and defines the three types of identification:

1) Identification prior to the choosing of the sexual object: identification with the ideal. This is direct and immediate identification prior to any cathexis on an object. Identification with the father prior to the father of oedipal law; cannibalistic identification, with an ideal, which establishes itself on the background of incorporation based on primeval myth—the pleasures of devouring the violent and jealous father, leaving all the females to himself, and casting out the boys (Freud, 1921, p.105).

The Consciousness Bearers

This is the initial establishment of the law and its consequences, which are connected with symbolizing the difference between the sexes. From this point the registry of the paternal metaphor and the function of the signifier "the name of the father" commence. The body of the Real father becomes missing, due to him having been murdered and devoured. From this missing object or lack, the potential for subjectivity is born. From that moment this initial identification has two destinies, which are interpreted retrospectively from the Oedipal complex.

On the one hand, the Oedipal complex works to subjugate the subject to the law of desire. On the other hand, primeval identification leaves footprints on the claims of the super ego, which can be cruel and violent.

Beyond primeval myth, the potential of subjectivity repeats itself through the oedipal killing of the father, upon the same background of lack, which leads to instead of incorporation of the father, to incorporation of his name or of symbolic law. This is the second point of identification:

2) Symbolic identification with a unique trait[12]. Freud shows that in certain instances identification does not affect the object as a whole rather it affects a unique trait of him. In neuroses the choosing of the object undergoes regression to identification. This is symbolic identification with the unique trait that Lacan developed to identification with the signifier or identification with the symptom.

The subject takes on identification with the trait of the

---

12 For example, many Germans grew a Hitler moustache during the Third Reich.

object as a symptom, such as, for example, Dora's cough (Freud, 1905a). This identification grants the symptom its aspect as a signifier, by taking the trait from the beloved object or from the opponent, the object sought after by the other. In the absence of a sexual claim by the other the subject can identify with the unique trait common to both him/her and the other, for example, the wish to be loved. Hysterical identification stems from displacement. Identification in this context occurs in relationship to a different trait. For this the subject is required to be logically empty, so the emptiness will be applied dialectically. For Lacan, since there is no final significance, any signifier can occupy this place. I contend that not all signifiers are equal in value to others—in relation to this the object of identification is of crucial significance.

Lacan shows us that the passage from identification to anxiety is often just one step. That step is the unique trait. When it fails for a moment, or the identification unravels, it can no longer fulfill its function, which is to preserve the subject in the face of the desire that is reflected in the gaze of the other. In his book *Inhibitions, Symptoms and Anxiety*, Freud referred to it thus:

"I am therefore inclined to adhere to the view that the fear of death should be regarded as analogous to the fear of castration and that the situation to which the ego is reacting is one of being abandoned by the protecting super-ego—the powers of destiny—so that it has no longer any safeguard against all the dangers that surround it" (Freud, 1926, p.57).

The apprehension that arises in the face of desire is experienced as anxiety. Anxiety is apprehension of what the other yearns for in the subject, as subjects we are ignorant of that desire (Lacan, 27/6/1962). The subject is captive in this gaze, captive to being the other's object of desire, without knowing what it is. He will try to be that same object of desire that identifies with object a.

Identification with the unique trait—the signifier—acts as a mediation that preserves the subject from that gaze. Simplicity, distinctness of the trait, is what we put into the Real, whether or not the subject wants it, Lacan says, and we become that trait. This is our being. This is precisely the fragile and rickety thing that stands between us and the Real, the field of the signifier. So who are we without the identifications?

3) Identification with a feeling or with a situation; The connection between the two "I's"; hysterical identification with desire as the desire of the Other. This identification is based on the possibility or upon the desire of the I to put itself in the place of the other. Freud brought the well-known example of the boarding school girls, one of whom receives a love letter and all of whom are infected with hysteria (Freud, 1921, p.107). One self creates significant identification with another at a particular point, in openness to a similar emotion in our example. The identification that is constructed at this point under the influence of a pathological situation is displaced by a symptom that one self-created and the rest were infected with.

The research on hypnosis, falling in love, and groups led

Freud to compare the identification that establishes or enriches the subject, with the opposing tendency—in which the object is placed in the position of the ideal self. For example, in the case of the leader that replaces the ideal self of the members of the group; where mutual identification starts occurring between the group members, but there is a pre-condition for replacement. A subject can identify with objects, i.e., with a person, with a human characteristic or with a partial object. Everyone identifies with others in relation to the position of the leader. In this context Freud defines "masses" as joint hypnosis + identification with other individuals who have a similar attitude to the object.

Regarding the torus, in his seminar "L'insu," Lacan creates three ways of inverting the torus and clarifies that these transformations occur in relation to the three ways of identification (Lacan, 16/11/1976). When he develops these operations with the aid of topology, he emphasizes the structural isomorphism of the three identifications and describes each one's uniqueness.

Identification with the Real Other is the hysterical identification with the desire of the Other. Identification with the symbolic of the Real Other is identification with the unique trait. Identification with the Real Other is the way to obtain the name-of-the-father; in this context, Freud describes the connection between identification and love (Lacan, 1974-75, 18/3).

In "L'insu" Lacan shows how love takes the place of identification in the primeval father—the place of the initial connection with the object. The identification is not with the unconscious, but with the symptom. In *The Da Vinci Code*, Mary Magdalene is Jesus' symptom. In that seminar Lacan says; man knows woman through bedding her, thus becoming better acquainted with his self. And how does woman know man? Perhaps through the womb, since the woman creates the man. However this answer does not suffice, since although woman knows man maternally, how does she know herself? What is identification with the symptom for the woman?

Now something may be said about Directing the Treatment and the future of psychoanalysis, as I see it. In his article "The Direction of the Treatment" (Lacan, 1966) Lacan shows Freud's confusion between identification and love, when he refers to the object of identification of the hysteric as the object of love—for example, Elizabeth von R.'s brother in law or Dora's Herr K. Only in the chapter on identification in *Group Psychology and the Analysis of the Ego* does Freud (according to Lacan) notice the third form of identification, which is conditioned by its function—supporting the desire. Freud shows us that the most trivial object can fulfill the role of the leader. Lacan uses the Christian metaphor (this apathetic object is the support of the object) devour my body, drink my blood. While passion remains the metonym of the lack in desire, the I is the metonym of desire.

Lacan is completely opposed to those psychoanalysts that contend that identification with the psychoanalyst indicates the conclusion of the analysis. On the contrary, he contends that not only is it *possible* to traverse the plane of identification (Lacan, 1964, p.273), but doing so is a necessary condition if analysis is to succeed. So the conclusion of analysis is characterized by what he refers to as dispossession of the subject. This refers to the moment when a question mark appears in relation to the subject's identifications, in such a way that it is no longer possible to maintain them in the same manner as before. At the conclusion of analysis it is preferable that identification is with the symptom—that same remnant of enjoyment, which cannot be interpreted, which enables a person to live.

In his XXII R.S.I. seminar, Lacan deserts linguistics in favor of topology. He adds one ring to the Borromean knot—a knot which cannot be described via the imagination, which is also beyond significance (Lacan, 1974-1975 7/12). Lacan develops identification with the symptom [Synthome], which is the holy man. In this seminar James Joyce is Lacan's example of choice of a holy man. By his rejection of an imaginary solution, he was able to conceive a new way of using language and organizing enjoyment.

Estela Solano-Suarez refers to identification with the symptom (Suarez 2001) as a new type of connection with the symptom. Psychoanalysis is a synthesis of knowledge gained from the appearance of the symptom. This is Real satisfaction of the libido. She asks, How can the symptom's attitude to the Real be touched? At the conclusion of analysis, what will the fate of the satisfaction of the drive be? What can occur to cause the symptom that represents what is most foreign to the subject to turn into identification at the conclusion of analysis. How can we be rid of the eroticization of thought? How can we stop getting involved with it and devolve it of its phallic value, with its enjoyment?

Julia Kristeva, in her beautiful book *In the Beginning there was Love: Psychoanalysis and Faith* (Kristeva, 1987, p.7) presents an etymological analysis of the word "analysis." From that it is perhaps possible to extract a Hebrew term for analysis—*the theory of separation.* On the etymological level, analysis is separation, from below, from above, lengthwise. Destroy, loosen, separate and pay. In Latin, pay is to atone for, to release. In Sanskrit, it is to cut, to divide, to annihilate. In Gothic, it is to lose. It causes the subject to pay the price that he/she is prepared to pay in order to discover that his/her complaints, symptoms, phantasms are expressions of love directed at an impossible other—deficient, regressed, incapable of fulfilling his/her demands and desires. Analysis then is the place that facilitates simultaneous separation as crossing (of the phantasm) and loss. The analytic symptom therefore separates between my identifications and myself.

An interesting statement is made in the forward of Polemus journal's edition on the subject of identification (Gesser, 2002, p.7)—"the subject does not find a satisfactory explanation for its existence. Therefore it must invent something in order to cope with this hole." Since it lacks being it will attempt to resemble someone and identify with that someone phantasmatically. This is what will determine its being. In the process of analysis according to Lacan, it is stated in a most pretentious way, that phantasm must be

Ruth Golan

crossed in order to bring about *the reduction of all of the person's ideals.*

At the conclusion of analysis the subject is divested of its identity. Various psychoanalysts caution us that this is liable to lead to mourning and depression, yet also to absolute loss of the boundaries of morality. In order to avoid this, Lacan proposes brotherhood of man, based on the most essential differences between us. Such a statement bears witness to the value of the perspective of identification—not merely to the shattering of identifications. So what is "brotherhood"? A new kind of identification? A new kind of ideal? What about Freud's contention in *Psychology of the Masses* where he enumerates the characteristics of the individual who identifies with the masses? Where he outlines the slackening of intellectual ability, the absence of inhibitions in expressing emotions, the inability to moderate and defer emotions, the tendency to transgress all boundaries when expressing and offloading emotions? Freud contends that these are different behaviors that reveal a picture of regression to an earlier stage of mental development. If that is so, what then of the intellectual and emotional regression that Freud speaks of? Perhaps there is a collective identification, which rather than merely creating a multitude, creates a higher level of consciousness?

To conclude I would like to consider this last possibility since to my mind it opens up the dead ends in psychoanalysis if, that is—psychoanalysis is prepared to consider it. In recent years more and more people have spoken of the experience of groups "connecting" with a different dimension, a new awareness, and an intelligence that is greater than the intelligence of each individual when separate—a kind of shared intelligence common to the group. This phenomenon is referred to in different ways—collective awareness, collective intelligence, enlightened communication, etc. This phenomenon is being encountered in groups and teams of varying sizes, in various situations and is being explored and developed by scientific researchers, business consultancies, social entrepreneurs, spiritual teachers as one. The phenomenon is occurring more frequently, apparently spontaneously in various groups and situations—from Jazz ensembles, competitive sports teams, work groups and even military units in critical situations. I have experienced it myself in various groups of which I am a member and I believe that this constitutes a new ring for the torus.

One of the researchers of this phenomenon, Robert Kenny, founder of the Consultation Institute for Leadership teams, describes it thus:

"When the group reaches a certain level of coherence, generally there's some higher level of order that comes into the room and it's very noticeable to people, It's like something has shifted. People stop fighting for airspace and there's a kind of group intuition that develops. It's almost like the group as a whole becomes a tuning fork for the inflow of wisdom" (Hamilton, 2004, pp. 55-57).

Another researcher, Otto Scharmer speaks of the phenomenon as encountered in management and development and innovative teams:

"More and more people are having this type of experience in the context of everyday work and professional settings. What's interesting today is that this kind of experience is something that no longer occurs in retreat from doing your real work, but in the midst of doing your real work—particularly when the work is related to profound social change and innovation" (ibid.).

The wonder of the implications of the phenomenon for realizing creative potential in team work, in a professional community, including the psychoanalytic community is evident in this account by a group participant, Laura Hartzell:

"I'm noticing a new way of working together, where our interest in what is possible—from the most creative to the most practical—comes deeply alive and our flow of ideas is like a dance, where we are each paying attention to one another, taking in the thinking and research that each individual has done prior to the meeting, and responding in such a way that we really come together. It is so far from any meeting I've ever had in any other work setting—and I don't know how it is happening—but we're able somehow to bring forward the ideas we have without being attached to them, and without our identity being wrapped up in them. It is as if this creative mind just sweeps down on us, and the more we pay attention to each other and keep open the space between us, something else happens" (ibid.).

Towards the end of his life, physicist David Bohm became more and more aware of the potential in the new kind of dialogue that he encountered:

"...[T]he possibility of transforming not only the relationship between people, but even more, the very nature of consciousness in which these relationships arise" (ibid.).

He referred to it as *dialogue,* meaning moving through.

This new form of dialogue is a key to a new form of mind, based on the development of a common discipline that can adjust at any given time in the process of dialogue. People do not oppose each other, neither can it be said that they are interacting. Rather they are participating in a pool of shared significance, a pool that is capable of unending development and change. The basic idea behind these dialogues is simple. A group sits together and explores a subject while meticulously observing a number of straightforward yet rather challenging guidelines such as temporarily putting aside one's opinions and ideas, listening attentively to what others are expressing and speaking authentically oneself.

By creating such a new form of collective intelligence a group can thus follow a thread of communication on a deeper level, a higher level of collective understanding that is coherent for the thought structures that underlie culture itself. Exploration of this possibility is likely to be essential for the continuance of civilization. Thus a higher human potential can be accessed, without the need to relinquish autonomy and individuality. Indeed not only are autonomy and individuality not suppressed in participating in such a group—they are strengthened.

Identification with the holy man will perhaps mean organizing enjoyment around identification with an evolutionary step forward of the consciousness beyond the private self. This is a new form of communication through identification and it still requires much study and research, spiritual, as well as psychoanalytical.

The woman's silence[13]

In the seminar Encore, XX, Lacan says: "*A woman can but be excluded by the nature of things, which is the nature of words, and it must be said that if there is something that women themselves complain about enough for the time being, that's it. It's just that they don't know what they are saying—that's the whole difference between them and me.*

"*The fact remains that if she is excluded by the nature of things, it is precisely in the following respect: being not whole, she has a supplementary enjoyment compared to what the phallic function designates by way of enjoyment.*

"[...] There is an enjoyment that is hers, that belongs to the 'she' that doesn't exist and doesn't signify anything. Here is an enjoyment that is hers about which she herself perhaps knows nothing if not that she experiences it—that much she knows. She knows it, of course, when it comes. It doesn't happen to all of them" (Lacan 1972-73, pp. 73-74).

I write this paper also as a woman, as the "excluded one" of the words, as she who doesn't know what she says. This

---

13 This chapter is based on the paper: "A Woman's Voice is Erva": The Female Voice and Silence – Between the Talmudic Sages and Psychoanalysis written by Admiel Kosman and Ruth Golan

is why I turn to male sources, to those who know what they say, and I read in the *Book of Numbers 5:11-31*, in a section called "the adulteress":

"...If any man's wife go aside, and commit a trespass against him, And a man lie with her carnally, and it be hid from the eyes of her husband, and be kept close, and she be defiled, and there be no witness against her, neither she be taken with the manner; And the spirit of jealousy come upon him, and he be jealous of his wife, and she be defiled: or if the spirit of jealousy come upon him, and he be jealous of his wife, and she be not defiled: Then shall the man bring his wife unto the priest, and he shall bring her offering for her... And the priest shall bring her near, and set her before the LORD:... And the priest shall set the woman before the LORD, and uncover the woman's head, and put the offering of memorial in her hands, which is the jealousy offering: and the priest shall have in his hand the bitter water that causeth the curse:... Then the priest shall charge the woman with an oath of cursing... And this water that causeth the curse shall go into thy bowels, to make thy belly to swell, and thy thigh to rot: And the woman shall say, Amen, amen."

What does the woman say during this event of testing and humiliation? "Amen, Amen." Her secret she does not reveal. She should be given the cursed water for it to come out. If she committed adultery her belly will swell, and if not, she will gain pregnancy and a male child.

Later, all along history, the minute the testing is not preformed any more but turns into a theoretical discussion

The Consciousness Bearers

between the sages of the Mishna and the Talmud or those who came after them, the ritual becomes one of humiliation and punishment in the form of measure for measure as far as the imagination and the enjoyment of men can go.

The discussion moved from being a divine religious test to a social punishment, from positioning in front of God to a positioning in front of the public. From a woman who sinned secretly, to a woman dripping with sexuality. The discussing men are carried away after their enjoyment without limitations.

For example, in the Tosefta 4a, the sages try to decide what is considered as sexual relations:

And how long is the duration in the matter of seclusion? Sufficient for misconduct, i.e., sufficient for coition, i.e., sufficient for sexual contact, i.e., sufficient for a person to walk round a date-palm. Such is the view of R. Ishmael; R. Eliezer says: Sufficient for preparing a cup of wine; R. Joshua says: Sufficient to drink it; Ben Azzai says: Sufficient to roast an egg; R. Akiba says: Sufficient to swallow it; R. Judah b. Bathyra says: Sufficient to swallow three eggs one after the other; R. Eliezer b. Jeremiah says: Sufficient for a weaver to knot a thread; Hanin b. Phineas says: Sufficient for a woman to extend her hand to her mouth to remove a chip of wood [from between the teeth]; Pelemo says: Sufficient for her to extend her hand to a basket and take a loaf therefrom. Although there is no proof for this [last opinion] there is an indication, viz., For on account of a harlot, to a loaf of bread.

This discussion sounds like a joke (Witz), like an absurdity. Metaphors of men standing impotent outside the closed door. One can feel the enjoyment of the Torah sages. One can see the drive peeping between the metaphors. They are carried away in their talking in order to make the woman's voice silent. The threat is constantly growing the more one puts borders and limitations. When the sages discuss in measure for measure in the ritual of the adulteress, they relate only to the sin of the body, and not to the emotional or spiritual cheating. For example, in Tosefta c' 5-4 the process of seduction is described in parallel to the process of ceremony.

I will quote only the seduction without words:

She stood at the entrance of her house to display herself to the man/ She wound a beautiful scarf about her head for him/ She beautified her face for him/ She painted her eyes for him/ She plaited her hair for him/ She signaled to him with her finger/ She girded herself with a belt for him/ She thrust her thigh towards him/ She received him upon her body/ She gave him the world's dainties to eat/ She gave him costly wine to drink in costly goblets/ She acted in secret.

In the section of "the adulteress" we find a construction of the erotic situation and turning the woman's body into a body full of drives—with no speaking. What happens to the adulteress? It seems that her main sin is the secret. The secret turns her into an erotic creature that drives the men crazy. We see in the Mishna and Talmud how they are carried away into plastic descriptions. The enigmatic erotic situation of the woman is threatening to disintegrate the symbolic order that is relying on the Law of the Father. What is therefore her punishment? To expose the passage between the erotogenic zones and the piece of flesh, to turn the drive into an animal instinct, to empty the woman's body from the symbolic order and return it to its objectal non-subjectal form.

Lacan speaks about the opposition between the body and the organism in terms of enjoyment, that is to say he puts the phallic enjoyment as opposed to the body enjoyment. At the beginning the hysterical body is unified, later it disintegrates according to the cutting lines that are determined by the Other. The body as Real shows itself only in an extraordinary way, for example in times of de-personalization. During this process part of the body becomes unrecognized, because the signifier is taken away from it. As a result of this procedure the subject needs to confront the Real of the flesh and the same with the uncanny who gives rise to Angst. The same process one can recognize in a hysterical disgust. If the body losses its erotic investment, its signifier, the hysterical subject responds in disgust to the Real in its own body.

The adulteress doesn't speak-the men don't allow her to have her own voice, since even a voice in a woman is Erva (nakedness). What, then, is the link between the feminine voice/speech and sexuality? Why was it often so important, even outside Jewish culture, to warn men about the dangers of the feminine voice and to try to repress it, as Sophocles concisely formulated shortly, "Women's glory is silence—and it is their beauty."

§ The threat of the "feminine" voice and music to "male" language and law

In a book on the history of women, the authors show how women's voices were scorned and imprisoned in an ethics that considered the sins of the tongue to be a source of lust and pride. Women who talked in public were thought to be diffusers of the poison of sins, and were condemned for it (Danielle Regnier-Bohler, 1992, p. 425). When in the Middle Ages, a quotation of a woman's speech was introduced in a man's text; it was often in order to emphasize its evil power.

One should understand that female voices were seen, not as the basis of significant speech, but as something that "transgresses the language boundaries," as they were defined by Regnier-Bohler. This point links us to a long-standing and general problem, when we look at the continuing struggle among different cultures throughout history with regard to music and voice. This struggle focuses on the demand that music and voice should not deviate from the words that give them meaning, lest the voice become meaningless and threatening, especially due to its power to seduce and intoxicate the spirit. Moreover, the voice "beyond meaning" is identified with "femininity," while the "meaningful" text with masculinity. The voice "beyond words" is considered as a meaningless, sexual and seductive instrument. It has an attractive and dangerous power, although it was also considered to be empty and frivolous.

In the Jewish sources we can find the strict view of the fourth century CE Babylonian sage R. Yoseph Bar-Hiya who states: "When men sing and women join it is licentiousness. When women sing and men join it is like fire in tow."

So, according to R. Joseph's interpretation, one should forbid women to participate together with men in a choir, because in his opinion, neither of the two possibilities, which arise, agrees with Jewish, sexual moral rules, even though the second possibility is worse.

This is how, for instance, Shmuel, who in the third century determined that "a woman's voice is Erva" (Babylonian Talmud, Ber. 24a). He makes a list of different things which are called "Erva," in a sense of exciting sexual provocation. He is inspired by The Song of Songs. In the end of the list he comes to the voice:[14]

Samuel said, A woman's voice is Erva, as it says 'For sweet is thy voice, and thy countenance is comely' (Cant. 2, 14). R. Shesheth said: A woman's hair is Erva, as it says 'thy hair is as flock of goats' (Cant. 4, 1).[15]

Rashi explains Shmuel's statement thus: "From the fact that the Bible is praising the beauty of woman in that way, we can deduce that this beauty is passion." That is to say, the fact that the sentence in the Song of Songs sees the voice of the beloved as a pleasant voice, and compliments it, means that this pleasantness can arouse sexual passion.

---

14 The term "Erva" comes from discovery and exposure, and was used in the original to mark incest taboos but its semantic meaning was enlarged to include any sexual prohibition or issue.
15 And in BT, Sanhedrin 45a they said that woman is totally Erva.

This statement, which identifies totally aesthetic pleasure and sexual arousal, is not obvious, and is not common to all ancient civilizations. Philo's position, for example, reflects a completely opposite position—one which maintains that the chanting of men and women together is not only prostitution, but even has in it an element of sacredness and religious sublimation. This duality passes through all of the different opinions in Judaism regarding of a woman's voice.

Because it was not possible to legitimize the female voice in society and law, interpreters and commentators described the spiritually provocative power of this voice in utopistic terms. This is how, for example, they could claim that a woman's voice is really a very spiritual voice for men—but it can be grasped only when certain conditions make it possible. These conditions will dominate man's world only in the future; when the sexual drive that serves to blur it will be canceled. This blurring prevents men from appreciating the spiritual vitality of a female voice. This blurring now is the result of male sexual fantasies upon hearing a female voice.

In this way one can present the fundamental tension between positions that see the woman's voice as spiritual and even divine and the positions that are threatened by this voice and present it as a seductive and dangerous voice.

In his paper "The Object Voice," M. Dolar (1996) cites

a few examples, which demonstrate that the voice was considered to threaten "the male order" of society, and music—like that of a voice without words—is considered to be feminine.

Already for Plato—as for most of the Greeks—the gender differentiation passes through music.[16] In Greece, only girls were allowed to play the flute, and the right audience for hearing this kind of music was women, because, when one plays the flute it is not possible to pronounce words. Men were expected to deal with philosophy.

We see later that the Christian tradition shared this conception. St. Augustine for example, writes that the voice is a source of danger and decadence, and that the cure for it is to adhere to the word—the divine word, of course—to make sure that the word will rule, and to get rid of the voice of that which is not connected to words.

Music in Christianity is considered something, which elevates the soul to the divine but can also lower it to sin,— "Delicta Carnis." In many texts, music represents the flesh in the most concrete way.

Opposing this rejecting conception, which sees music or voice without words as sinful and seductive, some of the Medieval mystics suggested a contrary paradigm. Music for them was conceived of as the only adequate way to attain devotion, because it aspires to God beyond words. This is

---

16 An early example is from the saying of the Chinese emperor Shun (2200 BC app.): "Let the music follow the sense of the words. Keep it simple and ingenuous. One must condemn pretentious music which is devoid of sense and effeminate."

the way to a limitless, eternal being. If God is the musical principle par-excellence, and of the word of God attains its true register only through the singing voice, then the radical result is that the word alone belongs to the "Satan." Hildegard von Bingen, a nun and composer of the 12th century, proposed this extreme conclusion.

Music can be the element of spiritual sublimating beyond this world and its representations, but it can also release, by the same token, the uncontrollable meaningless enjoyment beyond the sensual pleasures that can be represented. The voice, according to this conception, undermines every certainty and every institution of established meaning. It is limitless and is found of course on the feminine side.

J.A. Miller explains thus the contribution of Lacan to an understanding of the status of the voice as an object (Miller, 1989, pp.175-184). If Freud discovered the primal objects, the breast and excrement, in his study of neuroses, Lacan adds the objects "gaze" and "voice," in his study of psychosis. The voice appears as an object when it is the voice of the 'Other.' The voice is the element of language that cannot be assimilated into a part of the 'I,' so it is subjectively referred to as 'Other.' This is the haunting voice that represents surplus enjoyment. Castration means that one doesn't hear a voice in the 'Real,' which is to say; it is a situation of "deafness." So where is the instance of the voice when I speak? Not in the tone of speech. The voice lies precisely in what cannot be said. It inhabits language, it haunts language. It is enough to say something in order for it to become as uncanny as something that cannot be said. If we talk, chat, sing, and listen, it is connected, according to Lacan, to the fact that we try to hide what we can call "The voice in its function as 'object a.'" The voice contains the craving for the lost object, and it reveals what the words, which are part of the symbolic order, try to cover.

This strong tension between these two central conceptions of the voice in the Middle Ages was described by Regnier-Bohler (Regnier-Bohler, 1992, p.482):

"The language and haunting metaphors of pleasure provided a way of losing oneself in language while denying all capacity to use words. It was a sensual enterprise in which the soul, open to penetration, sought to make itself naked. The feminization of language resulted in the invention of a new vocabulary that expressed the absent through the extreme presence of the word. Humbly the mystics confessed that no language of love, no matter how determined to overcome the barriers of language, could fully express the joy of the mystical union with God. Courtly culture provided images and turns of phrase for expressing an emotion that no language could ever capture. Mystics therefore dreamed of discovering a more immediately comprehensible primal language; in so doing they developed a language of gestures, of inarticulate screams and cries."

§ The relation between "the voice of the father" and the feminine voice

In opposition to the feminine voice stands the voice of the 'Primal Father,' the voice of God. This is a voice that stresses the word, the logos; a commanding voice, which ties a bond and signs a pact. Lacan raises this issue in his seminar "On Anxiety" (Lacan, Seminar X, 1962-63), where he takes the sound of the *Shofar* as a metaphor. The sound of the *Shofar* is the "Voice of the Father"—the cry of the primal father of the herd, the "Leftover" that pursues and that also stands as the foundation of the law and seals it. The sound of the *Shofar* is the sign of the pact with the Lord that the community of believers signs. This is how it declares its recognition of the Lord, its surrender and its obedience to the Law. "Pure Law," before it commands specifically, is embodied in the 'Voice of the Father,' the voice that commands total obedience although it is meaningless by itself. The voice is a substitute for the impossible presence of the Lord, a presence that covers a substantial absence.[17]

---

17 The most significant sound of the *Shofar* in the Jewish tradition is the one that was blown on the occasion of the Sinaitic theophany. The *Shofar* in this establishing moment is what testifies to the presence of God for his people, because all they could hear was this terrible commanding voice, and only Moses could have spoken with the Lord and understood his sayings. The voice that is described in the Sinaitic theophany is a 'Real' voice: "And all the people saw the thundering, and the lightning, and the noise of the trumpet, and the mountain smoking, and when the people saw it they removed, and stood after off" (Exod. 20:18). *'object a'* in this instance was constructed in this impossible way from Voice and Gaze - the auditory drive and the specular drive blended together. To see the voices means that the voice has materiality, which it is of the "Real".

If the Word (logos) has to fight repeatedly with the voice as the carrier of the meaningless 'Other' of the 'Other,' feminine enjoyment, it can do so only by an implicitly leaning on this 'Other Voice,' the 'Voice of the Father,' which accompanies the law.

In this way the struggle is not between logos and voice, but between 'voice' and 'voice'—'The Voice of the Father' against the 'Feminine Voice.' Is the 'Voice of the Father' inherently different from the 'Feminine Voice'? Is the pursuing voice inherently different from the pursued voice? Dolar suggests the possibility that perhaps they are both identical (Dolar, 1966, p.7). There is only one voice object that attaches itself and splits the Other from the outside and from the inside. "And why not interpret the face of the 'Other,' the face of God, as supported by the feminine enjoyment?" asks Lacan in his late teachings (Lacan, 1972-73, p. 95).

And so, feminine and male positions are maybe two ways to approach the same impossibility—two related versions of the same voice which guards deliberate dimness.

The Ten Commandments were written in a speech act. This is the link between the 'Real' and the Word that is of the symbolic order. The speech act helps us understand the reference Lacan makes to the 'Real' in the symbolic and the symbolic in the 'Real.' Speech is symbolic and the act is 'Real.'

§ Conclusion: A psychoanalytic view of the relationship to the woman's voice in Jewish sources

It is possible to realize to what extent the tension between different approaches in the Jewish thought is a case study of the general psychoanalytic discussion relating to 'object a,' which is the voice.

The psychoanalytic insights of Freud and Lacan concerning the object of the drive can help us understand how this tension between the different interpreters in the Jewish tradition relating to the woman's voice, was created: a tension that we called: "a woman's voice is Erva" as opposed to "a woman's voice is Erga (craving)" (a play on words in Hebrew). As we have seen, this tension is not unique to the Jewish sources, but arises on the surface in different times and different cultures.

The Jewish sources, in referring directly and clearly to the woman's voice as carrying seductive sexual quality, help us understand the psychoanalytic assertion on the sexual quality of the search for *object a*, in this case the voice.

There is a threatening aspect to the 'Feminine Voice,' a threatening element to the symbolic order in traditional Jewish society, which is represented by the prohibitions that are related to the performance of the rituals while hearing this voice.

The Consciousness Bearers

On the other hand, we saw that many traditional sources relate, even though in an utopic way, to the woman's voice as carrying a "sublime" quality. Our claim is that precisely because the woman does not fall completely under the "Law of the father," she can represent a possibility of "liberation" which makes the touch with the 'Real' possible, a touch without which the artist cannot create, and the religious man cannot reach devotion to the Lord. The psychoanalytic conception of 'Feminine Enjoyment' as 'an-other' enjoyment also links the feminine voice and the artistic and mystical voice.

This element in the woman's voice is threatening for the symbolic male world quite as much as the sexual seduction, because it presents a kind of *transgressive craving* to disintegrate the accepted symbolic order. It is important to remember that even those interpreters who are ready to admit in the woman's voice a spiritual quality had to work to cancel its sexually seductive aspect.

There is a relation between 'object a,' which is the object of the drive, and the 'Other' which represents the Law, the ideal, and one can say that which represents the "male" God. The craving after the ideal, the belief that the 'Other' 'Has' it (he knows, he is potent, he determines) is responsible for most of the human suffering expressed in symptoms or in negative emotions such as envy and hatred.

In opposition to this 'Other', feminine enjoyment represents the psychic fact that the 'Other' doesn't 'exist' (and to the extent that he exists it is perceived as not whole)—an idea that Lacan developed in his 20th seminar (Lacan, 1972-73, p. 60).

Feminine enjoyment is seen in this context as the signifier of the lack in the 'Other,' as in Lacan's matheme S($\bar{A}$). So when one makes place for feminine enjoyment and doesn't silence it, the 'Other,' as whole, as ideal, falls and the possibility is opened for liberation from paralyzing negative emotions.

So, in light of these findings, it is clear that the 'utopic' description existing in the interpretative texts that we have presented on the possibility that woman's voice will lose its threatening quality in the eyes of men, that 'the time' will come when men will be able to see (through the screen of phallic search after 'object a') its spiritual quality—'The Infinite.'

This interpretation represents deeply the male 'craving' to that same 'utopic' situation—a situation where listening to the 'Feminine Voice' will teach men other spiritual possibilities which usually those who are under the phallic function are barred against.

part II

Psycho-Evolution

"The most beautiful and deepest experience a man can have is the sense of the mysterious. It is the underlying principle of religion as well as of all serious endeavour in art and science. He who never had this experience seems to me, if not dead, then at least blind. To sense that behind anything that can be experienced there is a something that our minds cannot grasp, whose beauty and sublimity reaches us only indirectly: this is religiousness. In this sense I am religious. To me it suffices to wonder at these secrets and to attempt humbly to grasp with my mind a mere image of the lofty structure of all there is."

A. Einstein

From Albert Einstein's *My Credo* (1932)[18]

---

18 Courtesy of the Albert Einstein Archives, Hebrew University of Jerusalem, Israel.

§ Psychoanalysis on the Ladder of the Evolution of Consciousness

When Sigmund Freud was a twenty-nine year old neurologist, he went to Paris to study with Charcot.[19] In his letters to his fiancée he wrote "I am looking for something new." What characterized Freud throughout his life and research was the constant search for something new, the desire to find a new way of understanding the human psyche. The short time he stayed with Charcot engendered in him a big shift. From a neurologist he became a pathologist and turned his attention from interest in research of the brain to researching the depths of the psyche.

Freud didn't underestimate the importance of the brain but attempted, in all his researches, articles, as well as his thoughts, to prove that the brain and the psyche are one.

Jacques Lacan, who was a psychiatrist that began to teach at the end of Freud's life, dedicated his teachings to what he called *the return to Freud*. In this apparent return, he literally anchored Freud's discoveries in a new context, thereby going far beyond Freud. Throughout his researches he hoped to create new grooves and his teaching never stopped evolving. One can see in his psychoanalytic inquiry the development of the context, the teachings, and

---

19 Jean-Martin Charcot (1893-1925, French MD, neurologist and a psychiatrist. He achieved international acclaim in the domain of psychiatry and neurology. In the Salpetriere hospital he established the first of its kind in Europe neurological ward. He contended that hysteria is a hereditary neurological illness, he used hypnosis to raise a hysterical state and he would show it as examples in his lectures. Freud of course disagreed with him.

the praxis of psychoanalysis.

What characterizes Freud and Lacan, throughout their many years of work, was therefore the ongoing development of their teachings, the fact that it was based on clinical observations and a search for the new. They even conceptualized the results of the psychoanalytic cure according to "the new," i.e., an invention of new knowledge about the psyche, an invention of new love, an ability to create the new and so forth.

I contend that psychoanalysis has no meaning without taking into account the context of the evolution of consciousness; when we look at the values to which the analysis is directed, those are the things that emerge: recognition of repetition compulsion, the fall of ideals, renouncing pathological narcissism, recognition of the partiality and limitations of various desires and cutting the identification with them—that is to say—freedom, taking responsibility for our enjoyment, the invention of knowledge and the invention of new love.

Psychoanalytic practice is focused on liberation from the personal complaint and enlarging the point of view to include the universal structure of neurosis and psychosis. What is the goal of psychoanalysis if not to stop repetition, to liberate oneself from fixations, to create space for the movement of desire, to raise the representations of the drive to new metaphors? This liberation can become the foundation for the emergence of a new authentic dimension. The main difficulty of psychoanalysis is to observe itself and its context of values.

One way of defining psychoanalysis is as a kind of psychic motion. To be more precise, psychoanalysis deals with the conflict between the dynamics of progress, regression, closed cycles, and deadlock—a dynamic of internal and external events of drives and representations, occurring within the framework of time.

Psychoanalysis is founded on three postulates: on the dominant influence of infantile sexuality on life, on the unconscious and on transference-resistance as a paradigm of relationship.

In parallel, **the concept of the Evolution of Consciousness is based on three postulates**: on the constant drive to develop, on the choice of Authentic Self instead of ego, and on the potential for development which is a result of the union between the autonomy of the individual and the communion between people which transcends ego. This theory deals with only one kind of motion—a spiral upward motion.

The psychoanalytical perspective derives from the relative dimension. The point of view of the approach that includes conscious evolution and is called "*Evolutionary Enlightenment*" is founded on the absolute dimension. It has neither boundaries nor limitations.

A well-known saying of Freud's is found in a letter to the prominent philosopher Binswanger. Freud made the distinction between psychoanalysts and philosophers stating:

"I have always lived on the ground floor and in the basement of the building—you maintain that changing one's viewpoint one can also see an upper floor housing such distinguished guests as religion, art and others...If I had another life of work ahead of me, I would dare to offer even those high born people a home in my lowly hut" (Freud E., 1960, p.431).

If Freud was still with us, I would want to tell him that life has taught me that the other way around is also true. Dealing with the sewage reveals its spiritual dimension, or more precisely the high/low division is another one of these apparent dichotomies that fall apart when examined closely. The human psyche has both its upper levels and its dungeons and our task is to choose the direction of ethical hierarchy, because the fundamental questions of each domain are of an ethical nature: "Who am I and how shall I live?

Psychoanalysis and the evolution of consciousness: points for contemplation

1. Psychoanalysis influenced self-awareness in a fundamental way. The way in which a human being thinks about himself and the world is immersed in the discoveries of psychoanalysis.

2. Psychoanalysis has no clear worldview as to the direction of change. Is it dealing with the way we should live our lives? with our position towards life? How do we want to relate to our analysts or to ourselves at the end of analysis? (not personally but structurally). Do we want to be able to be interested in life, to have the ability to be flexible, not to be stuck in pathological situations, hold larger perspective on life, and have the ability to control our drives, live without idealizations? Do we want to feel the wish to contribute to the further development of culture? less attachment to the ego—weakened narcissism and an enhanced ability to love? to know the weak points in our structure and to know how to avoid getting trapped in them? to reduce the repetition compulsion? to identify with our symptom, i.e., to accept ourselves?

In retrospect, after years of psychoanalysis, has all this happened to us? has it happened to our patients?

3. The invention of Psychoanalysis was a great evolutionary leap—but still partial. What happens when one doesn't stop when confronting castration anxiety? is a transformation of position towards one's own enjoyment the end of the way? or, what is the desire of the analyst? to help others reach all this? to deepen the ability of self-reflection? to broaden the boundaries of matter possessing self-knowledge?

4. Have fundamental transformations occurred over the years? Do we, psychoanalysts, even aspire for this to happen?

5. Within the individual we can observe a development of self-consciousness and evolutionary leaps—in his capacity to suffer and to embrace more complexity and larger perspectives. At certain points fixation is created and development stops; From a certain stage, if we don't act there will be no more conscious evolution.

6. What is the current context of psychoanalysis? What are its basic postulates in our times? The world hasn't stopped changing since the time of its establishment. It has been changing and that change is becoming exponential—at least where human culture is concerned.

7. We treat people who suffer from fixation in their self-awareness, and we try to liberate it so it can continue to develop. Lacan contended that one can bring someone else only up to the point where he does not want to know anything more about his unconscious. But there is more to know. The context can be enlarged. A spiritual context can be seen in the universe, a post-personal context. Why stop? There are those who are ready to continue—if the analyst is ready to continue himself. Personal example is crucial. Nobody can make another person go further than he himself has gone.

8. What are our therapeutic values? is it important for us for our patient to develop values? values such as avoiding hurting others, consideration for others, seeing the other, giving importance to where we are speaking from—self-image—or focusing on the subject of discussion, responsibility towards the other, towards oneself, transition from the consumerism that leaves us frustrated to the economics of giving.

9. Psychoanalysis focuses on the cut, on the split. The teachings of evolution of consciousness offer a perspective on world which goes beyond the cut. It suggests the possibility of union while cultivating autonomy.

What is evolution?

All time is one body and space is one book
—Sri Aurobindo

According to Webster's dictionary, the word *evolution* is etymologically connected to the Latin word *ēvolvere*, which indicates an act of unfolding or opening a scroll. Evolution is the transition in time from simpler modes of organization to more complex ones. For example—transition from sub-atomic particles which unite to become atoms. Atoms in their turn unite to create molecules, molecules unite to create cells, and cells unite to create organisms.

Other aspects of evolution are for example more complex and more branched interrelations with the environment, and the rule of simpler organizational forms included within more complex organizational forms.

§ Emergent Evolutionism

"Emergent Evolutionism is a doctrine first brought into prominence by Loyd Morgan as an interpretation of the history of nature (Morgan, 1923). It was designed in part to cope with the influence of Darwinism on philosophy by providing a way in of interpreting evolution without having recourse to mechanistic... ideas.

...Classical Darwinism assumed that all changes in living beings takes place gradually... Emergent Evolutionists maintain that such events must be discontinuous with what went before. Whatever comes to be for the first time must do so suddenly or abruptly.

The concept of emergence implies that the variety, divergence and complexity engendered by evolution are irreducible" (The Encyclopedia of Philosophy 1967, vol. 2, p. 474).

The process is irreversible. The lizard can never go back to being a fish. From time to time the evolutionary process creates things that have never before existed. This is true in regard to the level of human consciousness as well as the mineral/biological level.

Every emergent being brings something new to the world. When one relates to the characteristic that emerges as new, it doesn't mean only a new order of pre-existing elements or characteristics, even though this new arrangement can be one of the conditions which determine it. It means that the new characteristic is qualitative and not only quantitative, it differs from what has existed in cosmic history, and furthermore, it is unpredictable. The unpredictability of a new characteristic means that one can-

not understand the occurrence with existing tools. That is to say, we lack the suitable hardware.

The emergence of the new, according to emergent evolutionists, is a sign of radical contingency in nature. New characteristics always attach themselves to organic wholes, which are more than the sum of their parts. The existence of such wholes cannot be explained, or is perhaps the result of a primordial agency of "creating a whole" in the cosmic work. As we shall see, this description of biological evolution is wonderfully congruent with the evolution of consciousness.

Even when speaking about the evolution of consciousness, we mean that the more complex forms carry within themselves a higher consciousness, that is to say, a larger point of view. The changes are usually small, but once in a while big leaps happen. This occurs when elements from the former level of consciousness unite in a new kind of connection, at a higher level of consciousness.

§ What is Consciousness?

History is a split with nature that was created due to the emergence of consciousness. —Jacob Christoph Burckhardt

The interiority of the Cosmos
In Webster's dictionary, as well as in The Encyclopedia of Philosophy, consciousness is defined as human wakefulness

or self-knowledge of the human being. In the Hebrew *Even-Shoshan Dictionary* it is defined as awareness, the entirety of concepts, sensations and thoughts of the human being and also as his spiritual life system.

The teachings of the Evolution of Consciousness define consciousness as the interiority of the cosmos. Human consciousness is located in a continuum of consciousness and is a specific area in the cosmic field of consciousness. It can be also defined as the absolute element of reality or as a field which includes all that exists. In this respect consciousness is the universal subject, as well as the particular subject.

The evolutionary process is also a deep-time process of development and unfolding of higher levels of consciousness.

What is self-reflective consciousness?

In *"An Essay Concerning Human Understanding"* Locke defined consciousness as *"The perception of what passes in a man's own mind"* (The Encyclopedia of Philosophy 1967, vol. 2, p. 191).

Consciousness or reflection is a person's observing or noticing the "internal operations" of his own mind.

Through consciousness, human beings acquire ideas concerning different actions or mental states, like ideas about perception, thought, doubt, contention, knowledge and will. Thus we learn about our mental states at a given time:

"It might properly enough be called 'internal sense' because the understanding turns inward upon itself, reflects on its own operations, and makes them the object of its own contemplation."

This concept was embraced by the British philosophers, who started using the term "Introspection" around the end of the 19th century.

According to G. Stout for example: "To introspect is to attend to the workings of one's own mind" (ibid. p.192).

When one examines the history of the universe and human history, one inevitably comes to the conclusion that consciousness evolves. As for our times, it seems that human beings are the cutting edge of evolving consciousness, since only in humans consciousness reached a level where it has become introspective and reflective. At its current level, consciousness can know itself only through humans, so along with free choice and individuation, a unique situation has evolved wherein the new level of consciousness, the creative next step of evolution, can only occur if we freely agree to create it. That is to say—the continuation of the evolution of consciousness depends on us.

Consciousness is the pure subject. How do you think about a subject? how do you experience a subject? I, who am I? The child, until he is three years old, the sleeping man or the man in a coma do not experience consciousness, but it is nevertheless there. In every place where there is life. There are differences in the level and intensity of experience. The experience evolves. But does consciousness itself evolve or only the experience of it? Consciousness is primary. What of the unconscious? An inherent hole in consciousness—a hole that creates a difference.

From the ocean of consciousness pieces come out for embodiment in bodies, for self-knowledge, and then return to the ocean. So when we die nothing happens. Consciousness remains the same. It dis-embeds itself from the body but it is still present! The essence of consciousness is simultaneously whole and empty. It is absolute. Experience is an experience of knowing or of connectedness. What is this knowing in an evolutionary context? its intensity, width, depth are changing. What is the thing we know? the source of life.

To enlarge consciousness so that it will not focus on any object and then to return it to itself. To observe the observer. It has an absolute nature which is beyond the human being but exists also within as a part of him. I am part of that. Life's importance is as an expression of consciousness. Death loses its importance. Because consciousness endures. It goes on, it is opening, it knows itself more and more. It never actually goes anywhere. Thoughts, pathological neurosis, all pass to the background. The leading actor is consciousness. This is the meaning of the freedom of the one who is aware of that. The one who "dances with consciousness" is the universal human being who is part of the whole cosmos. Knowledge preceded the world. Knowledge was cast in letters, and then came the act of putting in place. Not all knowledge exists in letters. There are unspoken remains. This is why there is a hole. But in knowledge itself there is no hole.

A person is born into language. Language behind which lies the potential to know. God is hiding his face. Language bars to us the possibility of knowing without an object. Knowledge aspires to be known. For that it needs a place and a vehicle. Consciousness is the fixed and absolute thing in our life and beyond us. But there is a kind of consciousness within us, which is why we can identify it and feel ecstatic happiness or a sense of completion. Consciousness which precedes us needs and wants to be expressed. This is the reason it should be placed and enter language. On one side language alienates consciousness from itself, on the other side it allows it to get to know itself. Awareness is always partial and lacking, but there is knowledge of the whole. Knowing is the primal mode of awareness.

In consciousness without boundaries—the same encounters the same. We have from the One inside us (Lacan—Il y'a de l'un), and there is One knowing inside us. All that is needed is to listen deeply beyond the mind and the emotions. Simply. There is a direct and unmediated way of knowing. At a later stage the placing in language and space brings with it some mediation, but also facilitates. Consciousness itself is not a relation, it is not partial and it does not relate. Therefore the bond that is created between it and us is not a dual bond. We are it; Or as we can say—*the primary or central thing in us is consciousness. All the agencies—conscious, unconscious, already belong to the relative level. They arrive after it takes its place. Taking place creates boundaries and limitations. But there are sparks of the absolute. And there is a possibility of knowing what "to do with" (savoir fair—practical knowledge)—not with the symptom but with that very same knowing, or better still—to turn this knowing into a new symptom. There is enjoyment which is not tied up with pain—but still it's beyond our capacity to give it word or to give it significance. Recognizing consciousness, its absolute nature, allows me to feel safe regarding the question "who am I?" and after that comes "what is my role?" I can only be accountable to myself, but isn't this "self" also the one absolute consciousness?*

The transition from neurotic lack to the hole in the Real is not the end. One can go beyond it. When you go beyond the hole—you reach the whole, you reach consciousness. You cannot understand it only with your mind. There is an experiential dimension which is open for anyone ready to remove their attention from their full and complicated world, personality, actions and relationships—to an empty place—to stillness. How can one know what to do with this knowing of the pure subject?

The experience of consciousness, or the encounter with it, demands you direct your attention to it. This is the reason for the need for stillness and detachment, and most of all there is a need to peel layers of cynicism and apriority of knowing. All the fears and desires change their priorities, they pass into the background. There is confidence in the inherently perfect nature of life.

§ Some guidelines regarding the history of the evolution of consciousness

The idea of the evolution of spirit and consciousness was discussed by philosophers even before the discovery of evolution by Darwin. German idealist philosophers of the 18th and the beginning of the 19th century such as Kant, Fichte, Hegel and others were engaged with these ideas. It was clear to them that reality as a whole acts in certain tendencies in an essential way.

In 1697 Leibnitz wrote:
"A cumulative increase of the beauty and universal perfection of the works of God, a perpetual and unrestricted progress of the universe as a whole must be recognized, such that it advances to a higher state of cultivation.... As for the objection which may be raised, that if this is true the world will at some time already have become paradise, the answer is not far to seek: even though many substances shall have attained to a great degree of perfection, there will always, on account of the infinite divisibility of the continuum, remain over in the abyss of things parts hitherto dormant, to be aroused and raised to a greater and higher

condition.... And for this reason progress will never come to an end..." (De rerum originatione radicali, 1697).

In 1755 Kant wrote:
"The matter which appears to be merely passive and without form and arrangement has even in its simplest state an urge to fashion itself by a natural evolution into a more perfect constitution" (*Allgemeine Naturgeschichte*, 1755).

In 1800 Shelling wrote:
"Has creation a final goal? And if so, why was it not reached at once? Why was the consummation not realized from the beginning? To these questions there is but one answer: Because God is Life, and not merely Being. All life has a destiny, and is subject to suffering and to becoming... But in the actualization (of Being) through opposition there is necessarily a becoming" (Philosophical Inquiries Into the Nature of Human Freedom, 1809).

According to Hegel, the tendency of development is towards more and more intensive expressions of the Universal Spirit in a world of time and space. I will expand on Hegel's theory of development as an example, and I will consider it in contrast to the thinking of Levinas.

§ The Evolution of consciousness (Hegel) and of revelation (Levinas)

Without doubt Hegel was the dominant Western philosopher to engage with the evolutionary perspective on consciousness.

In *The Introduction to the Phenomenology of Spirit:* Yirmiahu Yovel says:

"In Hegel's own self-understanding, the social world and it's evolution, while crucially important, are embodied within a larger project, in which being itself is supposed to attain a more actual and manifest state" *(Yovel, 2000 p.3)*.

For Hegel, evolution takes place in both dimensions—the relative and the absolute:

"...absolute being, because it is a subject, is not immediately identical with itself, nor is it static, finished totality—as it is for Spinoza—but exists as a becoming totality. This means that the entirety of being—the immanent God—constitutes it's self-identity by becoming other than itself both in its otherness and as a result of its own development" *(ibid. pp.23-24)*.

Being for Hegel is not a noun but a path, a way, a verb. It exists as a process. It is not pre-given in its perfect state but gradually realized. Like being, the absolute entity is a result of the process of its own movement and self-becoming.

Yovel explains:

"...the movement in question is not only the movement of something in being, but the movement of being itself—its development toward higher levels of actuality. In its lower stages, being's subjective character, that is, its self-actualization movement, is manifest in the organic domain: the phenomenon of life. In its higher stages it is a historical movement—the movement of culture, practical life, social forms, and institutions, and the consciousness they express or embody. And at still a higher stage this is the movement of self-consciousness, pure contemplative cognition, and absolute Spirit" *(ibid. p.18).*

As I wrote previously, one cannot solve tension in a set of concepts at the same level at which the tension was created. The tension will be solved at the new level, that will also include part of the logic of the previous one.

Hegel writes:
"In this way, the activity of knowledge is the cunning which, while seeming to abstain from all activity watches how the [specific] determination is living it's concrete life in the belief that it is promoting its own particular interests and self-preservation, while actually doing the opposite, namely, dissolving itself into a moment of the whole" (Hegel, 2000, pp.170-171).

For Hegel, the whole is the real. This whole includes the process of becoming itself as well as the factor of entity, with which it stands in a dialectic relationship. The equation he constructs is whole=truth=good, and the good is also connected to the concept of urgency. He who receives the Good must respond urgently.

The Consciousness Bearers

Urgency is not a limit that bars freedom, but it testifies, more than freedom, more than the isolated subject which freedom establishes, to responsibility one cannot deny, beyond any obligation. In this respect begins the undermining of the totally separate subject. To be myself, for Hegel, means to be responsible beyond anything I have done.

Responsibility is also a central concept for Levinas, though Levinas argues with the Hegelian conception of the whole or the "totality" with his concept of ethical "infinity" which is "revealed in the human being's face." According to Levinas, the human face is not a phenomenon like any other phenomenon in the world. According to his description, when I see a human being I exist inside an ethical experience. The other's face is a supreme moral imperative for me, an imperative which constantly refers back to me. The "totality," i.e., the world's order which denies the "oppressed people's tears," is cracked, and the human morality is measured by his willingness to respond to the call and to say: *Here I am!*

To Hegel, the mind is a negative principle from which emanates the subject, whom he defines as a negating activity (similar to Lacan's subject, who is defined as a "lack of being").

Yovel explains:

"Understanding (the intellect) is the negative principle which constructs the worlds by undermining the compact monotony of being and generating distinctions, diversity and movement" (ibid. p.128).

Therefore, the mind is a principle of entropy. The mind is also the principle of split and tear in life and in consciousness; it creates a split within consciousness, between man and his world, between the finite and the infinite, between the subject and the object and so forth.

Levinas contrasts awareness (which is connected to the mind) and the innocent deed: he goes against the idealization of awareness in the Western culture.

"But opinion, recognized as the sole enemy because it takes advantage of credulity and ignorance, legitimates, if one can put it this way, this all-encompassing curiosity, this unlimited and anticipatory indiscretion which constitutes knowledge, seat of the a priori and of the fact. It makes us forget the unsavory joy of knowledge, its immodesty, the abdications and incapacities that were her lot in times of dangers and catastrophes" (Levinas, 1968, p.34).

In contrast to awareness he places the innocent deed, which he calls "the generous spontaneity in its pureness." The act is not conditioned by awareness but by what Levinas calls "Revelation," which in my opinion is another name for enlightenment—or for an act (in the psychoanalytic sense).

In this context he says:

"It may be, however, that the notion of action, instead of indicating praxis as opposed to contemplation, a move in the dark, leads us to an order in which the opposition of engagement and disengagement is no longer decisive and which precedes, even conditions, these notions."

This will lead us to Revelation: "Revelation...must comprise elements which no reason can discover. Consequently, these elements must rest on an island of fideism or in a blind confidence in the transmitter of these elements" (ibid. p.36).

The Talmudic issue that Levinas raises in the context of revelation interprets a seemingly innocent phrase from the revelation of Sinai:

"And they stopped at the foot of the mountain...Rav Abdimi bar Hama bar Hasa has said: This teaches us that the Holy One, Blessed be He, inclined the mountain over them like a tilted tub and that He said: If you accept the Torah, all is well, if not here will be your grave" (Talmud Bavli, Shabbat section, p.71-72, 88).

And Levinas asks:

"Is one already responsible when one chooses responsibility?"

Does freedom start in a state of freedom?

"The Torah or death," "the truth or death," would not be a dilemma that man gives himself. This dilemma would be imposed by force or by the logic of things...That which must be received in order to make freedom of choice possible cannot have been chosen, unless after the fact."

Free choice itself, which is the pre-condition for the free deed, is not revealed before the deed but after it—in retrospect.

"In the beginning was violence...Reason would rest either on violence or on a mode of consent that cannot be reduced to the alternative liberty—violence and whose betrayal would be threatened by violence. Wouldn't Revelation be precisely a reminder of this consent prior to freedom and non-freedom?" *(ibid. p.37)*

A revelation is therefore an act of memory. A memory of the initial agreement, similar to Freud's initial positive response to the beginning of life—his concept of Bejahung, similar to the initial "Yes!" which is the expression of the creative impulse in its essence.

This initial agreement signifies a third way which is other than wisdom and compulsion but is not identical to lack of wisdom. This is the meaning of act in psychoanalysis as well as in evolutionary enlightenment. Not only that joining precedes inquiry, but action precedes joining. It is located beyond freedom. As Levinas contends, agreeing to freedom not only expresses a human possibility, but it determines the essence of reality. The act of the people of Israel of agreeing to receive the Torah is the act that gives reality its significance. Receiving the Torah precedes knowing it. This is outrageous to one's sense of reason but according to Levinas it is the quality of every inspired action. Reversing the accepted timing of agreeing and knowing implies transcendence beyond awareness—a different transcendence than a return to infantile innocence.

Hegel implements his evolutionary teachings on human development in society and culture:[20] The process Hegel unfolds proceeds towards true consciousness that requires certainty. In order to reach certainty, the process of mutual recognition is required. For that a process of looking for

---

20 Written from a lecture by Adam Tenenbaum, Jerusalem 2002.

one's self in the other must occur, and with that a renewed recognition of one's self. This is a dual process of both the other and of myself. Hegel described this process as a life and death battle in which self-awareness and life are two dimensions, differentiated and split into two sides of mastery and slavery.

Mastery is not bound by particular thing in existence and it is not attached to life with any devoutness. It is characterized by willingness to risk life and bet on it. It is an attempt to transcend life and to look fearlessly in the face of death. For the master life is important for itself, for freedom, for awareness.

Slavery is a refusal to bet on life. It is an attempt to keep life and a will to preserve life as a result of turning it into a kind of service.

The truth of mastery is attached to slavery. Slavery is what gives significance to history due to the work of preserving life and meaning. Slavery makes history possible due to the imperative of the sacredness of life, work, postponement of pleasure, limiting danger, honoring death.

According to Hegel, the condition for any meaning, history and truth, lies in the dialectics of mutual recognition between mastery and slavery. The master wagers on life for his identity, and the slave enslaves his identity for life. This has significance concerning object choice and enjoyment. The master is the one who enjoys, and the slave withholds his desire and postpones the disappearance of the object of his desire. Instead of enjoying the object of desire, he preserves it.

The slave therefore cannot enjoy himself immediately, whenever he feels like it, but only after a process of work. Every process of work implies holding back desire and postponing satisfaction. In order to prevent the disappearance of the object of desire, the work demands the sublimation of desires. To work means to withhold and postpone enjoyments, to put limits on dangers, to honor death whenever one needs to face it.

Hegel contrasts meaningless life and death with meaningful life and death. The meaning is constructed in the process of molding the master's truth and self-awareness. Life becomes essential for self-awareness precisely as self-awareness becomes essential for life. A new concept of life is created, which includes abundance and surplus of enjoyment which digress from wisdom. That is to say, the mutual recognition and the collaboration of the master and the slave create a development of self-awareness and meaning. Essential life, meaningful life, joins the biological existence, restrains it, and recruits it to work for the establishment of full self-awareness, truth and meaning.

Real human freedom begins with the suppression of enslaving selfishness. This requires the undermining of the value of separate personal will, lowering the value of selfishness, of self desire. All these constitute a necessary stage in the molding of a human being. This is a taming which breaks the persistent will for freedom, for rationality and for preparing the human being for self-regulation. He who lacks courage to die for his freedom remains in a state of slavery. This is the negative side of freedom, while the positive side is in rationality, in reaching the post-personal generalness.

In Ken Wilber's words—the slave exists in the horizontal realm of translation and legitimating, i.e., enlarging meaning and the master exists in the domain of vertical transformation and revolution. [21] The slave makes the vertical leap of the master possible, while the master creates new possibilities for certainty and liberation from slavery.

§ The evolution of consciousness in the 20th century

In the 20th century, the prominent philosophers that were engaged in the evolution of consciousness were the Indian philosopher Sri Aurobindo, the French philosopher Henry Bergson and the French paleontologist and priest Teilhard de Chardin.

Bergson and De Chardin used the scientific understanding of evolution in order to follow the evolution of the concept of God through the cosmological, biological, psycho-social and transcendental domains. The main works in this context are Bergson's *Creative Evolution* and De Chardin's *The Human Phenomenon* (Bergson 1911, De

---
21 See "Horizontal and Vertical transformation" in the chapter "Eppur si muove!" in this book.

Chardin 1940).

Bergson (1859-1941) developed a philosophy based around the concept of "Creative Evolution." He describes the relationships between life and matter while differentiating between our conceptual recognition of the outside world and consciousness as we know it from the inside. The mind, when scientifically researching the outside world, uses two tools: analysis and selection. In order to make analysis possible, it is necessary to relate to the world as constructed from segregated elements that stand in external relationship one to another. In order to facilitate selection, it is necessary to relate to these objects as repeated emergence of the same types.

The result is that the world is understood in terms of limited number of types of separate elements, carried on repeated organizations, and re-organizations of space. Therefore, the mind relates naturally to fixed objects existing in a given space "side by side." It does not perceive fundamental transformations happening in time, but imagines these transformations as a continuum of static states, which extend upon a continuum of momentary spaces. Our self-awareness is radically opposed to the mind as such.

Within the boundaries of our self-awareness we experience time from the inside; we are not aware of a continuum of differentiated states but of our being, which means—our present is perceived as growing and rising from the past and turning into future that hadn't yet assumed a clear structure. "Time" in this internal experience is not the external time of the clock, but a real experience in transformation where stages of "before" and "after" interpenetrate. This kind of time Bergson refers to as Duration. He contends that this is not only a method of measuring the transformation of reality but the transformation of reality itself. This is a psychical state in which we are conscious of the quality of the flow of inner consciousness which is called intuition; It is a certain mode of unreachable consciousness which is free, even from symbols. Bergson compares the intuition to interior creative excitement, which allows the writer to meld his raw materials into one unified whole; Melding cannot be realized if the creator hasn't obtained the raw materials, and the obtaining is done by the action and the effort of the mind.

Bergson interprets evolution as a burst of the life impulse. According to his teachings, the wholeness of nature is the product of a power that creates itself in new unpredictable forms of organized structures.

From De Chardin's (1881-1955) point of view, it can be said that evolution goes forward through a series of "Creative Unifications." Complex and conscious beings are created through the unification of less complex and conscious elements. These creative unifications introduces to the being, something that did not previously exist there.

Since we can look back and see the repetitive pattern, De Chardin believes that it is possible to project into the future and to expect further creative unity, in which we humans will be the unifying factors. However, when Evolution meets up with our free choice, it alters its rules. We have the choice to pass or not to pass on to the next stage.

Sri Aurobindo (1872-1950) contributed a completely new dimension to this evolving field—he translated the concept of the evolution of consciousness into spiritual practice.[22]

"The time is ripe for the world to move towards a new and comprehensive self-fulfillment in an integral human existence for the individual and the race" (Aurobindo 1914).

In that very same year Freud wrote one of his groundbreaking papers which would change Western culture In "An introduction to Narcissism" (Freud, 1914). Freud defined the worst pathology of the human race—Narcissism, which developed and gained dominance in the 20th century (and which seems to have reached its peak in the beginning of the 21st). The cure for this pathology could be the result of the mutual efforts of a minority of human beings who succeed in awakening to and facing the threat posed to life in the cosmos, thereby participating in and advancing evolution at the level of consciousness itself.

Such a solution is also suggested by contemporary spiritual researchers and philosophers such as Ken Wilber, Andrew Cohen and others.

Ken Wilber

Ken Wilber is an American philosopher whose work focuses around an *integral approach* to human knowledge

---

22 After completing his studies in literature and philosophy in Cambridge, 1892, Aurobindo became a key figure in India's movement for independence, and he was even declared by the British empire as "the most dangerous living man." Eventually he left the battle for freedom in favor of devoting his life to a totally different kind of freedom.

organized as a complex set. An integral approach to knowledge is constructed, as he contends, from organizing all insights that emanate from psychology, postmodern philosophy, spirituality and empirical science into one complex set which represent a mapping of consciousness. Thus he presents a consistent integral model as a map of the evolution of the cosmos as an organizing principle. The integral principle actually gave birth to a new meta-theory which is offered as heir to postmodernism, i.e., a constructive postmodernism.

Andrew Cohen

Andrew Cohen is an American philosopher, spiritual teacher and visionary who teaches and writes about Evolutionary Enlightenment of consciousness. "Evolutionary Enlightenment" is a spiritual and philosophical teaching which places the traditional perception of enlightenment in a context of 14 billion years of cosmic evolution. This perception Cohen seeks to implement in the practice of life in the 21st century. Cohen sees the goal of life as transcending beyond pathological narcissism and as an awakening to the moral obligation of the people who recognize it to participate in taking forward the evolution of consciousness and culture, consciousness and culture being different aspects of the cosmos in general and human civilization specifically.

Andrew Cohen works by constant ongoing empirical checking of the theory; focusing, honing, checking the perspective from all angles—with close students upon whom he can rely. Searching for repeated proofs. Searching for balance between enlightenment and evolution. Direction, calibration, intention, self-examination, increasing awareness, a few inessential blind spots, readiness to die and as much transparency and integrity as possible.

§ The complex face of reality subject/object

What is the relationship between seemingly external objects and consciousness that can conceive of them? Every fact presupposes a subject who chose it from an infinite variety of possibilities. So every fact emerges simultaneously with its subjective creator. Therefore one can describe reality as Moebian[23] or as a projection of the self upon reality according to the pleasure principle—what is pleasant for me I interiorize, what is unpleasant I cast away onto "the outside world." In this respect the boundary between subject and object is an imaginary invention but if there is no real separation between object and subject one can also say that objects are projected onto the subject, i.e., the "world outside" determines our identity. We are not separate from the world; we don't arrive into the world we arrive from the universe. There is no being external to the

---

23 A Moebius band is a three dimensional form. It can be created by twisting a long strip once, before joining the two ends. A form is created where the passage between outside and inside is continuous. Describing reality as Moebian literally cancels the dichotomy between inside and outside, as well as other divisions (love/hate, truth/lies etc.)

The Consciousness Bearers

universe. Approximately every seven years the cells in our body have all changed—so who are we? A pattern of accumulating information? The separation between the world and us, that Lacan referred to as "the mirror stage" of our development is responsible[24]; this illusory image, which alienates us from ourselves and from the world, structures us as an imaginary bubble.

Our uniqueness as human beings is expressed in the fact of our awareness of two seemingly different dimensions—an objective external dimension of matter and a subjective inner world of thought, feeling, meaning and creativity. All our knowledge about the outside world is formed of deductions mediated by our neural system, our unconscious etc. Our subjective dimension is an ontological fact, or as Descartes believed—the only fact on which we can be totally sure. This is a mysterious fact, since no scientific knowledge, whether it be physical, biological and even psychiatric, can explain subjectivity.

One cannot analyze the part and join them together to create a whole. Wholeness is the primordial state of the cosmos. One cannot construct wholeness inductively from accumulations of observations. One cannot speak about a relationship between life and cosmos; one can only speak

---

24 The Mirror Stage is a developmental stage occurring at the beginning of the child's life. When he sees himself/herself in the mirror and his mother points to his reflection and happily says "this is you." This is how the imaginary relationship between man and reality and self-alienation starts to be created. He identifies with the whole image reflected to him from the mirror while his inner sensations at the time are still fragmented. The mirror stage describes the creation of the "I" through a process of identification. It is obviously related also to the development of narcissism.

about the *living cosmos*. A real whole is like a living organism. In order for something to be whole a hierarchical organizing principle is needed—a structure that will appear in each one of the parts. An intrinsic relationship exists between all the parts. The organism grows, differentiates and develops from the inside, in contrast to a machine. The organism is attached intrinsically both in space and in time.

In his book, *The Interpretation of Dreams*, Freud describes this by using a psychic model which resembles a comb (Freud, 1900, pp.537-542).

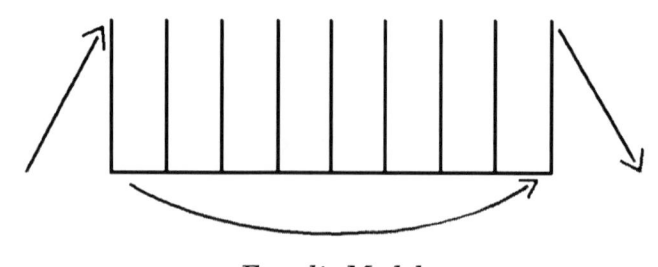

Freud's Model

From one side of the comb we perceive various stimulus, on the other side there is a motor or thought response; in the middle—the teeth of the comb, which are memory traces. Memory traces are located between perception and awareness, i.e., Freud draws a scheme which is constructed from a perceptive end and a motor end. The traces are in the middle, connected among themselves by associations of time and place. In order for the traces of perception to pass to the memory, they must be first erased from perception and vice-versa. If there is perception there is no memory;

unless it is attached to a word and then it becomes a representation, a symbol.

Descartes, who imprinted the immortal sentence that initiated the modern era of science and subjectivity *Cogito Ergo Sum* (I think therefore I am), caused Western civilization to associate identity with awareness instead of with the organism in its entirety. Following the Cartesian dichotomy between identity and body the experience of the "I" crystallized as a separate dimension, which "abides" within the body. The subject therefore does not exist as an essence that includes representations, qualities or characteristics, rather he exists only when he thinks and as such he is totally emptied of materiality. This is how a conflict was seemingly created between awareness and the impulses that are supposed to be controlled by it.

After thousands of years of confusion between outside and inside, between the mind and the world, in the last few hundred years a new mode of polarity between subject and object has developed. According to this polarity not only can the subject perceive the object with greater objectivity, he can also recognize a new spectrum of inner phenomenon, starting from neurotic conflicts and ending with the infinite nature of knowledge, i.e., of consciousness. New modes of objectivity and subjectivity have been developed. This development raises interesting questions concerning the nature of reality, like for example—how to differentiate between fantasy and memory?

Bertrand Russell, in his book *The Analysis of Mind*, defined a unique sense of reality which is expressed by a feeling of respect (Russell, 1922). According to him, respect is necessary in order for us to believe in the content of our memory. Russell's subject reality is everything he perceives. He respects this reality, says Russell, therefore he believes in the traces it leaves in memory. However the subject Russell speaks about is different from the psychoanalytic subject. Psychoanalysts treat the relationship between perception and reality differently. To them the stated reality includes the inner reality, which is also comprised of drives and from the unconscious.

Freud recognized the fact that the small boy perceives that the little girl is lacking a penis but he does not necessarily respect this perception, which is why he will not believe in the matching content in his memory. There can be perception without belief, conviction or certainty; we know that the psychotic subject does not believe—he does not believe in the name of the father or in the symbolic cultural order. On the other hand he has certainty—he is certain that everything in the world is a sign relating to himself.

The distinction between perception and belief is clearly represented in the German language. In German there are two different words for reality: *Realität* and *Wirklichkeit*. The second word is related to the word *wirken*, which means that something is working. So one can say that there are perceptions which "work" and become *Wirklichkeit*, and there are others which do not work so well or do not work at all. This distinction is especially important when we speak about the unconscious.

The Unconscious is a structure in memory who is created by a limited number of elements in language. These elements are called representations or signifiers. These signifiers and the structure they create determine the subjective—like the specific structure of the DNA. They also determine the relation of the subject to the other, since they come first and foremost from the other. When a child "enters" the world, the world of culture, the meaning of life is given to him in that he becomes part of the symbolic world of culture. He respects the arbitrary social rules. The parents are those who introduce him/her to the world of signifiers in placing him as a talking being. For example—they give him a name. Our first name is the sign of the other's desire for us. often this is a name that identifies us with one of the family ancestors or destines us to a certain ideal future.

Through the parents' discourse about the child, their desire for him, the future they plan for him, even before he is born, they mark him with the sign of culture. Through their demands of him, the limits they put on the satisfaction of his needs, they give him a place in the family and in the group he belongs to.

The subject also identifies with the language which is spoken to him and about him, as part of accepting culture. One can say that we live within an envelope of language. It is an envelope that creates a screen and defends us from what threatens to be an inconceivable relation to the traumatic Real. Lacan emphasized again and again the fact that language, or more precisely, discourse, precedes us.

In other words, language is what pre-designs the image of the subject. The subject exists first and foremost in the future—he will be. He gradually constructs himself in what can be called an anterior future—what he could have been.

The signifiers therefore, reach us from the Other—from outside. The baby "entering" the world emerges in the discourse of the Other as someone who will become. Of the subject's being, we know nothing. We can depict it as an X, and to this X we can put all of what the Other's discourse implies about him—his first name, his gender, his destiny. This discourse does not deal at all in the fundamental nature of the baby. It constructs a fantasmatic structure of identity around it.

This inscription in the symbolic order, which includes ascribing of qualities, in a certain sense precedes the assertion on existence or being itself. This is a result of a quality of language which is the ability to speak about something that does not exist. When parents speak about the child of their dreams, or the child they are worried that they will have, they speak about something that does not exist. A gap is created between the subject as it is spoken about and the being which is not defined but later will become unique.

As for language, we share a common illusion. Each one of us bears the feeling that language is a tool for us to use. It is the means which we use in order to express ourselves or to communicate. We have a sense that we make language our own even though it envelopes us from the beginning as a discourse coming from the Other. We are also helped by the daily accumulating experience of speech that is based on the illusion and strengthens it. For example, an experience of searching for words, where we feel that one word is suitable and the other is not. There are great historical and cultural differences regarding language.

The illusion is that language is a tool for communication, but a tool that carries with it many problems, i.e., not so comfortable to use. Often we feel that we do not control language. For example, when we complain that we cannot express ourselves, we cannot say what we want; the experience of lack of words exactly when we need them. There is also an opposite experience—words that force themselves on us. For example when writing poetry, in what is called inspiration, when the subject experiences something that is overwhelming, as if there is someone else inside his mind, even someone not human, even God.

"The dimension of being represents the un-manifest, timeless, formless ground of being which is spaceless. From this ground all manifest and creative process emerged 14 billion years ago. The dimension of becoming is the wholeness of that dynamic burning explosion in motion which is the creative process itself. Being exists before time. Becoming occurs in and through time. In order to experience being, one needs to transcend the process of time, and this happens with the help of the simple action of liberating attention from identifying with any object whatsoever that arises in consciousness. As much as we cease identifying with objects, the empty and infinite ground, timeless and spaceless, begins to emerge as that same ground of our unborn being. Every sense of boundary or limitation, including all memory and desire, dissolves in a glowing ocean of fullness and wholeness that always existed before the universe was born" (Andrew Cohen, Tuscany 2007).

§ The manifest and the un-manifest

Observation of the relationship subject-object, in language and outside it, relates to the reality of the world of exterior and interior manifestation. This is a relative world of time and space. Psychoanalysis mainly relates to this dimension, even though with the concept of the unconscious there is an invasion of an order which is located outside time and space. From a spiritual point of view, relating to reality includes the relative dimension as well as the absolute one. The absolute dimension includes all that exists, the "cosmos," and all that does not exist, which means a dimension that existed before the emergence of the cosmos and will exist after its disappearance. This is a dimension that does not evolve and is beyond time and place. The traditional teachings attributed the absolute dimension truth value, and the relative dimension they saw as an illusion or as a temporary state. The teachings of evolutionary enlightenment regard both modes of reality as two sides of the same coin. The manifest and the un-manifest, the relative and the absolute.

The un-manifest dimension is also conceived by certain scientists. Einstein, for example, was convinced that the immediate emergence of the laws of physics with the creation of the universe means the existence of an immaterial brain. According to the biologist Rupert Sheldrake: "If the laws of nature existed before the big bang, there must have been non-physical ideal beings, abiding in some kind of a fixed mathematical mind, be it the mind of God or of the cosmic mind or simply the mind of a body-less mathematician" (Sheldrake 2001).

A universe is therefore the realization of the transcendental laws which control it. What results from them is what our senses identify as matter. We cannot perceive these laws with our senses, only with our mind, in the eye of wisdom.

The evolving universe must be more than the sum of its parts, since a world containing prefixed laws can never be differentiated from its origin. There is a necessary element of chance in order for the new to occur.

The parts of the universe, as it is revealed in quantum physics, are related and connected in a way that each part can be understood to exist in a certain sense "inside" another part. One of the sensational discoveries of quantum physics is that the electron does not move in a continuum space, but emerges in certain positions in space for continuous duration. Those are called quanta. Matter has the nature of vibrations—on/off, like sound and light. Matter in this respect is perceived as a process in time. Time is not only duration without qualities, but the essence of creative evolution. The essence of all that "is" is change and participation in the creative progress of the universe.

Alfred North Whitehead contended that in a certain sense, everything exists everywhere all the time, since every location includes an aspect of itself in any other location, so that each space-time point of view reflects the world. The past is participating in the present, the present predicts the future, and the future can influence the part of the present that is not prefixed (Whitehead 1967, p.34).

Arthur Schopenhauer invented the term *Noumenon*, which alludes to reality itself, not colored by our perceptions. This is a reality that must be the Big Undifferentiated Other, which is known to itself in a direct non-cognitive way and not in the regular way of subject/object. The assumption of boundary between mind and matter, and the assumption of an objective world, totally independent from our consciousness, are mistaken assumptions. He writes:

"If we take away the thinking Subject, the whole material world must vanish; because it is nothing but a phenomenon in the sensibility of our own subject and a certain class of its representations" (Schopenhauer, 1847, p. 36).

While Aurobindo writes:

"At first sight it may appear that birth and death are attributes of the Life, but it is not really so: birth and death are processes of Matter, of the body. The Life-principle is not formed and dissolved in the formulation and dissolution of the body... Life forms body, it is not formed by it" (Aurobindo, 1910, p.79).

The relative, the absolute and the relationship between them

In his essay "On the Improvement of Understanding" Spinoza writes:

"After experience had taught me that all the usual surroundings of social life are vain and futile; seeing that none of the objects of my fears contained in themselves anything either good or bad, except in so far as the mind is affected by them, I finally resolved to inquire whether there might be some real good having power to communicate itself, which would affect the mind singly, to the exclusion of all else: whether, in fact, there might be anything of which the discovery and attainment would enable me to enjoy continuous, supreme, and unending happiness" (Spinoza 1662, [1],1).

When God created man, the angels complained: *For thou hast made him a little lower than the angels.*

Man was born almost as God; A lacking God (and as Lacan tells us, the Gods belong to the order of the Real). Instead of this lack, language appeared—man was the one to give names to all creation around him. This structural lack, which cannot be completed, man carries either weightily or lightly upon himself and he tries to fill it in various ways—through constituting a complete Other or an Ideal I, which include identification or falling in love, through creating symptoms that will plug the hole like a cork, or better still, by sublimating the drive, which leads to various types of creation. Is there another way?

Freud describes various vicissitudes or courses of the

sexual and death drive. Is there a course that Freud disregarded—the drive to create? the impulse to evolve? A person comes to analysis because he does not know (he is unconscious) what is his problem. He assumes that the analyst knows. The analyst moves during analysis the emphasis from the "problem" to the formations of the unconscious—something which creates effects of transformation in the subject's position. From here he can, with the help of the analysant, either attempt to solve the problem or go forward with the inquiry of the unconscious. The person can accept his "lack," continue his attempts to fill the lack with various objects or, awaken to the evolutionary dimension of consciousness and to the creative impulse which is precisely dependent on ceasing to make the effort to become or to find the missing part of being. In such a way there is a possibility of transcending the lack and reaching a place of stillness and abundance—this is a place where there is no lack. This way is called enlightenment.

To create and to develop from the place of abundance and not from the place of lack can be seen as a paradox; however, as in the solution of paradoxes, we know that the impossible at one level of consciousness is possible at a higher level.

I start from a few primary insights:
1. Knowledge in the world is one just as God is one—God as a force, as a drive as a universe creating intelligence. The creation of the universe is the beginning of the split—from the one to the many. The beginning is the beginning of the lessening of God—Nothingness and

God's spirit. The beginning is the split. The split from the One.
2. With the creation of the human being, alienation and split became more elaborate, that is to say, the ability of observation which is simultaneous with participation in the universe.
3. Realizing knowledge is an evolutionary process moving from the One and towards the One—the absolute. In other words, the evolutionary process is the absolute as such. Various teachings at different times attempted to describe or to understand the split by defining dichotomies— dichotomies at different levels. Division into two: matter and form, body and psyche, Eros and Thanatos, subject and object, full and empty. Sometimes the division is into three: the Christian trinity, Freud's structural model—id, ego, super ego. Lacan's dimensions—imaginary, symbolic and real. And so on and so forth.

The course taken in psychoanalytic practice I named the personal—the universal—the particular (or the singular). The personal relates to the complaint that causes the patient to come to analysis. The universal is the psychic structure which is revealed during analysis from the overdetermination of the net of signifiers. The particular is not just the unique manner of enjoyment of the individual and the invention of new love, but also the possibility to transmit knowledge. That is to say, through peeling away identifications, recognizing conditionings or "emptying" of the self, a possibility rises to receive abundance/knowledge and to transmit it further in a way that has a transformative effect on the listener.

Andrew Cohen sees the essence of spiritual inquiry as engagement with the relations between the absolute and the relative, between enlightened awareness which exists in the realm of the divine beyond time and history and the relative world of birth and death, time and becoming.

The East gave us the concept and the experience of enlightenment and of the dimension of the absolute beyond time but it didn't deal with the relations between the absolute and the relative—the reality of the world in time. In the West we researched the world that exists in time, especially concerning the concept of becoming or evolution.

In the ancient world the concept of time was cyclical. In the western world the conception of evolution developed and has inspired us for more than 150 years, i.e., the realization that all existence, including the speaking beings, is in a process of becoming. The motion of evolution does not exist only in matter but also in spirit. Or to put it more precisely perhaps—matter and spirit lose their dichotomy, very similarly to what happened in quantum physics.

As much as material evolution is a motion from the simple to the complex, so too spiritual evolution is hierarchical and progressive. The spiritual direction is a motion; an aspiration to higher consciousness, i.e., the movement or action of evolution is development at the level of awareness. In other words, matter becomes more and more conscious of itself. We are partners in this life process, which has become conscious of itself through us.

This is a new way of understanding our place in the universe. The "I" is part of this great movement of evolution, and the awareness of this fact makes it simultaneously empty—a vehicle—and present. That is to say, the "I" is matter becoming more aware of itself.

What is the connection between the absolute and the relative, between God and the human being, between being and action, between the one and the many?

In the absolute there is no possibility of measuring—there is no I or other or time or thought. There is nothing but—you exist there—an unlimited existence—a deep awareness of yourself, free from limitations. You cannot define yourself without a sense of a boundary—only when there is another object (difference). In the absolute realm there are no objects for comparison. The entire experience is that of existing without boundaries—unlimited self-existence. There is no time, beginning or end. There one feels liberation and freedom—liberation from the painful experience of non-absolute existence, which is defined by experiencing the fears and desires of the separate ego, as well as those of the dictatorship of feelings and thoughts.

The relative dimension is the experience of the separate existence defined by a sense of limitation, a fundamental boundary, experienced directly as fears and desires of the ego—fear of loneliness and of independence and an unceasing desire to escape from it all. The absolute and the relative are opposed to each other. In the relative realm the questions arise—where did we come from, where are we now and where are we going in our imaginary picture? We constantly try to locate ourselves in regard to all this and in regard to time. In the absolute realm there is only the experience of pure existence, independent from time. This is total freedom, as compared to total slavery. In the absolute there is no fear and no duality. The "I" is not aware that he has something to lode.

The connection between the absolute and the relative is a subject for spiritual inquiry. Between enlightened awareness—an awareness of the absolute dimension beyond time and history, and a world of relationships—birth and death, time and presence—reality.

The awakening of the spiritual impulse is an aspiration for higher consciousness, sublimated perception, which is expressed in that the spiritual impulse is the motion or the action of evolution at the level of conscious development. Usually we are unconscious participants, but when we awaken spiritually—we become aware of the process in which we participate. Life becomes more conscious of itself through us, literally. The motion of evolution itself is happening through our awakening—individually and collectively.

I speak of awareness in relation to three things: the realm of the absolute, the realm of the relative and the fact that they are identical. The evolution of consciousness occurs

The Consciousness Bearers

as existence becomes aware of itself through us.

"I" am part of this motion. Enlightenment is important not for the individual and his salvation but for the evolution of consciousness itself.

The question is, where your attention is directed towards, to the large context of the whole picture or to the narrow and limited one. One cannot silence all thoughts or ego. One can move attention to a different place. It makes it easier when one understands that "it is not about me." I am part of a whole exciting and fascinating evolutionary process, so how do I feel and how hard it is are not exactly important. The ego is like a defensive net whose holes are plugged so you cannot pass through them. Your ego is always more precious than the other's. We do not understand that the ego is one. In this respect the path and the goal are one. If you are in an enlightened place and your responses are unconditioned, if you are on the way, striving for it, and you are aware of your conditioned responses—it is one and the same, because what is important is what you do. A man (or a woman) is what he does. Only when we stop identifying with our self-image or when we are ready to be in the place of not knowing, we will understand that we are not the center of the universe. Otherwise our vision is reflected by a distorted mirror. Everything reflects back to you. The need to be seen (which is so essential for a woman) is the need to see ourselves in the gaze of everyone. Affirmation, self-value.

If you compromise, if you betray yourself and avoid coping with situations, it will gradually become bearable and even second nature. We distort our interpretation to the level of complete repression or complete denial. A lot of courage and humility is needed for looking truth in the eye.

There is a need to leave the repeated cycle of the ego's attempts to be and to be and to be, in order to reveal the leaving desire for participation in the evolution of consciousness.

§ Motion and connectedness

Spinoza's primary postulate is that God has infinite adjectives of which we know of two, and those are the ones which are active in the world—extension and thought, matter and motion or constant and awareness.

Between extension and thought there is the third factor—the factor of movement, action, and dynamics. The process of creation includes nothingness, God's spirit and the action of creation through saying: "...and God said." Even this motion can be divided into two—a circular motion and a directional motion, a motion that has cause and direction. Movement makes evolution possible; or perhaps there is evolution in movement itself. The principle of motion breaks the dichotomies and opens more and more courses beyond them. Development requires motion. I would like to relate the concept of motion to the context of matter, spirit and psychoanalysis.

The insights regarding motion in matter are based mainly on Frijtof Capra's inspiring book *The Tao of Physics* (Capra, 1966). The motion in matter I will describe through drawing some guidelines from quantum physics. I have no extensive knowledge about this domain but everything I read reminds me of the spiritual and psychological domains. The motion in spirit I will draw in a few and general lines from the teachings coming from the East, and finally I will describe in short the basis of motion or dynamics in psychoanalysis. The concept of motion is connected of course to the concept of non-duality or fundamental unity that characterizes the universe; it is a unity that cancels the separations between outside and inside, subject and object. In other words—motion relates to elements of interaction, connectedness and unity.

§ Motion in matter

"Heraclitus believed in a world of perpetual change, of eternal 'becoming.' For him, all static Being was based on deception and his universal principle was fire, a symbol for the continuous flow and change of all things. Heraclitus taught that all changes in the world arise from the dynamic and cyclic interplay of opposites and he saw any pair of opposites as unity. This unity, which contains and transcends all opposing forces, he called the Logos" *(Capra, 1975, p.20).*

Parmenides, as opposed to Heraclitus, spoke about the basic principle—being, and contended that it is one and unchanging.

In modern physics the world is experienced as a dynamic undivided whole which always and necessarily includes the observer. In this experience the traditional concepts of space and time, of discrete objects and of cause and effect, lose their significance. Quantum theory reveals the fundamental connectivity of the universe. It shows that we cannot disintegrate the world to independent units.

The concept of motion became central. The universe is perceived as a web of relationships which maintain intrinsic dynamics, wherein the qualities of the sub-atomic particles are structured only on the basis of the dynamic context: in terms of motion, interaction and transformation.

As Niels Bohr contended:

"Isolated material particles are abstractions, their properties being definable and observable only through their interaction with other systems" (ibid. p.37.).

David Bohm:

"...[We] say that inseparable quantum interconnectedness of the whole universe is the fundamental reality, and that relatively independent behaving parts are merely particular and contingent forms within this whole" *(p. 138)*.

Quantum theory destroyed the classical concepts of solid objects and deterministic laws of nature. At the subatomic level, the solid material objects of classical physics dissolved into wave like formations of probabilities, and these patterns finally do not represent probabilities of things but probabilities of mutual relationships.

Therefore quantum physics reveals the fundamental unity of the universe. It shows that we cannot divide the universe into its smallest discrete units of μB. When we penetrate into matter, nature does not reveal to us separate "basic building blocks," but is emerging as a complex texture of relationships between different kinds of wholeness. These relationships always include the observer. The human observer is the last link in the chain of the process of observation, and the qualities of a certain atomic object can be understood only in terms of mutual relations between the object and the observer. The Cartesian separation between the "I" and the world, between the observer and the observed, is not possible when the subject is atomic matter.

At the atomic level "objects" are perceived only in the sense of interaction between processes of preparation for measurement. The end of this chain of processes exists always in the awareness of the observer. Measurements are interactions which constitutes "sensations" in our consciousness.

As Werner Heisenberg says:

"Natural science does not simply describe and explain nature; it is part of the interplay between nature and ourselves" (p.140).

In Einstein's theory of general relativity the classical terms of absolute and independent space and time are totally canceled. Time and space turn into elements of language which a certain observer uses in order to describe the observed phenomenon. Matter is nothing but a form of energy. In this respect even a still object carries energy within its mass.

From Capra's book: Max Planck "discovered that the energy of heat radiation is not emitted continuously, but appears in the form of 'energy packets.' Einstein called these energy packets 'quanta' and recognized them as a fundamental aspect of nature...At the subatomic level, matter does not exist with certainty at definite places, but rather shows 'tendencies to exist,' and atomic events do not occur with certainty at definite times and in definite ways, but rather show 'tendencies to occur'" (pp.67-68).

So modern physics presents matter not as indifferent and passive but as dancing a constant dance the rhythm of which is determined by the structure of atoms and molecules. The particles in the sub-atomic world are themselves processes! Matter and its motion are not separable any longer. They consist of different aspects of space-time reality.

For the physicist Robert Laughlin, a contemporary Nobel prize winner, reality is a collective effect which is created when all the particles move together. When closely observed all know natural laws disappear—like in an impressionistic picture (Laughlin 2005).

So it seems that modern physics is based on two foundations which are parallel to the Eastern worldview: the fundamental unity of the universe and its intrinsic dynamic nature.

§ Connectivity and motion in the East

"[The natural] laws are not forces external to things, but represent the harmony of movement immanent in them" —I Ching (Capra, p. 221).

"The basic elements of the universe are dynamic patterns; transitory stages in the 'constant flow of transformation and change.'"—Chuang Tzu

The mysticism of the East contends to the same dynamic unity existing between emptiness and the formations which are created from it. The conception of the East on the nature of the universe is organic. All things and happenings which are perceived by our senses are connected to each other, and actually are different aspects or expressions of the same reality as such.

In this view the division of nature into differentiated objects is not fundamental and every object has qualities of transformation and flow. The cosmos is experienced as an indivisible reality in constant motion.

The two fundamental principles are unity and connectivity of all phenomena and the dynamic intrinsic nature of the universe.

Suzuki says:

"The central ides of the Kegon [a school of Mahayana Buddhism] is to grasp the universe dynamically whose characteristic is always to move forward, to be forever in the mood of moving, which is life" (p/ 190).

Ruth Golan

§ Connectivity and motion in psychoanalysis

Psychoanalysis is based on the dynamic principle of drive and desire and on the fundamental split between them and the demands of reality. That is to say, motion is fundamental, based on interactivity, and there is no unity.

Dynamics, (According to the dictionary of Laplanche and Pontalis) is defined as a point of view that sees psychic phenomenon as a result of conflict and a combination of impulsive forces which activate certain pressure (Laplanche & Pontalis, 1973, p. 126).

Freud distinguishes between his approach and that of Janet:

"We do not derive the psychical splitting from an innate incapacity for synthesis on the part of the mental apparatus; we explain it dynamically, from the conflict of opposing mental forces and recognize it as an outcome of an active struggling on the part of the two psychical groupings against each other" (Freud, 1910a, pp. 25-26).

According to Freud, the Libido is an energy which lies behind the transformation of the sexual drive as regarding the object (displacement of cathexis), the aim (sublimation) and the origin of sexual arousal (variations of erotogenic zones) . The word Libido in Latin means a wish or desire. The Libido is the element of motion and also the element of split.

Lacan, in his late teachings, began to act in the direction of the one. He repeatedly said—"there is of the one" (Il y'a del'un). Enjoyment—that mode of going beyond the pleasure principle, and even beyond sexuality, is related to the traumatic Real dimension, and connects psychoanalysis back to unity.

§ Connectedness and movement in Evolutionary Enlightenment

The definition of evolutionary enlightenment is the integration of two seemingly contradicting worldviews, or between two modes of motion.

The Concept of Enlightenment	Evolutionary Enlightenment
Originates from traditional teachings, mostly from the east.	Originates from modern and postmodern insights.
Experiential perception of the wholeness and unity of the world.	Deals with development in time—from the beginning of the universe, the big bang, and onward.
The movement is from the many to the one.	The movement is from the one to the many. It indicates multitude and divergence.
One must transcend what is called "ego."	Transcending ego enables the emergence of Authentic Self

Andrew Cohen unifies these two motions into one teaching that is Evolutionary non-duality. These two currents as one are giving new meaning to spirituality as it is expressed in the 21st century. This is a new answer to the eternal questions—who are we and why are we here.

Enlightenment is a way of seeing—when subject becomes object. It is a mode of detachment and contemplation from a big perspective. What is the real nature of the cosmos? Evolutionary enlightenment is the recognition that we are part of the evolutionary process, which means that we identify with the process which aspires to create ever higher levels of consciousness.

Radical positivity and wholeness in an inquiring group of people speaks from the place of this positivity and the joint will to go to a new place—an authentic action that leads to a rare place in our world. Awakened listening, that looks to advance and go deeper and does not judge you. Trust in the authentic self and in right action is connected to this acceptance, to this ecstatic intimacy that has nothing in it of the personal. When someone is speaking he does not own this speech as well as the listening. And then the two opposites—the absolute and pure action—balance each other and deepen each other and somehow meet and depend upon each other. When communication is a way of action one can be in the stillness of the zero point, in this delicate space, and yet act relentlessly.

Therefore, evolution according to the teachings of evolutionary enlightenment is a developmental motion that began with the big bang and has continued ever since and will continue in the future. The human being today is at the edge of the evolutionary trajectory. He is the leading edge of this motion. For us, humans who recognized the fact of evolution merely 150 years ago, two parallel movements are occurring: a retrospective motion—we realize in retrospect deep time development starting from the first cause, or from moment of the beginning of the universe —this is the process of awakening; at the same time a movement forward should take place—the realization that we are creating the continuation of this movement in the future—from the highest evolutionary place that was reached by consciousness—the ability to know itself.

The central point that should be remembered is that we are not separate from this motion; The point in time where we awakened is a virtual point. Actually we are that motion itself.

Another thing that should be emphasized is that this is not only theory but also, principally a way of life. That is why the emphasis is put on both intellectual awareness and emotional experience. We need both of them because we have to know ourselves at the virtual crossroads. Actually this is a continuous process, which includes quantum leaps along the way. The crossroads is our realization that we are the process or the motion itself. Just as psychoanalysis introduced the subject to a process of introspection, and following it science did the same, thus Cohen introduces the self into the heart of the process. That is to say, the authentic self is the expression of the process, the trajectory of the creative impulse that passes through us.

We are situated now only at the beginning of this insight

and its implications that matter is only now becoming aware of itself. The interiority of the cosmos—of which our interiority is the most developed—only begins to emerge now, so long as we become aware of it. "I am the universe evolving now. My consciousness, as un-perfect as it is, is the edge of this process in these times" *(Andrew Cohen, 2008)*. When one realizes this, seeking is over and one cannot hide any more—God is walking in the garden asking "Where art thou?" and answering at the same time "Here I am!" This is because the question and the answer come from the same source. The ability to develop the interiority of the universe is a result of the evolution of life itself—it is inseparable. There is no difference between biological development and spiritual development—both are parts of the same evolutionary process. One of the consequences of this realization is that the impulse to become more conscious is immortal. The recognition of the immortal element in the subject, which like the creative impulse itself continues to roll along in the universe and find new grooves through which to express itself.

Consciousness can develop in two ways—depth, a deeper experience of the self, or broadening of perspective. We all live in a universal context, but what do we identify with? According to our identification our perspective shifts. The evolutionary impulse at a high level is the spiritual impulse.

It can be said metaphorically that God is returning to the picture after we removed him from it, not as an other, not as something outside of us but as "I," as part of me.

Usually we relate to the awakening universe as our own awakening to the awakening of the universe, or the awakening of the universe through us. In all those cases there is still the dual relationship I-you. It is difficult to get the "I" out of the picture. It is difficult to think that I am the universe awakening to itself. The "I" attempts to own the process for itself. But the process is not personal at all. It is not I who am awakening, but matter is awakening to itself *through* me. It has taken matter 14 billion years to organize itself in the evolutionary process in such a sophisticated way that it can awaken and also know itself. Actually, it is enlightenment as such.

The ego and the authentic self are not personal or individuals but phenomenon, impersonal motions in consciousness. They are motions with which we identify, and with this identification we become one with them. The motion in consciousness is an impersonal force. The ego is an inert principle as opposed to the authentic self, which is a creative principle. The ego has no wish to evolve or to engage with evolution, and we try to escape from this significant realization and the demand for integrity it implies.

When we observe the process we can see its directionality—from the simple to the complex, from the less developed to the more developed—and for that a sufficiently big perspective is required; for example, the shift from paganism to monotheism was a stepping stone in the evolutionary process, as was the development of print or the French revolution. In the developmental process, Cohen sees not only directionality but also intentionality.

The intention of the creative drive to awaken to itself.

Cohen calls this intention "Kosmic narcissism": "I am the universe that decided to awaken and turn from matter to spirit. This universe is my plan. Finally I have a vehicle to lead it from the inside. We are at the top edge of reality. I was there in the beginning. I am the process of time."

The integrative model
Psycho-evolution

"The human phenomenon is a unique biological, collective, and global phenomenon, whose past, present, and future is intimately bound up with the formation, life, and ultimate transformation of the Earth. [...] But once the whole of the human is integrated—the "inside" as well as the "outside"—into a coherent representation of the world, the human comes to be seen as the very axis and arrow pointing the direction of evolution itself" (De Chardin, 1940, p. xviii).

I will try now to present all that was said until now regarding the two dimensions of the universe: the manifested and the un-manifested dimensions—and the relationships between them. In addition I will try to present the absolute and the relative points of view in a schematic mode. This model tries to position the psychoanalytic theory in its relation to the teachings of spiritual evolution. I would like to emphasize that I am not trying to merge them into one theory. But in a wide context one can delineate both of them as describing the human psyche and spirit in two hierarchical unparalleled dimensions. The evolutionary impulse includes the sexual impulse and the creative impulse and brings them to a higher level. It can become conscious and deliberate, that is to say, to be directed by the subject from the very point where the psychoanalytic research finished its task. The psychoanalytic insights are not refuted by spiritual research, but by discovering the series of values that lie- below them they can receive a different context and continue to evolve.

The Consciousness Bearers

The Normal-Neurotic Triangle

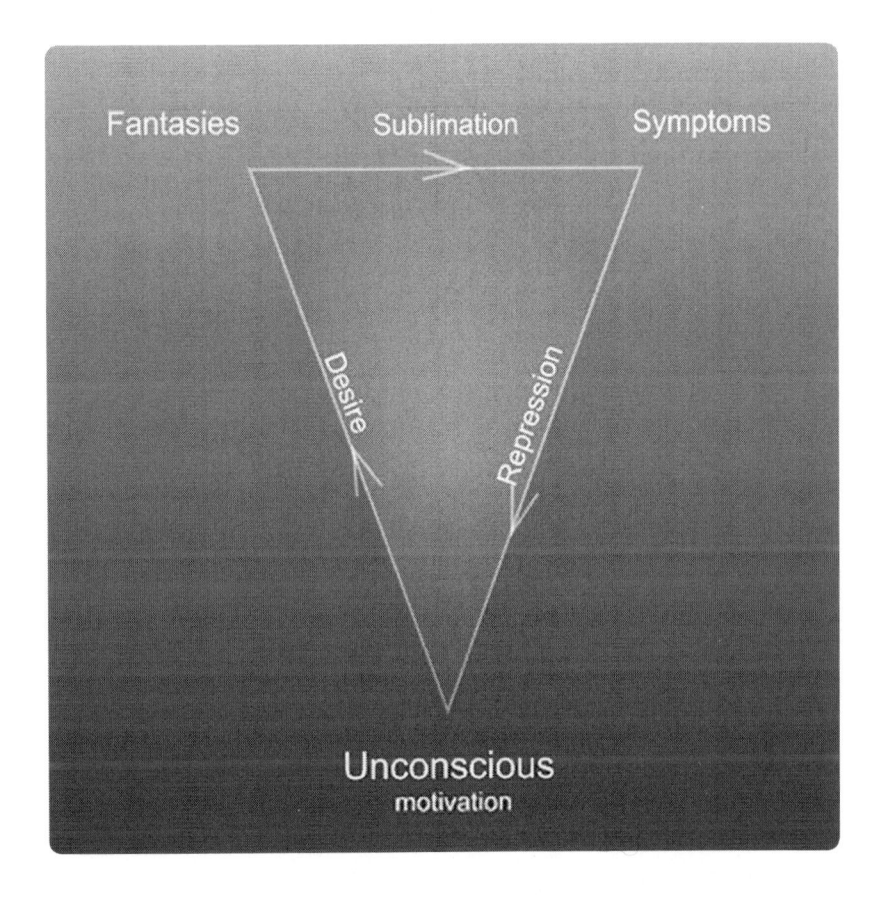

Fantasies — Sublimation → Symptoms
Desire — Repression
Unconscious motivation

For much of our lives we follow the course of this triangle, without even being aware of all the other possibilities and potentials embodied within ourselves and in life itself.

This dimension is heavily influenced by the formation of the separate narcissistic ego. The ego is an object formed out of the building blocks of "identifications." It functions as a shield or screen intended to protect the subject from unmediated encounters with the bodily, the spiritually or the worldly Real.

The ego serves as a defense in the face of the dynamic uncertainty of the subject of the unconscious, its inherent Otherness and the sense of the uncanny that accompanies such encounters. Because of the imaginary fixation on the ego as our identity (fixation is referred to by Eastern wisdom as "attachment"), the ego resists movement or change in one's desire. In analytic practice, the ego is considered to be a source of resistance and fixation. Reinforcing it merely serves to increase resistance. The attachment of the ego is considered the personal, imaginary perspective of one's psyche, which puts a stop to motion.

By undermining the attachment to the ego, psychoanalysis tries to restore the movement of desire and of its dialectic and to open up free space in which the subject can dwell and move more freely through life's contingencies.

§ Unconscious motivation

The tip of the triangle is that part in us that is simultaneously the most intimate and the most alien. Freud named it "the other scene." Lacan named it "the Other's discourse." That is to say, the Unconscious is something in me but not *of* me. It is an agency or function that covertly influences most of our being and action in the world as well as conditioning our reactions. The Freudian unconscious relates to the causality which motivates human behavior. We recognize the unconscious through actions that are caused and conditioned by other actions of which we have no conscious knowledge. This is evidently a blow to human narcissism. The ego is not even master in its own domain, but has to be satisfied with fragments of information that reach it about what happens in its unconscious. We can also see the unconscious as the subject that appears unexpectedly in the gap between the motivation, and what the cause is operating upon. It appears as an obstacle which implies that there is a hole in the fullness of our life. Thus in order to be liberated from the conditioning of the unconscious we should know ourselves, and for that we should recognize and know the unconscious.

Freud says: "No matter how difficult it is, there is a necessity to go there."

The Unconscious is the place of the drives. The drive is a concept representing the motivating force, the motion. A distinction has to be drawn between drives and biological needs. The Drive is disconnected from biological need and it can go through different vicissitudes depending on the culture. A drive is always striving to reach satisfaction, without necessarily relating to an object. In the drive there is dualism. Freud distinguished between Life drives—*Eros* (sexual drive), and *Thanatos* (death drive). Freud called the energy that motivates the erotic drive *Libido*. The death drive is the tendency of every living creature to return to an inorganic state. We usually find the two types of drive mixed together.

The drive, like the unconscious, operates according to a rhythmic principle of appearance and disappearance. It circulates around an object and aspires to get satisfaction. It's movement is a horizontal cyclical movement. Along all Freud's theory, the drives are describes in a dualistic manner. At first Freud claimed that the sexual drives are opposed to the ego or to the self-preservation drives. The ego drives are the self-preservation drives of the individual. This is knowledge embedded in the body. This knowledge usually controls the body. The sexual drives support the ego drives by giving them energy, but at the same time they evade its (the ego's) authority or this order of self-preservation. The dialectic is between the unifying of all the drives under the control of the ego and the multiplicity of the partial sex drives that are not integrated into a unified sex drive.

When Freud understood that the Ego drives are also sexual in their nature, he constituted the dualism on the opposition between life drives and death drives. He saw the life drives as a tendency to unity and acting according to the pleasure principle, while the death drives act beyond the pleasure principle towards disintegration and destruction. In real life we will seldom find these two drives completely separated from each other. We will find rather every emergence of the drive as a combination of the two. Without the Erotic drive, the Death drive would not have been felt because it is a drive that acts in silence. Lacan keeps this duality even though for him every drive is simultaneously both sex drive and death drive, because every drive, beyond

The Consciousness Bearers

a certain limit, is repetitive, creates enjoyment, and finally is destructive.

There are two principle ways for erotic drive to attain satisfaction. One way remains within the limits of "the law," thereby avoiding transgression of the pleasure principle (i.e., we accept that which gives us pleasure and reject that which causes us displeasure). The other way combines the two drives in a way that causes the law to be transgressed, (going "beyond the pleasure principle"). The latter way is called Enjoyment. Enjoyment is a satisfaction derived from painful experiences but also from ecstatic ones. This experience exists in every element of life, in sexual orgasm as well as in symptom, speech and even enlightenment.

While the human subject that is described in this neurotic model is fundamentally split between the drives and the demands of reality, enjoyment is a movement towards the One.

Enjoyment is also dualistic—most of the enjoyment known to our western civilization is phallic enjoyment connected to power and conquest. The human being has the possibility to experience a non-phallic or another mode of enjoyment.

The second mode is unlimited feminine enjoyment which cannot be described in words, since language fundamentally belongs to paternalistic law and phallic culture, but can be experienced as ecstasy or sublimation, as in the case of poets and mystic sages.

Lacan contrasts Enjoyment beyond the pleasure principle to the pleasure within the pleasure principle. For him the pleasure principle constitutes the phallic principle, and phallic or sexual Enjoyment always stays in the realm of the signifier. The non-phallic, psychotic or 'being' Enjoyment exists in opposition to that realm. This is Enjoyment that is outside language and beyond sexual differentiation. It belongs to the body as an organism. Every woman has potential access to this other Enjoyment, because not all of her is subject to the phallic principle. If we go one step forward we can see evolutionary potential in this claim.

The relation between these two kinds of Enjoyment consists of limits, regulation, and defense. Phallic Enjoyment regulates Enjoyment since it includes a limit channeled by the phallic signifier. The other enjoyment belongs to the body, and it exists outside the symbolic order. As Lacan claims: "Phallic Enjoyment is the obstacle owing to which man does not come (*n'arriver pas*[25]), I would say, to enjoy woman's body, precisely because what he enjoys is the enjoyment of the organ" (Lacan, 1972-73, p.7).

Phallic enjoyment is a defense against body as an organism. Enjoyment, which includes the abandoning of the symbolic, which means the death of the subject and its disappearance from the symbolic order. Phallic enjoyment is always partial, separating between people, releasing tension and acts through orgasm. Orgasm results in separation from which the subject develops. Feminine Enjoyment is holistic, enmeshing, arousing tension and results in symbiosis. One can describe it in Lacanian terms and say that

---

25 To come – also in the sexual meaning.

the subject disappears in the Other, or one could say that this mode of Enjoyment can open a possibility of experiencing the absolute.

The drive is completely cut off from needs. It is a cultural-symbolic construction. It goes round the object in a cyclical movement. It emanates from the erotogenic zones and returns to them. Freud named different partial drives, each having a different origin and a different erotogenic zone. Lacan constructs a list of drives: oral, anal, scopic (related to seeing), and invocatory (related to the voice). He emphasizes the partial nature of the drives and that as far as sexuality goes there are only partial drives. While Freud is hesitant concerning the existence of a genital drive, it being the highest point of development and integration for the drives, Lacan claims that the drives are not partial in a sense of being part of a genital whole, but that in fact they represent sexuality in a partial way. They represent only the enjoyment aspect of sexuality and not its procreative aspect. According to him, there is no procreative drive.

Lacan emphasizes the cultural aspect of the drive rather than its organic aspect. For him it is not a question of biology but a question of the symbolic order, the action of language on things. Never the less the drive touches the Real. In the constant movement of the drive around the satisfying object, which belongs to the realm of the Real, something of the Real penetrates the symbolic order. For Lacan the death drive is not a separate drive but an aspect of every drive. Every drive is striving for its annihilation, every drive ties the subject to repetition and every drive is an attempt to go beyond the pleasure principle towards Enjoyment which includes suffering. That is to say, the drive is sadomasochistic in its essence—it revolves around the relationship between pleasure and pain, and the other is only an object of pleasure or pain.

§ The arrow of Desire

Drives always strive to achieve the primal satisfaction they derived from primal objects like the mother's breast. Since these objects are lost, a track of indestructible desire is created. In this path any object eventually turns out to be disappointing, which leads to searching for another object. Thus desire is a result of a lack. From the psychoanalytic point of view, this lack is fundamental to the structure of the psyche, and can be fulfilled only temporarily, through fantasies, symptoms and sublimations. Psychoanalysis therefore deals with what is lacking in the experience of being and in the subject. Desire is never satisfied, it always wants something else. All needs can be satisfied, all the objects of demand, except for the object of love, the search for which is the motivation of desire.

St. Augustine calls the dimension of desire "Will." For him the will is the praxis, the act:

"For in these things the ability was one with the will, and to will was to do;....The mind commands the body, and it obeys instantly; the mind commands itself, and is resisted. The mind commands the hand to be moved; and such readiness is there, that command is scarce distinct from obedience. Yet the mind is mind, the hand is body. The mind commands the mind, its own self, to will, and yet it doth not. Whence this monstrousness? and to what end? It commands itself, I say, to will, and would not command, unless it willed, and what it commands is not done. But it willeth not entirely: therefore doth it not command entirely. For so far forth it commandeth, as it willeth: and, so far forth is the thing commanded, not done, as it willeth not. For the will commandeth that there be a will; not another, but itself. But it doth not command entirely, therefore what it commandeth, is not. For were the will entire, it would not even command it to be, because it would already be. It is therefore no monstrousness partly to will, partly to nill, but a disease of the mind, that it doth not wholly rise, by truth upborne, borne down by custom. And therefore are there two wills, for that one of them is not entire: and what the one lacketh, the other hath" (St. Augustine, 401A.D. book VIII).

§ The arrow of Repression

Repression is activated whenever there is a threat of forbidden wishes appearing in consciousness or an eruption of drive which the ego cannot stand. The concept of repression represents the process through which certain thoughts or memories are deported from consciousness and are limited to the unconscious. Freud distinguished between primary repression (a "mythical" amnesia of something which was never conscious in the first place, a perennial "psychical action" that constitutes the Unconscious), and secondary repression (concrete action of repression, where an idea or a certain perception that were once conscious, are deported from consciousness). Since repression does not destroy the ideas or memories which it deports, but only limits them to the domain of the Unconscious, the repressed material can always return in distorted forms, in symptoms, dreams, slips of speech, etc. (the return of the repressed).

For Freud, repression always had two aspects. One aspect is the ego's repressive force. The ego represses the drive and blocks its accessibility to consciousness. The second aspect of repression is also the defeat of the ego. The multiplicity of repressions is similar to the multiplicity of fixations.

In his later teachings, Lacan, similarly to Freud, combined the drives with the ego. In accordance with Hegel's philosophy, they both saw the relationship between the drives and the ego as war of life and death, constituted by repression and the return of the repressed. Does psychoanalysis attempt to make peace between them or does it try to find a different level of consciousness where war would lose its effect?[26]

Repression uses a warlike representation because it

---

[26] The driver is in the place of the master and the ego is in the place of the slave. See more in pp. 70-71

deals in a combat between representations that prevent awareness to other representations. The repression principle according to Freud is a war of representations. There are stronger representations, which force themselves on other weaker representations. The strongest group of representations is the group that constructs the ego. The ego is defined as a group of representations that have the power to repress other representations.

§ Fantasies, Symptoms, Sublimation

Those are three modes for facing reality, defensive ways that enable the human being to compromise between the often opposing demands of the drive and the demands of reality in accordance with the pleasure principle and enjoyment. These modes draw the upper flat line of the triangle and enable the subject to go through life without going beyond a certain level of consciousness, which the subject can experience as threatening and provoking anxiety. Going beyond this level can lead to disintegration of personality or transformation.

Fantasies

Fantasy is an imaginary scene in which the subject is a protagonist, representing the fulfillment of a wish (an unconscious wish). In this way the subject can fulfill his desires without endangering himself in any way whatsoever. Fantasy assumes different modes: conscious fantasy or daydream, unconscious fantasy (or phantasm). The reality we experience is constructed mostly from fantasies, so it is easier for us to face it.

Fantasy is uncovered by analysis as the structure underlying the manifest content. Phantasm is the particular way each one of us constructs his relation to the traumatic thing, to the Real. It is the defensive answer of the subject facing the Other's desire—the answer to the question "What does he/she want from me?" but to which he does not receive an answer. That is to say it includes our self-image and identity.

Symptoms

The symptom is the result of a compromise between repression and a return of the repressed, a consequence of a partial success of defense. It functions as a representation of a memory that seems lacking in symbolic signification. That is why interpreting the symptoms gives it retroactive meaning. Generally there are body symptoms related to the Hysterical structure—that is to say the body becomes ill from the truth concerning its repressed sexuality, and there are compulsive symptoms related to the Obsessive-Compulsive structure and expressed in thoughts or actions. The Hysteric (usually a woman) looks for the Other's desire and questions it; the Obsessive-Compulsive tries to eliminate the Other's desire. The Hysteric defends herself from enjoyment while blaming everyone around her; the Obsessive-compulsive is attracted too much to enjoyment, while feeling guilty.

Lacan divides the symptom to "an envelope" and "a nucleus." He calls "envelope" the symbolic meaning the symptom has for the person who suffers from it. This meaning is in language, connected with words, which is why it can be interpreted. Despite this, the nucleus of the symptom cannot be interpreted, since it is situated outside of language. "The nucleus" contains the element of enjoyment in the symptom which is related to the body, situated in the psychic Real realm. "The gravity force" of enjoyment gets stronger the closer one gets to the nucleus. That is the reason we repeatedly witness patient's having enormous difficulty in giving up their symptoms, even after interpreting their significance. The human being is attached to his suffering and will not renounce it easily, especially if he/she feels a victim of it.

Even if the nucleus of the symptom is related to language, it is a language that is used first and foremost for the Enjoyment of the speaker and not for communication with the other. Symptoms show stability and the ability to survive much more than other formations of the unconscious.

The symptom as a body event is related to the fact that the human being "has a body," which is different from saying that "he is a body." There is no identity between the body and the entity in man, since even if he identifies with his body he turns into a subject through the signifier, that is to say he is split and lacks "being." This "lack in being" as an effect of the signifier separates the "being" from the body and reduces the body to the status of "having." Due to this fact the human being suffers also from symptoms with which he cannot identify with. The uniqueness of the human body is that there are always events that leave traces in it and disturb it, and those are the events which are connected to speech and discourse; those are the ones that create a symptom.

Apart from the subject, which is an effect of the signifiers and of language, there is also the individual who is influenced by the unconscious; the individual who is influenced by words and does or does not do deeds that cause him guilt and the need to repress. The effect of the signifier is not only to signify but to create an affect in the body. The influence of the affect includes the influence of the symptom on the body. The symptom allows for drive satisfaction. The body or the thought turns into an origin of drive satisfaction through the symptom.

Sublimation

Sublimation is the process that deals with the challenge of satisfying drives not by affecting the drive itself, such as by repression or subjugation, but by changing the object.

Sublimation means displacement of the libido: Drives cannot be subjugated but objects can be shifted in ways that will grant legitimacy from the social aspect.

Sublimation also involves resistance—the resistance of culture to the original satisfaction of the drive. Sublimation of drives enables the higher faculties (scientific, artistic or ideological) to become active—to play an important role in cultural life.

The Consciousness Bearers

In this there is an attempt to grasp the rope at both ends: On the one hand the chances of authentic gratification and on the other hand, objects that are endowed with collective social value which have undergone development of the imaginary and phantasmic dimension. Sublimation is usually compared with de-sexualization, with the libidinal investment displaced from being a crude object (which is supposed to gratify basic drives) to a higher and more cultured form of gratification, for example—writing poetry instead of having sex.

In fact though, sublimation and de-sexualization are not connected at all. The sublimated object is an ordinary day to day object of no importance, elevated to the glorious level of the Thing. It is the embodiment of nothing-at-all.

Therefore, a sublimated object represents the paradox of the object that can only exist in the shadows, mediated, veiled, hidden. That is to say, represented by something else—language. Lacan called it "The beauty behind the veil." The moment one tries to reveal the essence by driving away the shadows, all that is left is a simple and insignificant object.

Full sublimation is not possible: Something wild is always left out, impossible to sublimate, attempts to totally sublimate drives are always prone to failure. Such attempts might even lead the person to attempt to commit suicide, whether physical or spiritual, as in the case of many artists.

Sublimation is a horizontal movement of widening and adding significations. The philosopher Ken Wilber calls this movement "translation." Horizontal motion only serves to reaffirm and reinforce the self. It cannot bring about a change in our level of awareness. It cannot liberate us from the ego. He opposes this movement to the vertical one which relates to radical "transformation" and liberation. This kind of movement is characteristic of a tiny fraction of the population. Instead of reinforcing the fixated ego it has the potential to destroy it. Emptiness rather than fullness. Vertical motion puts the very process of translation in doubt, shatters it. With translation, the self finds new ways of thinking about the world. Transformation means changing the world rather than translating it.

That is to say there is a different mode to dealing with reality and drives which is related not to sublimation of the drive but to their transformation.

This brings us to the second triangle—the model of The Authentic Human Being.

The Authentic Dimension

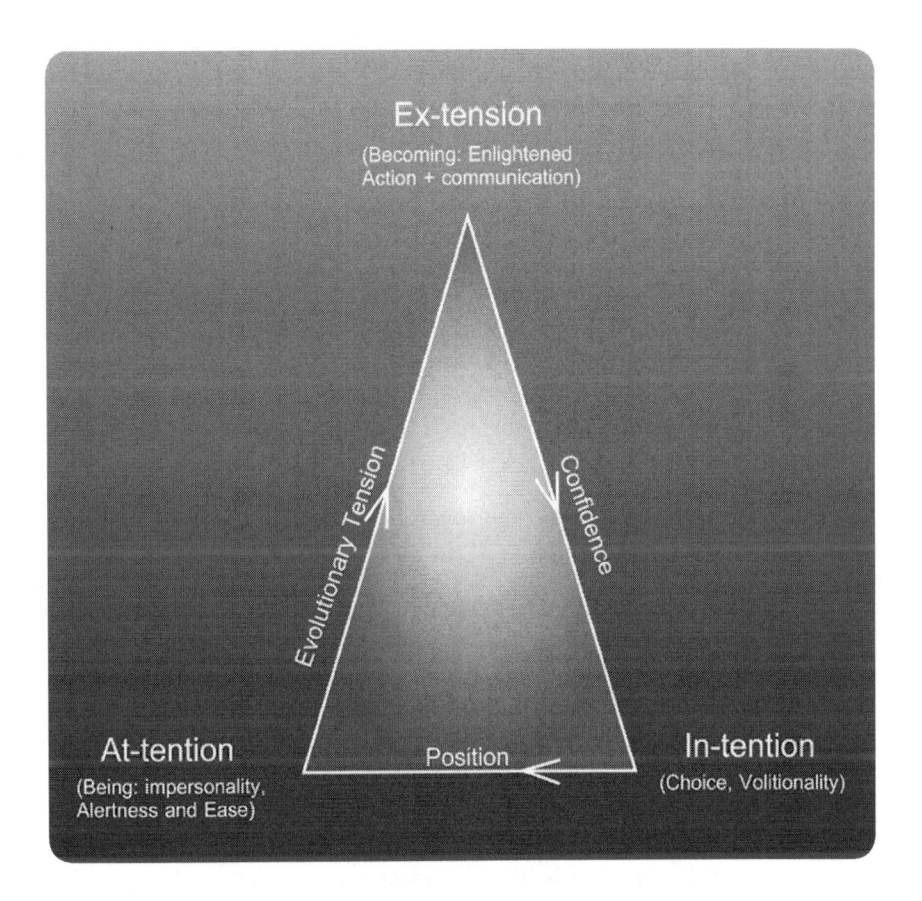

Ex-tension
(Becoming: Enlightened Action + communication)

Evolutionary Tension

Confidence

At-tention
(Being: impersonality, Alertness and Ease)

Position

In-tention
(Choice, Volitionality)

In his article—The Subversion of the Subject—Lacan writes: "In other words, a strain of psychoanalysis that is sustained by its allegiance to Freud cannot under any circumstances pass itself off as rite of passage to some archetypal, or in any other sense ineffable, experience. The day someone who is not simply a moron obtains a hearing for a view of this kind will be the day all limits will have been abolished. We are still a long way from that" (Lacan, 1960, pp. *283-284).*

This dimension appears occasionally, as a result of an awakening which leads to contemplating the Cosmos, life, and the place of the human being from a wider perspective, or as a result of extreme experiences, or of continuous discontent which compels the subject to look for a new meaning beyond manifestation.

At the beginning of *Life Divine,* Sri Aurobindo notes the "constant aspiration of mankind to reach the wisdoms concerning God, Light, Freedom and Immortality" (Aurobindo, 1914). Those ideals are persistent throughout history and can be reached by a revolutionary individual effort or an evolutionary general progression.

Andrew Cohen investigates the evolutionary journey of consciousness and our faculties of reflective consciousness and free choice in order to participate consciously in this vast process of the evolution of consciousness from the lower dimension to a higher one, from the gross to the subtle, the personal to the impersonal. For this to happen we are required to liberate ourselves from the chains of the fears and desires of our narcissistic ego.

It could be said that the practice of psychoanalysis also focuses on liberation from the personal complaint and the widening the perspective to the universal structure of neurosis and psychosis. I state that there is no real sense in psychoanalysis without referring to evolution as its aim: recognition of repetition compulsion, falling of the ideal self-image, renunciation of pathogenic narcissism, recognizing the partiality of various desires and their limitations and detaching the identification with them, which means liberation, assuming responsibility for one's Enjoyment, invention of new knowledge and new love. What is psychoanalysis for if not to stop the repetition compulsion, to liberate from fixations, to create space for the movement of desire, to elaborate the representations of the drive to new metaphors?

This could facilitate the appearance of a new authentic dimension. The main difficulty is that psychoanalysis fixated itself on the perspective of the relative, while evolutionary enlightenment is founded on the absolute and is limitless.

Therefore someone who is introduced to the possibility of such a dimension to exist can enter a new realm of existence and action. In the base of this triangle the individual position is situated and is constructed from his attention and intentions. This position emanates from the recognition of an absolute factor in the Cosmos of which we are part.

In his 20th seminar (Lacan, 1972-73), Lacan caused a revolution by going beyond Freud and almost reaching a spiritual dimension; Being is located beyond the subject. The a-sexual enjoyment can seem to be spiritual enjoyment. Feminine enjoyment touches upon the infinite. There is no sexual relationship but there is a relationship of identification with thoughts, ideas, with our memories. This identification inhibits our development. Anxiety indeed touches the Real, but something lies beyond anxiety: The

Real of love. Not the love of the Real but the Real in love. A human being can renounce his enjoyments when he finds another enjoyment, a spiritual one. The ego spoils love because it turns love into a place for bargaining and inhibits creation.

§ Attention

Evolution of Consciousness means the appearance of a new dimension in being. In order for it to appear we need to develop a different kind of attention than the known. It is attention which is directed simultaneously inwards and outwards, it is actually a kind of detachment from the chatter of thoughts, emotions, images etc. To be able to listen thus freely we need to agree not to already know what we are listening for.

In psychoanalysis as well, one of the main tools is "free floating attention." Freud recommends to the analysts not to know beforehand, not to understand the patients too much, so they can listen attentively. To listen in as free a way possible from conditioning and from dealing with their own narcissism. This is necessary in order to facilitate a space in which the unconscious of the patient can appear before his consciousness. In this way he can face the truth about himself, about the dead ends of his identifications, his compulsive patterns, his illusions and his enjoyments, to assume responsibility for his life and to change.

Andrew Cohen sees in the position of not already

knowing the opening that can lead us to form a new, enlightened perspective in relation to the questions "who am I and how should I live?", enlightened in this respect meaning as broad as possible and unified. This is a way to apply the free floating attention in life.

The tool which enables us to develop and deepen such attention is Meditation. The combination of deep ease, liberation from existential tension and a high degree of alertness characterizes the enlightened position.

Through meditative attention one can discover that the lack which psychoanalysis sees as necessary is actually only relatively necessary, only at a limited development level of consciousness. Because from an absolute perspective, nothing is lacking. "Meditation is the gate to the feeling of infinite liberation and unity."

An attention such as this leads to the insight that the human experience is an impersonal one. That is to say, it is a universal expression of life and of consciousness itself which strives to evolve and know itself through all sentient beings.

We are meditating in order to be able to transcend beyond our separate personal identifications and so that the authentic self will be able to emerge and influence the evolutionary process. In meditation we let go of our conscious thoughts, as well as our unconscious ones; Since we are still, we don't act and we go beyond them to the profoundest depth—to the very source of consciousness. The place that was never unconscious, that never sleeps. There are infinite ways to contemplate about this but it is hard to define in words.

It is clear that if there is in our body a part that is not created, like DNA or atoms that merely change shape but are not born and do not die, there is no reason to think that there such a part can exist in our soul, a part that includes regular consciousness but is linked to a higher one. One can connect to this part through meditation. The whole issue concerns how to leave this innocence open, to cultivate it and not to bury it. There is truth beyond the truth of the subject. The truth of the Real is the truth of the impersonal, of the structure. What fixates psychoanalysis is the fact that we don't understand this truth, we don't really believe in it, and therefore we don't implement it on ourselves and we don't incarnate it. The stance of the analyst is not one of technique. It constitutes the only possible way to live and to reach a higher place—a restraining of narcissism—by not acting from the ego and from free floating attention. We don't really believe in our own theory which is profound and simple. We are drowning in complexes, in symptoms and in our enjoyment of them, and we don't see what is right beneath our noses. If we don't perceive this truth we put barriers on our patients' development.

It is really amazing! To be in touch with something which is beyond concept and form our consciousness sees or feels this presence yet it doesn't have a correlating image, a concept or form. The force of life is one. On the surface we are all separate, we think we are important, but originally, in essence there is only One. There is unity.

This kind of revelation creates an obligation not to be egocentric. The fire of life disperses the fog and confusion concerning the reason for our existing in this world. New love. Is this the most important thing there is? I say yes! Even if all would be taken away from me. Even in Auschwitz!

There is a limitless foundation to all this—taking this seriously means to succumb to the infinite. It liberates from boundaries and limitations of thought and understanding, interpretation and desire.

The liberation is not an emotional one, but liberation of one's gaze and knowledge. Without this there is no meaning.

I accept what I always knew in glimpses—or in flickers of light in all my paths of life—and have always forgotten, or divested my attention from it. I am referring to the glimpses of freedom, inner liberation, and independence from the ego which creates psychic and spiritual suffocation, especially when one is concerned with problems all the time-with limitations. All this is emanating from our endless rummaging in ourselves. This rummaging has an immense attraction.

In this situation of disconnection from thought and morbid engagement with the self there is freedom. The analyst's stance is that you become master of your own des-

tiny. Things are not only "happening" to you—you are an active participant in what happens. This absolute truth is revealed only after one throws away one's ideas and move from the known to the unknown—this is also the situation of creation.

It doesn't matter how much the demons bedevil you—you sit still and do not act; you don't do battle with them. It makes no difference if you are in a state of peace and transcendence or in a state of confusion and distress. The mental position is the same. The mind recedes to the background or appears in the foreground, the position is that of "no relationship." People think they fight all their lives but this battle is not a real one but a battle of self-pity. A true battle has nobility in it.

Can one profoundly renounce the past? Can one renounce sorrow and happiness? Isn't the aim of analysis to turn the Name of the Father into a simple name? I understood this and yet did not understand anything until today.

To choose your own destiny—to understand that this place of freedom is not a peaceful, stable and fixed place, but very dynamic. You exist in continual and fragile insecurity. Since in the secure place you only go to sleep and all the demons cunningly sneak in.

The hole is the heart of the subject and anxiety is Real but the heart of being is whole and the real there is infinite.

The Consciousness Bearers

Until now I stopped and became frozen when faced with anxiety. The more you sacrifice to it and for it the more aggressive it becomes. Fearfully I cultivated it, and the belief in my courage disintegrated.

To focus on Zero, not to know, to be no-one, no-person, to be emptiness. When one connects to the 'no-relationship to thoughts,' one reaches choice and clarity. In a higher place there is no choice at all—there is freedom or death.

'No relationship with thoughts'—to think about nothing—to stop engagement—to agree or realize no-knowledge. The "I" is usually much identified with everything it is doing. To clean one's hands from the blood of all the actions that cause suffering.

The ease of being that is reached in meditation opens optical space. The scope of view is wider and hence response is more adequate, more peaceful. One's problems define identity and that is the reason one needs to hold on to them, because without them something disintegrates and you are left exposed. Here there is a battle against this conditioned need.

For women it is more difficult to follow and analyze the process of their thoughts because the death of the ego means annihilation for them. They cannot concentrate on Zero. For men it is more difficult not to know (to renounce the phallus).

Who is the observer? Who is the one that focuses? Who is the one that sees the movement of thought? It doesn't have an image or an identity. It is cut off from the self, but it is the self. We are caught in fixed images of ourselves in rigid identity. Rigidity reduces the scope of our world. Freedom comes with flexibility and with the disidentification with the image we have been concerning ourselves with. We do not need to know. This makes one's response more spontaneous and liberated. And then we save the world from ourselves.

We are inhibited in our creativity. We are inhibiting our actions since we are limiting, closing, knowing in advance. This is dynamic. One cannot grasp it. One should not grasp it. Why can't we leave things open? Why can't we go beyond knowledge? We need to let this happen all the time—to be in a place where nothing before happened and therefore there is no problem. To be in a position of profound interest and acceptance. In this Zero everything can happen anew again and again. We are dead within life when we stop the evolutionary impulse.

From the absolute Zero the movement of time begins which is the fourth dimension. The Zero in movement, in the ground of being, is one we can know in our being but not in our mind, when we assume inherent limitlessness. This is the original and basic Freud's Bejahung. The wholeness and absolute goodness of life. And what if this essential positivity is not veiled by our defensive needs that construct our self-image?

Meditation is a metaphor to an enlightened position in life, a liberated position which is constantly aware of the true and absolute nature of life. A position that sees beyond the relative. All the time, without movement. When everything is what it Is. Nothing has happened and everything just wants to live and to evolve. The firmness not to move irrespective of what we experience. To let the storms pass without moving and without identifying with them. To be true to this truth, never to betray it, and not to derive any conclusions about ourselves. This is transformation. There is the intention, there is joint deepening, the enlargement of consciousness and perspective, and then there is clarity—readiness, availability (the readiness to disintegrate to a thousand particles and to disappear in an instant, together with a strong experience of being). There is intention also in keeping silence and stillness when it is spontaneous and automatic as well as when it is one big storm. The position of interested investigation into happiness as well.

The idea is to renounce the compulsive fascination with the content of thought. With ease...with no-relationship with thought—I exist where I do not think...to connect to that...to stop the engagement with the content of the chattering thoughts that are the cause of so much suffering in my life. Like the place where poetry emerges. With ease. And I wish to receive into my being this gentleness, this sublimity, with ease, with softness and with relaxed holding.

What does it mean—without relationship to thought? Freedom. To be outside time and not inside time. The thoughts flow in their own rhythm and I am disconnected from them. Especially the thoughts about suffering, poisoning, lack. Not to lose something but to receive a kind of deeper and more sublime way of seeing like something that is opening. The sense of martyrdom disappears, so that in times of complexity, perplexity and confusion one can, clearly see the way.

To show interest in the meaning of disconnection from thoughts. To lose the sense of time. To understand that thoughts are not me. This is frightening, but one needs to take a risk. The ego is the feeling of separateness and supremacy over the other. A compulsive separateness. If this is absent we could merge. We recognize the differences but they are not important.

Thought rolls like a stone that doesn't collect anything on its way. This is the fearless being. If I give up the feeling of separateness that led me all my life and go towards the whole, what does it mean about my whole life?

One needs to renounce the fascination about knowledge. Knowledge that raises a false sense of control. I lack the belief that knowledge will come from somewhere when

I need it—to be ready for every catastrophe of abandonment. To be still is to renounce control.

§ Intention

Intention is conscious motivation. It is the part in our position that decided to choose freedom at any price. It is that determined will to be free in order to be available to participate in the immense responsibility that is put on our shoulders as human beings to take the lead in the evolutionary process of consciousness.

As Andrew Cohen says: "Having no doubt means that you are not only philosophically committed, but most importantly of all, you are emotionally committed. You see, the transformation I'm speaking about ultimately depends upon your emotional conviction. What that means is that even under the pressure and intensity of challenging emotional states like fear, confusion, frustration, or desire, there's no wavering about your bottom line. The big shift is actually getting to that point in your own evolution where you want to be free even more than you want relief."

One of the means enabling this freedom is renouncing the victim position, or in psychoanalytic language—renouncing enjoyment from suffering. This is a radical step in which we are ready, for the sake of liberating ourselves from the fears and desires of the limited and separate ego, to assume responsibility for the consequences of actions that hurt us and made us suffer, and of course also for our reactions. That is to say, to understand that we have free choice.

The secret is to want to be free. Free even from "being loved." Free from the happy or morbid narcissistic party. To renounce all that. And then you stand in front of the question: Who are you? What are you doing in this life?

There is a desire inside us—a desire-craving-need to connect to this process. For that one needs to make space—to clear space from all our narcissistic identifications.

Positive freedom is always for a higher purpose. Otherwise there is a falling back. The end of the road—the need to be free more than anything else, for life and for the evolution of consciousness—now. Negative freedom is a result of the modern ego.

Knowing—evolution of consciousness is the development of our capacity to know. The enlargement of our capacity to know is not connected to a higher capacity to understand a larger amount of information, but to the experience of knowing itself that means recognition of conscious freedom from specific information. When we experience the enlargement of our capacity to know, we become aware of experiencing a different level of consciousness. The human being is in touch with himself, with his heart, with life. A mysterious depth is starting to reveal itself.

The Consciousness Bearers

To be free—as a higher value than any other, when it is related to the experience of transcendence, wholeness and stillness. To turn it into the supreme value where all other values are positioned below it. This is the work that needs to be done. To stand behind your healthy self and to make it whole. The connection of the desire to be free with the high dimension of the self is an evolutionary leap. All of life and other wishes change, and therefore—there is different differentiation and different integration. A gap is created between you and your self-image; The self is the one who wishes first of all to be free more than anything else, and then he wishes for other things and checks them according to the supreme desire. The trajectory is going forward towards simplicity as opposed to complexity. Simplicity means dignity and trustworthiness. The wish to be free is expressed in all the important choices in life.

Like the Archimedes' principle, that raises the world. Or like Escher's hand that draws the hand that draw's the hand, freedom has a reference point outside yourself— you are conscious of your consciousness—this is where freedom is. This is what puts everything in order. One simple law harnesses all the horses to the carriage in a certain order so that it can move.

In Sublimation, the object is raised to the honor of The Thing (Das Ding). In Evolution, the I is raised—the center of gravity is increasing and the importance of objects is decreasing. The I is changing in a qualitative way.

Ruth Golan

It is like a feeling of falling on your knees. Maybe the surrender means being completely obligated—first of all to ourselves. But in relation to the whole. This is what life is about. The delicate nature of this process necessitates growing and deepening and infinitely evolving. "Thy will be done," but this time, by me. There is simultaneous surrender and obligation.

When we relate to freedom primarily, we are not making important mistakes as a result of inattention and we confront the truth about ourselves and about our lives. Our lives become simple and transparent.

If I want to be free, and it is more important to me than anything else—first and foremost I assume responsibility for all the consequences of what has happened to me. I also assume responsibility for all the suffering I caused to others by ignorance, selfishness and cultivating the sense of the separate I. The more one identifies with the ego and with anxiety—the more the fixated and un-free trajectory of our life is strengthened. What about the unconscious drives and repetition compulsion? We are not bound to act in accordance to them. When consciousness is enlarged attention also gets more focused. Attention outside of oneself as well as inside strengthens the capacity of choice. Most of us are mechanically conditioned and our personality is mechanic—we are alike in sensations and responses. The question is: how does one get out of all this? With awareness and understanding of the Nothing or of the One. The will to get liberated from all this is also the will that gives life meaning—we become the expression of freedom and enlightenment in the world. We become the image of God.

The goal and the path are identical. Speech and the act are one. Everything else is worthless. This is why freedom and love are one. Only thus can we understand what love is.

The minute falling in love and passion awaken, the ego claims them to itself—because in them there is the sense of the absolute, and every joy becomes pain. "Healthy" love, un-narcissistic love, is related to the relative dimension and is in accord with the will to be free and do not harm that will. The feeling is one of stillness and not of great passion.

Usually passion and love are in conflict with the will to be free not by their very being but because they are easy prey to the action of the Ego.

It is obvious that my task is to break the chain of cause and effect, or the chain of Karmatic consequences, and not to continue in the conditioned response of the victim. It's not that I will not suffer. Suffering is sometimes necessary, but I will liberate the world from the suffering that I cause.

Erotic love is usually the only ecstatic and deep feeling that people feel. When it disappears they search for anoth-

er deep feeling or they blame their partner on its disappearance. This search for erotic love is not equated with an impetus to reach liberation, but the other way around. It is fixated in the illusory dimension.

One should differentiate between unconscious drives or motives and using them as an excuse to our actions. The minute we act—we know. There is choice according to Freud, and it is true even for psychotic people. The unconscious is changing. The more we become conscious the more we can control our behavior and be humble in front of the impossible.

§ The arrow of Evolutionary Tension

The evolutionary tension is a different dimension of the same drive that psychoanalysis refers to as the erotic drive. It can be called the Life drive—the drive to evolve, to fulfill the potential that is inherent in life which aspires to manifest itself—the drive that expressed itself at the beginning of creation with the big bang. It continues to express itself in the aspiration for higher and more complex forms of harmony and integration.

Andrew Cohen writes: "In a more profound sense, it is the awakened compulsion to manifest the ecstasy and the simplicity and the wholeness that one discovers in the spiritual experience itself... But the degree to which you have transcended ego is the degree to which the evolutionary tension is going to be the source of ecstasy itself. You're awake, receptive and interested, and you always want to give more. Why? Because that's what your purpose is."

The essence of existential tension is the relationship to the other, abandonment anxiety, for example. This is why, when we reach zero, the absolute, where there are no relationships, there is no reason for existential tension. Instead one can feel evolutionary tension. Existential tension is really inhibited evolutionary tension.

So, it is possible to differentiate between three levels of the *creative impulse—sexual, creative, and spiritual.*

One is referring to the same impulse. The same Eros. A creative person—an artist, a scientist, a philosopher or a social activist—is burning with the need to innovate. The irrational impulse to create the new is essential to the human being, and it is expressed by various creators of culture as a compulsive impulse. When we are deeply inspired to create something, the feeling is of an external force that takes over. We do not want to eat or sleep and we forget about ourselves. The aim of the drive on a spiritual level is to awaken and evolve a new consciousness in the world.

When the impulse to evolve emerges, evolution demands conscious beings and conscious participation and is dependent on it. Evolution will not happen without conscious cooperation. There is no turning back, as there is no turning back from sexual reproduction to cloning. If you have been a fish and have been turned into a lizard, you cannot go back to being a fish.

The position of the authentic self is: "This is what we really are." We are the ones who write the poem or draw, or enlarge consciousness. But it doesn't mean that it is the "I" in the Ego sense that always finds excuses for postponing things. The embracing of the evolutionary process is not necessarily related to a certain insight or feeling that. The embracing of the process means admitting and recognizing the fact that the process is happening through us, that we are the evolutionary process: at least the part of us that is the Authentic Self that wants to go forward and evolve in the present is part of the evolutionary process, while the part of us that is Ego wants to postpone it.

The Authentic Self is not the positive part of our Ego. The Ego has its own positive parts. It is a result of a relatively late phase concerning the development of individuation. The ego's problematic part is created when it focuses too much on itself and on its own survival. The Authentic Self is the impulse that emerges from us when we enable it to. It emanates from what Andrew Cohen calls "the moral Kosmic imperative." This imperative is not related to us but to the infinite need of the Cosmos to evolve.

The liberation of the creative power in the individual is a very powerful act in itself, an act that is expressed in enhancing and deepening the experience of the creative power in art, science, etc. But the liberation of the creative Kosmic power in humanity itself—and the understanding that we have the capacity to develop this power by identifying ourselves with the Authentic Self—is causing us to feel obligated and morally responsible to the whole process.

There are two levels of motivation or two fundamentally different modes of "lack." There is personal desire—emanating from the lack in the satisfying object; Here one's desire is to fill up and receive—more and more recognition, love, satisfaction—but the lack never disappears. There is "another" motivation emanating from the wholeness of the impersonal dimension. This motivation constitutes the evolutionary tension that pushes us forward from an Ex-time location (which is simultaneously exterior and interior). The essence of freedom means connecting to an objectless space. Here there is freedom from all experience, or rather from a relationship to experience and from an adherence to experience. One needs to listen to a non-relationship to thoughts. From that viewpoint, one's perspective is completely different. It is free. This space constitutes ex-time and that part of infinity in us. Its expression is equated with impersonal interest, and with curiosity, which is the meaning of life itself.

Nothing is more important than this inner freedom. Not even love. We are all conditioned robots. I, too, am also conditioned by my own anxiety. Because the pain of anxiety is stronger than the strongest physical pain, I surrendered to it. The more I acted as a result of this anxiety, the stronger it became. To be in the world with open hands, with nothing attached to them. To hold on to nothing. What is more important to me? Knowledge, control or freedom, or liberation? And most importantly—there is no turning back. The path leads only in one direction.

§ Position

The individual position is situated at the base of this triangle, combined of attention and intention. This position emanates from recognizing the existence of an absolute factor in the Cosmos, a factor which we are a part of.

So the two elements—intention and attention—create a new position towards life. This can be visualized as a process of cleansing oneself by meditation, in a bath of emptiness. This meditation enables us to disconnect from all fears and desires, and reemerge with the right relationship to life. We re-emerge as the intelligence and energy that create the eternal Kosmic process.

This position connects between knowledge and ethics, whereas usually there is a gap between them—between what someone says and what he does, between a spiritual experience and the way of being in the world. From here it is possible to formulate three definitions of the "I" which is not ego:

The self-absolute—ground of being

The Authentic self

The choosing function—this function is impersonal and it is apparent when one has an emotional tendency towards something yet chooses against this tendency. Choice determines the intensity of the soul. One can lose the soul or enlighten and awaken it.

Ego choices eliminate more subtle energies or at least block them. They develop emotional sensitivity instead of energetic awareness.

This position demands not knowing anything in advance and not attributing anything personal to information one receives. This does not mean the erasing of knowledge or memory but rather this means discrimination between Ego and knowledge and creative sharing in the field of consciousness. One's interest in this discrimination will cause the position to develop.

So here three possible perspectives concerning life are posed—The narcissistic position of anxiety and desire; The disconnected position of non-relationship to thought which is the "spiritual" position; The position where everything is measured by the will to be free from the Ego and by the will to maintain evolutionary tension. This will frees us from conditioned responses and enables us to see the effects of conditioning and its karma-like consequences after the response occurs... This leads like an arrow straight to a higher being in the direction of the Absolute.

I = the one who chooses

Ego	Authentic Self
Survival	Evolutionary
A constricted and self-absorbed perspective	A universal perspective
Constructed from past fixated identifications and conditionings	An expression of the creative impulse
Threatened by change	In constant transition. Aspires to create that which is new.
Acts according to fears and desires	Free

Instead of positioning the central axis of "I," here a space, emptiness, and a question mark are positioned. Emotions exist here, but they are surprising. One does not expect them. Now. One is like a new born baby. If I have nothing, I am nobody, if I know nothing I am like a liberated butterfly, I am weightless. But when I meditate I feel an enormous weight that pulls me down. An enormous weight that pulls and pulls at me and which I jump out of. How does one get out of the known and the habitual into the unknown which is full of possibilities?

The Ego always wants more time, in order to be ready, to have an escape pathway. The ego is holding onto time.

I discovered my inner compass. This compass knows The way. I do not need it to answer all possible wise and sensitive questions. I believe that in the position of "no knowledge" there is an entity that is directing the way. In this position of not knowing one has all needed preparation for confronting catastrophes. This preparation is more profound than in knowledge. Knowledge exposes us to the possibility of breaking down—because knowledge constitutes an illusory control. When we are ready for anything we become lighter than air. The frightening, dangerous and difficult agent is the Ego that makes us forget, that twists our soul and that brings us down again and again.

The Ego exists in the judgmental self-consciousness and is used as a wall between ourselves and life. It is a de-

fensive wall that blocks vulnerability or presence. This constitutes neurotic regression. The victims whose Ego is the strongest are un-trustworthy people. They have "good intentions," but meanwhile they live in falsehood and fabrication.

To restrain narcissism and not to respond from the Ego. To take feelings and sensations inward and to burn inside—because of wanting to be free—this is what purification means. There is a part of us that is beyond the mind, a part that was not yet born and not yet created that is pure because nothing ever happened and nothing ever was done there—it exists beyond thoughts and is in the place of not-knowing. And there is the human part—the self, the Ego on which one needs to take responsibility only if one wishes to be free and full of Eros energy. Then it is important not to consider our feelings but the consequences of our actions.

Evolutionary energy has only one motive—to burst into the world through us. We are the filter, and we should clean this filter, and also we should not get intoxicated from the power we feel when this energy passes through us. Freedom is inherent in us and what we need is a subtle presence in order to reveal it, in order to see it.

The deeper we go and the more space we embrace, the more things are opening and we are able to get into contact with a higher subtlety.

Ruth Golan

The capacity to sit still and not to control the experience not to develop any relationship to it but to witness it. To be aware of awareness is necessary to the freedom we later have in life. To stay still in front of the machine—to be quiet in the midst of a storm. Not to identify with content. This is what transformation is. The change in the contents themselves is much less relevant.

Creating a hierarchy of values with the top value being the will to become free. Everything becomes clear and simple when there is one choice. This is something that really threatens the Ego. Simplicity doesn't allow one to hide behind a fog of possibilities. There should be a resolute decision that one always chooses the part that wants to be free, even while confronting hard opposition or seduction from the part that does not want to be free.

Other expressions of the Ego are manifested in walking on the edge as a goal in itself. One wants to feel special, original, not compromising, when actually not having initiated any revolution. We neurotics long to be crazy, to lose control. We are excited by these feelings—as long of course that the fort stays whole. One's biggest confrontation is with inertia and with adhering to what exists, even if it means misery. One is afraid and resistant to change. Here the possibility of change is suppressed. Life hides from us the fact that it is constantly changing. Nothing stays the same, yet we hold on to this suppression until something Real wakes us up, we are shocked and we almost collapse.

To be the self that is uncreated and unattached to the world but attached to the absolute. To be the one who acts. To initiate a difference. To take responsibility for the consequences of one's actions and to act in the world from a motivation that is free from the Ego.

Not to be a collector of spiritual experiences but to connect experiences to real life. All the time. To liberate the world from my Ego. To pass this way of being on. Only I can walk on my highway and there is no guarantee what the outcome of this will be. Freedom from the imprisonment of thoughts, imaginations, wishes, frustrations and hunger.

People behave in a repetitive pathological way that makes them suffer. They go to therapy because of this—because this is a narcissistic blow. They come in order to strengthen their narcissism. They ask for caresses and recognition. The analyst directs them towards assuming responsibility on their karma—a further narcissistic undermining and moving from a position of a personal victim position to an impersonal spaced position. He directs them to detach themselves from previous identifications. Then they can choose if they want to be free. They discover their evolutionary compass—so that they can evolve to a different level of being.

Andrew describes an opposite process. First the will to be free is recognized and after that all the rest emerges. There are two trajectories that move in opposite directions towards a similar goal. Most therapies stop in the middle because people are reluctant to give up their victimized self-image or their narcissistic investments, and the analyst is in a similar situation. He did not renounce his narcissism in his own life. He is defeated. He hasn't uncovered the evolutionary tension inside himself, thus making place for a different entity to emerge.

Looking for objects that change in a metonymic way constitutes our unfulfilled desire. This unfulfilled desire is constructed on a lost object and on an irreducible lack. The desire for liberation, on the other hand, comes from a different place. It is sustainable and it is not dependent on objects. On the contrary,—it is the desire to be free from any object. It is not a feeling; or rather it is a positive form of feeling. A feeling that doesn't lie, like anxiety lies. Instead of desire one can substitute passion, conviction, drive and intensity.

Evolution takes place not in the energy itself but in the mode of its channeling. The ego is like a barrier, like mud on the energetic track. Desire that doesn't come from the Ego constitutes vertical calling or pulling. Something is pulling at us from above. From the inside up. If we recognize this and commit ourselves to it we feel are being connected by a hidden string. This sensation is a more focused one. It is like a laser beam of enlightenment. Thus one feels less free.

The bounding of liberation means that many sacrifice themselves for the sake of the One. There is a sacrifice of many wishes, desires and fears, for the sake of the will to be free from all these wishes, desires and fears. In this position of the will to be free for the sake of something bigger than me, one arrives at caring very much. Because of this type of caring, one stops before and not after the fact. The questions then that one may ask concern how many mistakes and how much karma I can prevent from myself and from the world when I arrive at this caring position.

To look at the human experience from an absolute point of view and to remain there turns all of life or the position towards life upside down. This is an experience of being simultaneously inside and outside. Connected to life but also disconnected. Being in nothingness. What does this mean? Being that nothingness, being in a dimension apart from the dimension of birth and death. It is only God. Everything is created all the time yet nothing happens because there is a stable place that is beyond up and down vicissitudes. Mainly not to enable the Ego to take control or sponsorship over the experiences. Infinite wakefulness.

Ruth Golan

§ Extension: Enlightened Communication and Action

"Three things are needed for human being's happiness. Friends—cooperation, trust, Freedom—a feeling that he is the master of his life and decisions, and Time—for thought." —Epicurus

"The three points that a triangle has consist of self, truth, and life. A man who aspires for life is working from his Ego, from appropriation, and from consumerism. A man who turns to sacred and absolute truth—is connecting to life because truth and life are inter-connected." —Pythagoras

The tip of the authentic triangle represents the form in which the position of attention and intention is realized through action and communication in the world that is external to the psyche. Contrary to the normal-neurotic triangle that is characterized by repetitive defensive actions, here the action is vertical transformative, which aspires for the new and is not limited by fear or desire. Thus the action emanates from the self who is free from fundamental contradictions and selfish motives, enabling the human being to assume full responsibility for his actions.

Enlightened communication happens when human beings come together with the purpose to create something new in consciousness. The group attempts to journey together beyond the limits of the known. The wisdom which reveals itself in such communication is deeper and wider than the wisdom of each of the group members. This is a new foundation for human relationship which is not based upon the separate sense of self, but on the authentic self which is impersonal and free. In this way one can find new and creative solutions to problems and conflicts that threaten the continuation of existence itself.

In Enlightened Communication, the ecstatic intimacy that is created between people makes the Zero from which we develop and about which we try to talk manifest. The humane here is considered a positive thing, not as a negative entity. The Zero is movement with direction and without fixation. Fixations are a result of presuming limitations to one's communications.

Words are a mode of consciousness. They comprise the effort to be simple—to express oneself simply, and to listen inwardly and outwardly simultaneously. Without limits. To touch the new, always to touch what is new and fresh without fear and together with one another. This is the Authentic Self. An ecstasy exists in this passion if it doesn't become a manifestation of vanity: one can contemplate about it, be interested in it and investigate what it is. This is a different and new mode of communicating between people where words are no longer a wall or a weapon or a barrier but rather, a way of connecting. The person becomes a mode of response, without inner obstacles of self-consciousness.

Ruth Golan

§ The arrow of Confidence

Enlightened action and communication in the external world feeds the authentic psychic position of attention and intention, empowers it and the evolutionary impulse that aspires always to evolve and move beyond the known to new realms of creation and knowledge. This confidence is necessary to build a different momentum than the influence of narcissism and inertia, and is important to strengthen and stabilize the spiritual enlightened dimension.

The Ego is that part of us that draws conclusions on the basis of the quality of the experience—pleasant, not pleasant. This exemplifies the morbid, neurotic and narcissistic part of us. A possibility exists to choose not to be there, and more than that—not to enforce this on others.

The Authentic Self is what there Is; the Ego is self-created. When we do not construct our identity, not only what we know disappears but also who we are disappears. When this happens the Authentic Self is expressed—it is expressed when one cannot hold and cannot know anything unless it is through the effect of our actions in the world. This is a radical transformation in conceiving what is possible and the potential way to live differently. The Authentic Self is transformation. It is movement and relentless desire; it now includes the past and the future. It has direction. This transformation is evolution itself. It is actively passive. The evolutionary trajectory is not an integration of a great thing into our petty lives. This constitutes revolution.

The name of the game is evolution, change and transformation and not self-acceptance or empathy. For the above to occur, one needs to renounce many things which are connected to the Ego. We do need to compare ourselves to others, but we need to raise the standard of comparison. We will not make do with complaisant mediocrity. We invest an enormous investment in knowledge in order to avoid confronting zero and to avoid the empty center of not-knowing. Women are afraid to disappear into this empty center, but men demand knowledge in order to inflate the Ego. To be in the place of not knowing means to stand there with open hands, then you cannot lose anything and no one can catch you.

The relation to experience is what is important and not the experience itself; this means not knowing, not creating problems, but rather to be at point zero. One is not to contemplate about it but to be in it. The relationship to the experience is absolute.

Freedom is not a feeling of transcendence or joy or becoming one with the world. Freedom is to be in zero and in not knowing. Actually this is a position of attention—free attention, without knowing, without interpreting, without limiting and without enforcing anything.

To be in the nothingness or in the non-being. I relate to moments where all the commotion of the ego quiets down, but knowledge exists that the nothingness is there all the time. Like an under-current. Like a pleasant death. The Ego consists of holding on tightly, being attached to things, settling in one's self image and being demanding. Authentic Self=creation. The wish to create the interior of the Cosmos=the conscious future. The Ego is conservative and a coward; it does not want to know anything new and it is attached to what it already knows. This is what constitutes repetition compulsion. We simultaneously choose something and become what we have chosen. There is no separate identity.

The inter-subjective field of research does not surrender to the known, but always aspires to the unknown. Researching ourselves and the discourse between us and others are always creating a new space for consciousness. One can search and discover new territories. We are interdependent in order for this to take place. The Authentic Self is the incarnation of the creative energy in us and the Ego is merely a distorted screen.

The interiority of the Cosmos is at the same time our own interiority. Our awareness of this equality is to our advantage. This exemplifies the enlightenment of our capacity for choice: To be less in love with life's image, consistency, balance, seriousness and trustworthiness.

One needs two things in order to walk the path—a profound understanding in the truth of these teachings and confidence in our ability to walk this path.

The results of our action clarify to us what it is we really wanted to begin with. This truism is so simple that it is frightening. One reaches this knowledge when one is all alone—there is no guarantee whatsoever that what one perceives as the results of one's actions is what is really there. Nevertheless there is the inter-subjective field that can give one feedback into what our actions mean. Choice of action also gives one confidence because it is backed by the clear knowledge of what is really important. Morality, values and the meaning of life emerge from these choices and these convictions. When there is no pretense there is presence.

THE AUTHENTIC HUMAN

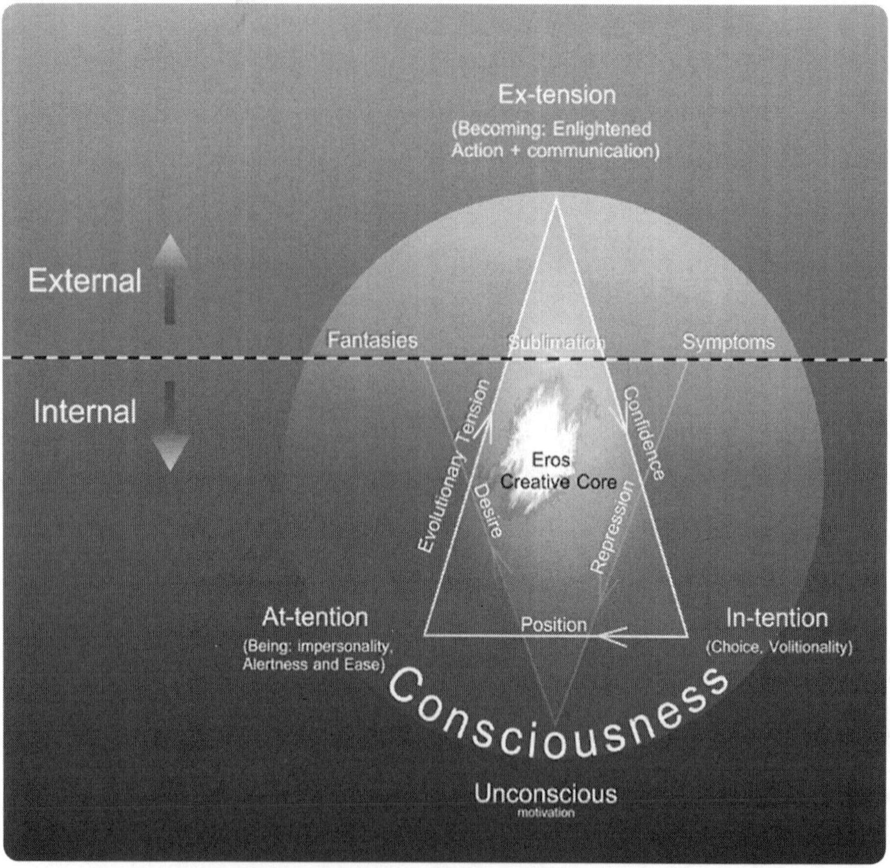
Ex-tension
(Becoming: Enlightened Action + communication)
External
Internal
Fantasies
Sublimation
Symptoms
Evolutionary Tension
Confidence
Eros
Creative Core
Desire
Repression
At-tention
(Being: impersonality, Alertness and Ease)
Position
In-tention
(Choice, Volitionality)
Consciousness
Unconscious
motivation

The Authentic Human is a combination of the two dimensions-triangles. When the authentic dimension has evolved, the less developed dimension—the dimension of the separate self—doesn't disappear. It loses its power and like in the schematic drawing it is subjugated to the authentic dimension. It is useful as what represents the human uniqueness and individuality but only with the condition of it being harnessed in the service of the evolutionary process.

Andrew Cohen says: "The authentic self is already free! This Authentic Self doesn't need therapy or spiritual practice to enable it to let go of unwholesome conditioning. It's a part of the self that has never been hurt, wounded, or traumatized. Why? Because it emanates from a more subtle level of manifestation, a level that can be seen in this world but is not of this world. It cares passionately about life and truth and evolution. And its manifestation is always spontaneous. While the ego is an expression of the personal and historical dimension of the self, the Authentic Self is an expression of the evolutionary impulse in consciousness, which is always impersonal and universal. When awareness, due to ignorance, is trapped in the gross realm by the ego's fears and desires, it is impossible to experience the peace, bliss, and fullness of the Self Absolute or the ecstatic life-affirming passion of the Authentic Self."

The meaning of spiritual practice is to face everything and to avoid nothing, that is to say, to practice a free relationship to experience. Once you stop paying attention to the self-image, attention breaks free. Attention is directed to experiences. Attention is a central axis where nothing has yet happened. That is why it does not matter what the desire or the fear of the Ego is, even if they are unconscious. With the help of liberated attention we can feel that nothing has happened. One can stay disconnected and not act from fear and desire. It operates also on the unconscious, on the condition that one wants to become liberated, free and enlightened. We do not need to defend ourselves any more to deny or to repress anything. All we need is to hold onto the stance that nothing has really happened. One should get out of the center of the stage and cultivate an evolutionary tension that exists between the relative and the absolute, and then something else will happen, something bigger than us. The evolutionary potential that is beyond us and beyond the capacity of our perception will emerge through us. Here it is the relation to the experience and not the experience itself that will emerge. The minute we do not wish to be someone, we do not need to defend and to guard our self-image. When we renounce this attachment to one's self-image, the whole defensive structure disintegrates or at least changes.

When one tries to change, the Ego ceases to be a defensive mechanism and becomes aggressive. If one does not face this aggression it attacks itself in a more and more morbid way. It does not stay static. Again and again the illusory confidence is severed; one's anxiety gets stronger and the mistaken choices that one makes from this anxiety and the desperate search after a defense from reality become more and more pathological. This is so dangerous that people revert to anti-depressants and anti-anxiety drugs and then what we see are deadened people who are still alive. The Ego is a fake shelter.

The Consciousness Bearers

How can one to aspire to become whole and have a right relationship to one's thoughts? One can do this when one is honest, serious and, inattentive to the Ego's fears and desires. One does not act as a result of these fears and desires. One needs to understand that the differences between people are relative and redundant. Of course, structure is what stands behind all that is personal. To relate in an impersonal way creates a stronger intimacy in the end because all differences disappear. When we are solely within our personal experience, we are alienated—this position is even aggressive. Where we pay attention is crucial. If we do not listen to the constant current of irrational thoughts and we don't make karmic choices, everything starts to look different. If we listen to the spiritual call to become whole, we start to look backward in time: two hours, two days, two weeks, two years, and this route begins to start to look good—evolutionary. It connects itself to the source of life. The source of life=the world and I are one. There are no divisions. To be in the 'not already knowing' means that The Ego is a deaf-mute, blind, and suffocates. This is the place of enlightenment. If attention is directed towards fears or anxieties—the feeling is of suffocation. But if we do not escape back into the little box, suffocation disappears and instead new spaces and new dimensions appear.

This is the difference between fear and awe. Fear comes from the Ego. Anxiety comes from the unconscious and awe belongs to consciousness. We feel awe when we face truth—the wholeness of everything: "Be joyful while trembling." To die to the world. To die to the Ego. Not "freedom or death" but freedom as death—and then we return, not belonging to anything. Blessed non-belonging. We need to detach ourselves from all materiality—including the materiality of thoughts, feelings, and knowledge.

The relationship to life is expressed in our choices—it determines our destiny. What is important is not to respond in a conditioned way; especially when confusion, anxiety, desire and doubt are strong—one should not respond. It is then that we usually tend to respond and choose—and there are consequences (miserable consequences) to these choices. If we succeed in maintaining a no-relationship, we will gain a lot of confidence, more than in times of peacefulness, joy and easiness. When attention is liberated from the efforts to get confirmation to self-importance and self-appreciation—we can see reality as it is—not deny it and not dive into it, just see it. Without avoidance. From a liberated attention which enables awareness to sharpen and be empowered. Then we will see how much all our "personal" experiences are mechanical and that the more we act only in our own interest—there will be no meaning to our lives. When one guards the motivation to be free, one can do all this and go forward. The evolutionary tension drives us further.

What does it mean to "be Real?" it means going in an unsplit direction. The Ego feels autonomous with this split.

It is not committed to what it says or does. To be Real means that a minute is a minute. There is no future. Every minute is the last minute. This is a total obligation to life and to choice. There is no middle road.

The recognition that it is not about me and that I am not the center of the picture—culminates in ecstasy. It liberates a most overloaded baggage. This is a winning combination. The Authentic Self exists in all of us—it is Real; To be in touch with this means to be in touch with the part of us that was always free. Freedom always exists but is covered in hard layers of the Ego. It is like the flower of the Lotus that wants to open up inside us and needs to remove the spiritual impurities around it.

The qualities of the Authentic Self
- Freedom: from the Ego and its fixated identifications.
- Responsibility: about our actions and responses. Renouncing the position of the victim.
- Confrontation: know thyself.
- Connectedness: awakening to the non-separation that exists between all of us.
- Giving: living in order to take the evolutionary process itself forward.

§ Eros, Creative Core

Both the dimensions of the authentic human are nourished from the same fire that is responsible also for all the creation in the world. It is the creative principle or one can say it is life itself which are not concentrated in the individual but in the life process itself of which the individual is a vehicle. It is also the source of the evolutionary impulse and its derivatives, i.e., the drives.

In the words of Andrew Cohen: *"First there was Nothing (Being), then there was Something (Becoming). Who and what we are is both of these things—Being and Becoming. Something and nothing, manifest and un-manifest, form and emptiness, human and God."*

For him God is the intelligence and energy that created the Cosmos, that is to say, God is Eros. In psychoanalytic terms we would say that "Eros" is that immortal Libido that creates the tracks of drive and desire.

Perceiving God as Eros is a non-dual perception of the divine, in the same way as Spinoza saw it. But contrary to Spinoza there is creation in the Cosmos. One can describe it as the absolute place where there is no time and space but there is a vibration of potential.

The potential is infinite like the void, and when the spark was ignited—the spark made the world burst into becoming. The spark is God. God is the cause. Our aim is to help him continue to be revealed in the world through our own consciousness and its evolution. In the un-manifest realm there is no otherness and no I. This is precedent to the subjective existence: that same thing to which we long to return—the oceanic experience. In the beginning there was The Difference. Before The Difference there was The One.

For Freud, renouncing the drive is the key to the establishment of God. The source of God is enjoyment, but the kind of enjoyment that one renounces or denies. This is the place where the prohibitive agency and the super-ego abide.

For Lacan God is the Other. It is the same divinity that is established due by way of language: by way of speech. Here one finds the logical and scientific face of God. The other face of God is related to enjoyment; this is God as the small object a. What psychoanalysis calls God is a condensation between these two aspects the signifier of the master and the object of the remains.

There is God of the law and prohibition and there is God of feminine Enjoyment that is limitless and infinite. In his "Seminar on The Ethics of Psychoanalysis" (Lacan, 1959-60), Lacan suggests that the object of desire is in its essence a forbidden object. We desire what is forbidden to us. The law defines the prohibition that is the condition for desire. The Name of the Father supports the prohibition, but with the disintegration of prohibitions in modern times even the Oedipus Complex is endangered. Eros became therapeutic and culture lost its sense of tragedy. The pleasure principle prohibits enjoyment and becomes the Name of the Father in relation to infinite enjoyment.

Ruth Golan

The aim of evolution is "to reach God"' and to build a world whose aim is to know itself better and better. This includes ourselves and our awareness of our capacity to participate in this creative process as we could participate in the process of creation. We have powers of creation and make space for them when we empty ourselves from Ego.

The post-postmodern aspect of Eros is the encounter between subjects. Consciousness recognizes itself in a way that elevates human beings.

Post-postmodern art that is influenced by this kind of an Eros is not concentrated on creating objects or indicating lack any more. It does not tempt us to the gaze or to reject the gaze, but is a creation of new metaphors that express consciousness itself in its encounter with itself. This part in the artist that is part of consciousness creates a form to this consciousness through which it encounters itself in another consciousness which is the spectator's. This encounter is contingent on the spectator's being in touch with this consciousness. That is to say—this is an expression of a pure subject.

This is a process that is between fixation and transformation. The potential for transformation of being exists in every one of us. In childhood this is very apparent yet at a specific time this potential is blocked. A fixation in thoughts and in the status of a being begins to exist. These are conditioned responses. One can make changes in these responses towards less suffering and more peacefulness, yet they still stay in the framework of fixation. The impulse towards transformation can awaken after an encounter with the Real or with a living, non-dual freedom from fixation, thought or being (yet one needs to be in a certain level of wakefulness in order to recognize this). Fixation kills our soul while we are still alive. Transformation directs us to the absolute and enables life. What does not exist in the current of transformation—dies. Fixation creates lumps of dead matter that accumulate and destroy the flow.

The psychology of liberation operates from top to bottom—from the One and the Non-dual and no difference to the bottom of the many and the split and the lack. The I which is on top is always free and it is impersonal. This is where ecstatic intimacy occurs. Our task in the evolutionary process is to actively participate in this liberation and the inclusion of it in our lives and our environment. To look from top to bottom and not vice versa—this is the opposite of what Freud said. To raise the center of gravity—this is what is new and fascinating.

How does one pass from one status to another? What is the motive for opening up and evolving when we are abiding in the darkness of egocentric consumerism? From where does the light beam enter? Is it an event of grace or a result of trauma? Where does the crack begin? What leads one man to transformation and the other to depression? Is it a born ability? Are there different intensities to different souls? Why are there people that appear hermetically closed?

The totality of reality—part of it being and part becoming, and inside it—the interiority of the cosmos. There are four aspects to the I—the authentic, the Ego, the choosing capacity, and beyond time and space—the absolute emptiness. I represent all of them, and this is why I am responsible for their development. My evolution develops the heart of the Cosmos.

The extreme narcissist alienates the I from its moral dimension. The psychological I is alienated from the process and from others, and it wrongly presumes a high level of moral development—both good and bad. This is a horizontal developmental line as opposed to a vertical one. The status of the soul is the sum of all our negative and positive experiences and our responses to them. Moral development leads to action from a moral conviction regarding life. A sense of moral obligation creates weight and depth. This is the real liberation. Moral development is the development of the individual. I make the choice to evolve from my alienated self to my Authentic-Kosmic Self. This is the only way I would be encouraged to develop morally. We choose to take unconditional responsibility for every traumatic event that happened to us on the level of the soul. The minute the essence of our soul emerged and was individuated, a window of opportunities was opened to evolution because of our intention to take the process forward. The capacity to choose, gains empowerment from the Authentic Self which is the serious part of the psyche.

The marriage between the Authentic Self and the capacity to choose begets evolution. The Authentic Self as a stirring force and as grace bursts out as a creative impulse, and the choice of responsibility. All this liberates us from dependence on different feelings and situations.

§ Consciousness

Consciousness is that energetic infinity which is actually immortal Life. Without consciousness what exists is only matter. Even concerning matter modern science is claiming that there is more or less hidden energy embodied in it.

In his article: "Narcissism, an Introduction," Freud writes: "He [the human] is the mortal vehicle of a (possibly) immortal substance—like the inheritor of an entailed property, who is only the temporary holder of an estate which survives him" (Freud, 1914, p.37).

The Authentic human recognizes his being a vehicle whose aim is to enable universal consciousness to know itself and to empower itself.

In the Eastern teachings Consciousness is the unmanifested. It is both emptiness and fullness. That which was never born and will never die. From that place the becoming self is conceived as a temporary illusion. But evolutionary enlightenment recognizes both the immaterial liberated being and becoming who is more and more aware of itself.

Consciousness is related to reality because one poses a question concerning the location of consciousness. If one looks at the way a baby is developing, it is obvious that consciousness is located in the interaction between the baby and its mother rather than in the minds of each one of them. Today Even scientists admit that our brain does not develop as a closed set, but rather that from its birth the baby is focused on the human environment in the same way that this environment is focused on it. (On this subject Lacan already has said in the beginning of his teachings that the human subject is born into a symbolic realm and not into a void. And more than that, the only way to become human is to be embedded in an abundant inter-subjective environment.)

The earliest social interactions are engraved into our biological structures that mature during the maturation of the brain in the first two years of life. Winnicot went even further and said that there is no such thing as a baby; Since the baby comes into the world without solid psychological boundaries there is only the liquid, changing, unifying space between a child and its mother. In this virtual intermediary space he locates his mind, with the help of a responsive sensitive parent. According to the Lacanian mirror stage there is also the other who points to the child who sees himself in the mirror, saying "this is you" with a joyful expression.

The Consciousness Bearers

It is possible to claim that as much as consciousness exists in an inter-subjective space, the "I" also is an inter-subjective product that emerges from an earlier stage where there is someone who responds- and who "reads" the baby's mind. This enables the baby to "read" the minds of the others who surround him when he grows up. This is a manifestation of the capacity for empathy. This — also is the origin of the capacity for transference.

The "next step" on this path is the understanding that Earth is not the center of the universe; that the human being is not a master in his own home; that the external Other collapsed, that God is dead and that he/she returns in full colors through our consciousness and our impulse to evolve it. The latter represents the impulse for knowledge. We find out that God is not the Other at all but that he/she is in the realm of the One; That he/she is not a small or a big object but a subject. This is why one cannot talk about "him." Freud's speech about the impulse for knowledge is related to primordial knowing. The human being is not a master in his own home because he is enslaved to the unconscious, that most intimate entity that is one's ultimate stranger. Beyond this lies universal consciousness. This ultimate stranger consists of the most ex-time (a mixture between intimate and exterior). Here, consciousness does not belong to me or to anyone else. We are vehicles—we are part of the evolutionary process—we are consciousness bearers.

One should let go of all the past in order to clear a place for consciousness, consciousness is always free and does not adhere to the past. Attachment to the past can create an illusion of fixation and a lack of change. One should let it go in order to give up membership to the unconscious or to turn the Name of the Father into a name on one's identity card. In addition, one should give up any cultural, ethnic or historical attachments. The latter change the past's location and its importance.

Consciousness affects us with abundance, and all we have to do is open ourselves up as containers and receive this abundance. But where does abundance exist? This abundance exists in our selves. We are filled to the brim, we boil over and we affect others. One's faculty to choose might be considered the conscience. The faculty gives one direction. If one chooses the Authentic Self—it develops the conscience and creates a momentum of choice in the same direction. If one chooses the Ego, conscience deteriorates. The best choice is done from a sense of freedom and of moral ethical obligation.

The Authentic Self also contains feelings, desire, and passion. It acts against the rational mind that can be distorted by the Ego. How can one connect with these feelings, desire and passion? We go back to zero and to the perspective? There is a hierarchy of knowledge, feelings and impulse.

The leading edge creates new grooves in consciousness, and then others can walk in them, thus creating the new and not adhering to a static state. Is the chooser part of consciousness or part of the vehicle? It certainly is part of consciousness that knows itself. When we make choices we design our destiny with our own two hands. But since we are only a link in the chain of consciousness, we are designing the destiny of humanity and maybe even the destiny of the whole universe. The exception here is the ground of being, that also lacks meaning if there is no consciousness that experiences it. To return to it and to exit from it reproduces again and again the act of the first creation—which constitutes the big bang.

Ruth Golan

Collective New Being

"Individuals belong to the community; they complement each other. In every human being there is something unique and rare that is unknown to others. Every individual has something unique to say: a special color to add to the communal rainbow of colors. So when a solitary man joins the community, he adds a new dimension to the communal consciousness. He contributes something that nobody else can contribute. He enriches the community. He is irreplaceable [...] Because of this uniqueness; human beings are coming together, complementing each other and reaching unity." —Rabbi Soloveitchik

"Collective reality is more real than some of its parts. It has a mysterious unity and is an active force in itself. Human belongs to this category of birth, revelation and endings. There are no isolated entities; there are only elements of a whole in process." —De Chardin

The next stage of the evolution of consciousness will not happen within the individual, but in a group—among people that aspire together towards a common objective. When individuals who are awakened to the absolute perspective are ready to stand behind that recognition and the knowledge they have acquired and to come together in an authentic way with a joint intention to lead an evolutionary process of consciousness, what begins to be created is a new collective being. This has enormous potential for the transformation of human civilization, for infinite possibilities. In order for this to happen two essential conditions are required: The first one is unity and communion between people, and the second one is the autonomous individual.

What is created is an organic interested and participating group structure, and from it a new being is growing naturally. This new being is constructed from the collective and from each of the participants who are without split and without Ego. This is a new experience in human evolution and we have no clue to where it will lead. What creates such a new structure is not related to the personal character or quality of each individual. It is only related to his/her willingness to abide in an unknown place with all that he/she has and without worrying about himself/herself and without self-consciousness.

Who am I without this persona? Without my personal part? I am a part in a marvelous flowing process. I am a servant of Kosmic consciousness. Here there is a lightness connected to collective being.

Our ability to act from what we recognize as right and not from what as a reaction to our feelings is revolutionary. Here a possibility exists to adhere to a decision even if it is in conflict to our emotions.

When one does not speak from the personal or from the abstract—speech is full of vitality, it is focused and straightforward. The question of love is of course complicated—love without attachment, desire or narcissism, is love that does not get anything back in return. It is very demanding but it liberates one from dependency on any object whatsoever. If I can say that there is One without there being a second one, I can also say that love is not separate from that One and it recognizes only itself. It recognizes only the big Self and not the small one. It does not recognize the Ego. It recognizes itself in the other. There is nothing to hold on to, no reference point; there is no point to lean on, When we speak in an impersonal and non-abstract way, we awaken, and we understand the depth of our sleep.

What does it mean to go beyond the personal? It means going from a lower level of consciousness to a higher one, from the old to the new, from the personal to the universal. How does one manage responsibility in an impersonal way? Presence. Freedom from history, freedom from inertia, and most of all—there is something in identification that turns everything to the personal, but actually it is inert, habitual, accepted, and not really personal. To go beyond the personal means to go beyond what is dictated—to a new and unknown place. It is so difficult to stay there! The personal attacks you with all its power—especially in matters of love—which really is not love at all. And what about creation? What about uniqueness? One should connect to the spirit through creation—to say something personal that will touch everybody and will raise them one level upward. This is the greatness of creation. This is the new that goes beyond the old. To peel oneself from the personal is to go nearer to God; to bypass the fact of death and entropy and to give meaning. The personal is what grounds you— to the feet of the evolutionary mountain. Romantic relationships are also ropes that tie you to inertia, to the ground, and to the Ego. When one is liberated—everything opens up. There is active and conscious participation in climbing the evolutionary ladder—when attention is directed upward and is deep and less prone to temporal fallings and blows. This is a ladder whose head is in heaven and whose feet are in the individual and in the group.

To go beyond the personal does not mean surrender or giving up but rather an entrance to something much more meaningful and fascinating. The mission of the evolutionary revolution belongs to each person. Evolution in leaps does-not mean annihilation of knowledge and history but going beyond them, towards the new and the unknown. Emptiness and form are two sides of the same coin. Form is constantly changing in relation to emptiness. Traditional religion is based on remembering and conserving, the new religion is based upon—letting go and continuing to walk.

Is there really a possibility to live without neurosis; to live without lack? More concrete than the will to be free is the will to connect to something authentic which simultaneously is mine and not mine.

All subjective experience is actually impersonal. That is to say—there is a subversion of the subject. Awe and liberation are one and the same. How should one be and act? How should I act from the understanding that I have responsibility for the creative principle since I am that creative principle from the very beginning? That I have responsibility for the whole process? There is radical autonomy and communion through the collective field. One cannot achieve this alone; a team is needed as is a field. If one gives one's heart to God, everything else will align with that.

You cannot own freedom or enlightenment. It is not something you have and it is not something that you can accumulate.

§ Communion

The experience of communion occurs when there is no sense of separation between people who come together. When they communicate among themselves as the authentic self, an awareness is being created concerning the breaking of the usual boundaries between the self and the others. (In resemblance to the description of Martin Buber of the unmediated experience of I and Thou). And then they can be an incarnation of the Absolute Unity.

Andrew Cohen: "Perfect communion is the experience of ecstatic intimacy—of merging, beyond ego, with the other as yourself."

Wishing to put order into chaos, to introduce sanity to insanity. Otherwise enlightenment becomes materialistic acquisition. If you attain it you feel important of course.

When one abandons the adhesiveness of the Ego, that is to say being attached to ownership and to acquisitions, what miraculously arises is a great caring and great love.

A natural hierarchy that exists between people with different levels of development liberates each one to be where he is. This pulls one upwards. When this happens in a group what is created is collective intelligence. A new being is created that one can actually feel. What is revolutionary here is the attentiveness to the investigation of truth and not of the self. Each person has freedom to speak exactly from where he is, and also to listen and want to know.

In order for collective development to occur each one of the participants should be at the edge of what he reached in knowledge during his own development. What we create in a group are new structures in consciousness—the field itself begins to evolve through us. For this to happen one needs to care very much for the process itself.

Consciousness wants to know itself. We are at one with the transformation. When we are at one with evolution our inner being does not disappear, but it aligns itself behind it and becomes part of what is going on. Then, if we investigate our inner world in the group, it is for everyone, it is for evolution. Something mysterious is also happening concerning a consciousness that has effects beyond a specific group. There really is a kosmic consciousness that passes through us.

§ Autonomy

"Therefore man is alone—he was created alone, he lives alone and he will die alone. The individual cannot be or walk like... For to be 'like' something means he is not alone. And that that is not alone is not human. Aloneness has nothing to do with the well known aspiration to be original. To be original is human instinct; it is in fashion...It means doing what no one had done before you. This instinct is not an original one. Many people are basking in that instinct and succeed in deceiving...themselves.

"Aloneness does not equal originality, it is not exclusive. Both aloneness and originality are nourished by man and by his humiliation in order to survive...Aloneness is the capacity to live and produce from yourselves what then develops into you, what is appropriate for you, and what only you can create and produce. This is a truism even if you were the first human being on earth. This is true even if there was nothing in the world besides yourself. You must live your own life, and be nourished by the reserves of your own truth, without being a spiritual parasite. Supervision, yes learning, yes. A rabbi, yes. But do not choose someone to do the hard work for you. One needs to work, to perspire, to fail, to try again and again. Without lowering your head in despair, without paying attention to what anyone will say."
—Rabbi Menahem Mendle from Kotzck

The choice of freedom and radical authenticity is a resolution of the individual who stands alone.

Andrew Cohen: "Autonomy is the expression of your own individual creative freedom—the powerful, unrestricted freedom of the individual to flower in his or her own potential without limit.

"So in evolutionary enlightenment, for what I call perfection or heaven on earth to become manifest, one has to directly experience the ultimate non-difference between powerful autonomy and profound communion within oneself. The evolutionary goal would be the manifestation of a miraculous context where autonomy and communion were ultimately inseparable. In that context the extraordinary creative potential of each individual would fully flower consistently, and yet no individual would be taking any position in being special or unique or superior in such a way that would prevent the experience of communion emerging in the ecstatic recognition of no difference whatsoever."

To conclude, these are the basic rules for a good life:
- The wise one—learns from every one: attentiveness, to be in the unknown without fear.
- The hero—conquers his drive: self- restraint, directing the drive to higher goals, without ego, with awe.
- The rich one—is happy with what he has: He is not identifying with an ideal, he can be happy with what I have; he crosses his fantasy and directs his Enjoyment.
- The respected one—respects people: not for his own sake but for the sake of the whole. He lets everyone express his essence. Love.

In the vicinity of Andrew Cohen

§ Notes from one workshop in Foxhollow, Massachusetts

The notes you are about to read include part of what was written during a workshop in an evolutionary enlightenment workshop in Andrew Cohen's world center in Massachusetts. The notes were written in a free association style, and they represent the experiential-personal mode of the writer. I met Andrew Cohen a few years ago and since then I have participated in many workshops. These notes wish to transfer not only information about the teachings and insight that the teachings awaken but also the experiential mode. On one hand those are personal experiences and on the other hand these experiences a significant impersonal real is also reached. The way I experienced the workshop of course represents the place I was in at the time and the phase of development I had reached. Part of the text consists of the way I understood Andrew's talks in the meetings and part of it manifests an inner dialogue.

Since this teaching is evolutionary in character and its aim is the transformation of the individual and of the whole, the dynamic flow never ceases. Therefore, in another time and from another position different things would have been written.

First day

Moments of pre-workshop and post encounter. The meetings with people are joyful but I don't really have anything to talk to them about. I am always weak in social talk. My actual wish is to be part of the organizers, not part of the guests, to be part of the doing for others.

The light comes up a blue-gray—The snow is here as are the trees, but where is the lamb that should be sacrificed?

I would like to ask Andrew about ethics and day to day life. How do you participate and take forward the evolution of consciousness in your own life, when you are not within a community of spiritual students? What are the social ethics? How does one act in the world and continue evolving? The beginning of the retreat consists of silence, no relationship to thoughts. There is no relationship.

How should I write? My world is receding rapidly. One cannot actually write when one has no relationship. Or maybe one can. The thought of relationships as a work of art like embroidery or knitting repeating chains of nonsense that create a whole.

Outside it is freezing cold and the sun is shining. There are divine variations to the light. Somebody is reading in a tent; she is small and alone in front of a memorial to the revolution.

Every man or woman to himself or to herself. In the end every man\woman is to himself or to herself. In the ground of being nothing has ever happened, but one can't get in touch with it in communion. You are totally alone there, because there is no relationship. One can't really share meditation.

We sit facing the sun—part of cosmic consciousness. We are part of Becoming.

Being created, Becoming, comes and goes, comes and goes, repetition and evolution. And the feeling of humility of the part in front of the whole: And the peace and quiet of course, to be where sacred and huge things are happening.

Before the afternoon meeting

"No relationship to thought" leads me in inevitable circles to the death of Rafi, to the moment of death, to where he exists, before and now, to all my former life. And I "think." The thoughts are the dead part. Being now and forever—is the living part. The heart is aching even physically, and a question rises—will I die here now? Does any part of my life exist?

After the meeting

Being is present in the ground of being—in the purity of seeing, in depth and width. What is important is not the aloneness and the non-relationship to thought, but the consciousness of which you are part. A sacredness of light, color and sound. All the "problems" are dissolved into the true reality of things, their realness. An almost unknown lightness emerges. The lightness of being, not the lightness of value. Not to observe thoughts but to let go of them. The thoughts do not have an "I" essence, I am the one choosing to identify with them or not, mostly with the awakened consciousness.

Partially I am happy, partially I cry about Rafi, about the anticipated death of my loved ones, partially I am merely peaceful.

I skip dinner, not only because of spiritual issues, but because of the cold and dieting, and my stupid mind also distances itself from me. Not to be dependent on it is a happy thing. I certainly moved forward in the last two years but my mission now is simultaneous attention/as much awareness as possible/stillness and lightness—and this mission is flowing inside and outside.

It is freezing and snowing outside. Inside is the sweet and good spirit of Andrew, to which I haven't yet connected. But I will not even follow this thought.

Second day

Meditation on zero. One cannot grasp the Real. It is always new. To return to the place of before the beginning in order to be born again. I talked with Andrew on the experience of detachment that brings with it a much more intense sense of death and loss, and from there, in touch with the ground of being one can reach beyond life and death. There is no birth and death there, I am totally alone, and yet totally together, something of Rafi is there with me.

One cannot build anything on this zero; it nullifies every experience, including inertia and repetition. It is the opposite of repetition! And its depth is infinite.

Yesterday a white moon appeared in the center of the window of meditation hall. It was big, almost round and completely white. Reflecting the shades of snow. And now the skies are clouded, but we are in a different place, in a place of retreat. Simplicity. The whiteness is appropriate to simplicity. Slowly I lose my fatigue.

The stillness. Being with the primordial stillness. Awakening to the Real to its absolute dimensions. To include the joy, the emotionality and the sadness and to transcend them. To evade the manipulative and shifting ways of inertia. "Now when the storms subside"—to become from the place where nothing ever happened. *A break in the sabre dance.*

An installation: And in the center of the snow pool there is a memorial contoured by candles and flowers, and by a chain of tiny lamps. Opposite them there is an orange tent. From the tent a woman's voice is heard. Day and night she reads about autonomy and communion: The intensity of autonomy within the greatness of communion. But it is not an artistic installation but people on a spiritual journey—so what is art? What is the Real in art?

Wakefulness is getting stronger along with the stillness and peacefulness, consciousness is getting wider. "The unconscious is opening up like a hand-held fan" (Yona Vollach).

So what is this ground of being? This no-place which is full? What is the consciousness that includes all consciousnesses? What is this place to which we come devoid of our deeds and of our personal life history? The place where all identifications fall away? It is just there. Being there/here. Devotion. To die to the world of intentions and direction. I don't know who I am—what a sentence! The ground of being is the infinite point in the sea of finitude, or maybe vice-versa. I stand on one foot, oscillating back and forth on a piece of a finite cloud that floats in a deep ocean of infinity.

Life is around me. There is no poem in me, no knowledge; all of me without context, totally still. In a movement of breath the zero is widening and retracting, or being created, or being welded, but not solid, mostly rubber. How improved is my lot.

The zero is a place without time and space and movement. The empty place full of vital potential which is inherently positive; *Totally positive.* Only recognition of this truth—and conviction—will lead to transformation. Otherwise we are led by fear and hunger of the soul. These kinds of people, full of hunger and fear are not trustworthy. One can never know what they will do.

Every therapy should begin with returning to this zero point, and to be reborn from there. Isn't there an

element of faith here? And what will I do with all those who approach me without any trust, faith or access to this positive potential? For whom life really stinks in its worst case, and is meaningless in its best case? That what directs them is cynicism and lust behind which there is great fear?

To be reborn time and again in this infinite context of the ground of being. A repetitive experience develops the confidence in its truth; in the existence of potential in the nothingness from which everything can emerge. Only than one can face life's tests.

Is identification with the potential, with the vibrating nothingness, the ultimate identification? The importance of experience is in the opening of the possibility of transformation.

The evening is descending; the branches of the pine trees wander in the wind, wishing to give shelter to the birds.

The reason retreats are important is their allowing an intense awakening without the need or the attraction to sleep. They make a safe place possible for which one can return to zero and go beyond, to make one more step forward.

Evening

Disturbing thoughts—if the ground of being includes the potential for everything, and its essence is completely positive, where does "evil" come from? Does it come from our life choices? From the un-manifest positivity—rebirth is always to a positive place (+1). The confrontation with the stresses of life leads us to the Ego (-1). If I should be with "no relationship to thought," to focus on "zero," I should not relate also to these thoughts, to rest in the positive and that's it:—to choose the positive. Here—there must be an element of faith and trust.

Third day, twice as good
The air is cold, but vital, not freezing. The snow on the ground is friendlier. The sun is shining and everything is well. This is simply the situation.

People experience transcendence, sacredness and ecstasy. The question from yesterday hasn't disappeared, but it is let go. Also Andrew in his way answered it without me asking. Zero—this ground of beginning, of a little before the beginning—before death and birth—is completely full from *a human perspective*, it being an ego-less place. The ground of being itself is maybe without any qualities.

"And you shall choose life"—this is a positive place in the sense of bursting creativity.

For this I am going, with two hands, two legs, and with my whole heart.

The origin is sacred. Before it we are the humble of the land and to it we give respect. "Evil" or "distorted" emerges from our ignorance, or from the ignorance of others. My question also arrives from the place which refuses to directly experience the pure contemplation—the "non-relationship" to thought.

There is nothing more important, there is nothing as important.

Until my physical death—to breath and to experience in the zero, in the nothingness—the sacred with certainty.

Freedom has no history. There is no past to freedom. Every minute, every day, to come new and humble to the possibility of freedom—this is the real enlightenment. I experience the strongest experiences of meditation through writing—speaking to myself and as myself. I am in touch with subtle frequencies, with the vibrating depth—it is easy for me to be "there" and not to worry about what will happen next. The vibration mostly awakens love.

My love for Andrew is deepening. "Your love for me is more miraculous than the love of women"—and men.

During meditation and contemplation—my head is like a broken radio full of noisy stations. Let it go! Let it go! All associations are so free, binding me in an infinite circle, "the star over the woods is blue and shining" (Alterman)—my inner star. I am attentive to the sacred center. Naturally there are a lot of religious associations. The fruit exploding with seed is inside, outside and beyond me.

Before me, after me, on all my sides, under me and above me.

"For the man is the tree of the field. Like the tree he aspires upward" (Nathan Zach). But his responsibility is much bigger than that of the tree of the field—not lightness of being but joy and a very heavy responsibility: "and I don't know where I've been and where I will be"—from zero to zero, intoxication spaces. From the narrow place, from the one exploding point—the entire world is in perspective.

Passing by a lake on which one can walk with safety. Not a problem for Jesus or for others. Through the snow ice pools appear, and where are the fish? And what about the light? It is just that. The same perfect zero. It is just that.

Afternoon

The questions return and bothers me immensely. I am in touch with the depth of the creative, with unity. With the potential and abundance, but where does the death drive come from? I remember the pessimism of Freud and the Americans' rejection of the concept of the "the death drive," and then I remember Freud's initial positiveness—the *Bejahung* (affirmation in German) which is necessary for the development of the baby before any negation. This is the initial identification with the life drive, with the un-fixated libido, with that same flowing of creation. Wow. There are transformations in consciousness that result in changes in reality. Different priorities; the collapse of guilt in favor of commitment and responsibility. De-identification that leads one to bounding oneself to freedom. Not to live life without an ideal and not to attach to an ideal without life. To move from an anxious love life to an independent love of life. To put a limit to self-love and to liberate oneself from self-consciousness. This removing of obstacles is like flowing waters as opposed to a standing swamp.

The Consciousness Bearers

What is the nature of the positivity of the ground of being? I want to say—a reservoir of creativity, like fire, boiling lava to which the true part of me belongs. He didn't let me speak and it's not really important. All the Ego thoughts passed and there was no paying attention to them. The question disappeared since it is obvious that in this potential place there is only positive power. The evil comes from elsewhere.

There are two principal things: *knowledge and gravity.* Knowledge without an object. Knowledge which is wisdom and a gravity force that one wishes to jump into and stay there. The issue is calmness, peacefulness and infinite joy, because nothing ever happened and there is no problem. Andrew asked us to continue paying attention to that but not to think about it. For me it is a creative vibration where I am totally me, without desires or fears.

It needs one level of separateness and abstraction to contemplate it—it needs minimal duality in order to separate the capacity of contemplation.

He spoke with contempt about the concept of "love" that people tried to raise from time to time. He is right. Love—an overused and non-evolutionary word. He spoke about the mentally ill as opposed to radical mental health. What is the problem?—Self-reference, self-centered. Gravity force towards the inside and not the outside—it is simple. But opening the perspective can change the whole picture if a person wishes to see it.

His accuracy, the research, the endless curiosity, the

going beyond, the non-compromise around clichés. He is talking about pure knowledge and not about pure consciousness, and this is an important difference.

To connect with this ocean of potential from now and forever. Beyond life and death. Just to be there.

This is where Andrew is abiding and this is where I shall be—without intermission, forever. It is exhilarating.

This free fall into the sea of potential, this "being there" is the true way and this is the only way to enlightenment! And there is all this even before there is any relationship to evolution.

Fourth day

The illusory spring ended. The sky knits snowy wool for us and the cold is getting stronger. And at night the dreams come. Violent—strange dreams. Who said that dreams don't come from the Ego? The entire dream = Ego.

Interestingly Andrew spoke today about the bad attitude towards life in the manifest domain. The bad relationship to life which is the narcissistic egoistic relationship, and asked us to differentiate between this and the will to participate in the evolutionary process that for a lack of a better name, he says, he names the "Authentic self." *The impulse to become is embodied in the manifest world.* From nothingness that holds all the potential, which is essentially positive, something is emerging—the entire manifest, the becoming—and because it emerges from it, it has essentially the same nature—a positive nature. It is very hard to see this but it is logically sound.

I examine my aging and wrinkling hands, and I am happy that I chose the path I am walking in. I am happy and I thank every minute, and I look back at all the instances of falling and sliding to narcissism.

It is difficult for me to sit for long periods of time, peacefully and with closed eyes—without doing anything.

Values—Andrew spoke about the way in which the value system that comes from the narcissistic place is completely different and is in conflict with the value system of the good attitude. (virtue = the good attribute).

To what depths can I reach? To what self-annihilation? Being consciousness. Can I touch? It touches me; it is calm and stormy, frozen and burning hot.

From where does the Ego derive its power? Initially it is an organizing principle of action and regulation. Then it becomes identifications, fascination, and our ability to be in a place of ignorance and denial. *As much as there is no limit to knowledge, there is no limit to ignorance and the modes of negation and estrangement.*

Noon

Suddenly it happened. A deep meditation the like of which I never experienced. And I felt exactly what it is about—I connected to a totally passive place, still and full. I wanted nothing; I didn't want it to end. I was ready to let go of everything and to remain only in that

place. I was this zero and it was wonderful.

The important and new thing in the differentiation between black and white, between the Ego and the Authentic self, is directionality. The Authentic self is the embodiment of the creative impulse and it is interested *only in the future*. In what didn't already happen. It doesn't recognize the Ego whatsoever and it is indestructible. The Ground of Being is the eternal moment, an ongoing present. The ego is dealing with limitations, security, freezing and conserving. From the point of view of the Ego—the impulse of the Authentic Self is wild and dangerous. Its radicalism is expressed in a constant movement between zero and one, while avoiding the -1.

There is no gradual process with Andrew. There is no development. There is a vertical leap. Most people can't go forward without first disintegrating the Ego defenses, to recognize them for what they are. For Andrew it is *evolution in action and not in insight*.

Andrew is a horseman galloping without a saddle. He doesn't look back. He is the knight of transformation and the new. And I? What about me? Do I take upon myself the commitment to act according to my understanding? I am thinking about home, about the future, about what needs to happen. This is not the right time.

The Ego is the lazy part in me, the part that is satisfied with the way things are and feels impotent, and always waits. The place from where the poems are written is the

The Consciousness Bearers

Authentic Self. No doubt about it. This is the point of certainty facing the spaciousness of being and wondering.

It is night. The skies are full of stars and faraway a layer of clouds is lit up in a refractive light. I discover islands of divine stillness. The zero is erotic! This is what Andrew says. The zero holds in it a creative potential—what is it if not Eros? Nothing is missing and yet the impulse exists—amazing.

Fifth day
As usual Andrew is more transcendent and more profound than all of us. He really thinks. He is the fire horseman who never looks back. He is like the Authentic Self that he really is the image of. He engages only with the future—he is the creative principle in person. That is why the future is his.

The Authentic Self is the soul—this is where evolution happens. There is no soul in the Ego or in the Ground of Being. One can manage in life with both of them, but the excitement, the creativity, the ethical challenge of the soul—they are all in the Authentic Self.

When I'm in Ego I build a fortress from stones of accumulating knowledge. The walls are made from my self-image, from perceptions and concepts, and inside it, it is suffocating and lonely. When I am connected to the Authentic Self—the Real part in me is the creative principle—that destroys every fortress, that doesn't act according to former knowledge but in opposition to it, that is connected to that profound knowing that exists in the ground of Being.

Sometimes I know the reasons for action only in retrospect, but the action is always correct. And there is certainty in it. It is an ethical act, a soulful act. There is no loneliness in it because there are partners to the road—even though there is aloneness or a readiness to be alone.

And now I am the *free agent*—this empty space that chooses what to identify with or "what to be," which amounts to the same thing. What is this I? From where does it arrive? Is it completely unique?

The Authentic Self has no shadow of self-consciousness. It doesn't think about itself but about what needs to be created.

Andrew's way of talking leaves me breathless (and full of soul)—galloping forward.

There is no silence nor peacefulness in the Authentic Self, there is an infinite demand for change and creating the future—and not just any future but an evolutionary one. And it is totally simple and not complicated.

And it is beautiful, so beautiful and clear, lucid and sharp. It is a sunny day and during the short walk I took I went outside the fence of the retreat and I sang old childhood songs. I also conversed with a red-headed robin that escorted me part of the way. We chirped and twittered to each other. He almost let me come near him until he despaired of my minute ability to twitter and moved on. Andrew's house was leaking icy swords.

Entering the meditation hall I saw some of the people sleeping, whereas some went deep into themselves; some were wondering about and some were abiding in transcendent realms.

The end of silence

Andrew is enlarging his talk on the free agency—the choosing agency. It is especially important to recognize this if one wants to transform and evolve.

He lets us speak together about the teachings, asks us to listen to each other, to come from a place of not knowing, not to impose our opinions upon each other and to leave each other alone.

My sense is that the choosing I certainly exists, but not as a blank board. We become what we choose. That is why the minute we choose Ego—we put weights on our free will. The choosing faculty therefore is not symmetric but it exists, and of course one needs to recognize it. *Here there is a breaching of the fortress.*

Suddenly when it was permitted to talk—I was filled with fear and unwillingness. Well, I don't need to always express my wisecracks. Humility! Just lately I told Andrew that I trust him a hundred percent and do I already have doubts? No, I will take responsibility for my choices. I want to participate in the evolutionary process. I already chose that! And after the last months I am even more determined.

As always— the act of talking causes the social game to enter. Who chooses whom, how to connect, who is

the leader. In the meantime I prefer a little more of the silence, the self-contemplation, the conversation with myself. It is mostly difficult to stand the American way of yakity-yakity-yak. I will talk soon enough. I will listen soon enough, because one can't act while meditating.

Andrew says—In the Ground of Being there is no 'chooser,' no separation, no parts. The 'chooser' begins the minute one passes into the manifest world. It also answers the question—when the One starts to divide, to become the many, the possibilities begin, as well as free will.

One impersonal enlightened conversation and my entire forlorn mood changes a little, all my excitement returns.

This is so important!

To understand that in the first step beyond the Ground of Being, in the beginning of our becoming, we are that same free will, that same liberation. Before we are someone, before our choice, we are that freedom. That saying Yes to life. We are the reason for the big bang, that is to say—because of the creative impulse there is revelation or embodiment in the first degree of separation.

From our point of view as human beings—we are bursting with creativity. Otherwise nothing would have been embodied. Everything is perfect (like in a beginning of a love story), what is missing is creativity that aspired to the new and to the future. We are so used to being victims and not recognizing this freedom.

Every minute one should take a step backward in order

for it to be possible to choose Authentic Self. It doesn't matter how many choices we made in the past. It is not a process—it is always possible, and the choice comes from abundance, and not from lack.

Morning. I really don't remember what day it is.

A lot of egoic "personal" thoughts. Thoughts about status. Am I loved or not, does anybody pay attention to me. Calm down and don't relate to it, not even with humor or cynicism, what is all this nonsense?

This understanding, that you are your free will at any given moment, that you never lose the possibility to choose between the different identifications. And if your feet are rooted in the Ground, that is to say in the eternal potential to create, and your head turns toward the future, then between these two a single current is passing, one line which is the evolutionary-creative impulse. An arrow bursts through your body, the vehicle that was given to you before you submerge back into this full and vibrating origin of nothingness.

So in order for the perspective to rise from egocentric to nation-centric, to world-centric, to narcissistic-centric, to kosmo-centric, one should assume responsibility for all Karma, starting from the personal one and continuing to the general. Since we are part of the evolutionary principle or the creative principle, and we have only this life to act in.

Suddenly he speaks so much about the unconscious, about how we don't see our choice. Even if it looks like we do, for somebody else it is much easier to see where we are than for us.

If you are not sure that you are the chooser, assume that you are and see what happens. Imagine that you know perfectly well what is the right thing to do at this moment—what is this thing? The knowledge appears when important issues are at stake. All other indecisions come from the Ego.

It is Friday evening. Today—Gong!—The bell of conditioning is ringing—call Mom.

The sky is blue and the land is white. A non-freezing cold is enough in order to breathe in vitality—this is an ideal combination for a retreat or for the evolutionary process to move forward—even if this process shouldn't be dependent on the weather or on the color of the sky or on the freshness of one's breath. All this self-engaging and my getting insulted are Ego choices. The minute I renounce them and dive into a conversation, the joy and sense of wellbeing immediately return.

The chooser is the individual.

Andrew is developing, the teaching is evolving—because forever—is about an arrow towards the future, not about being in a circular orbit around the self and its sensitivities. The feet are in the eternal ground, the head is in the future and everything flows upward. Repetition compulsion is retreat into one's shell.

Emotional maturity—this is what I lack. The gut fear about non-recognition—I see it all clearly.

He strongly emphasized the soul dimension—one perhaps can say the depth dimension—this gut knowledge, from a non-intellectual emotional place. Maybe the soul gives the Authentic Self the strength to act, the desire. The soul is already convinced it can say "No" to the Ego, it can evolve.

The soul is part of the divine—when the issue is the soul or God, my reference point is Judaism.

With Andrew one could have raised a revolution—what a man! What a prophet. He gives so much of himself—he told us that he was afraid of failing, afraid to waste his life with the wrong choices.

The importance of meditation—to submerge in the Ground of Being, to be in touch with zero, and also as a practice of total relaxation—not to respond in a conditioned way. This is a kind of necessary precondition—because if one can't sit still, how will we respond during action?

Between meetings I try very hard not to think about myself and just join the conversation. Without arrogance and without Ego.

Saturday

Going deeper concerning the soul. He let me speak the minute I vowed to myself that if he doesn't let me then...I had had enough of cynicism. When I am truthful and align myself behind my decisions I recognize the soul. *When I betray myself my soul- is estranged from me.*

A few important statements:

In the soul we know that we know.

One should enlighten and cultivate conscience in the chooser.

The battle with Ego is not by killing it but by opening the perspective.

A creative enquiry = together.

A new meaning to enlightened intimacy. *The intimacy that is created when speaking about the soul has a completely different quality and is much stronger than when speaking personally.*

At the soul level there is no time. There is the urgency of life and death.

The values of evolution are connected to the new, to change.

It is a new theology that you want to preach from the roof-tops. I am completely responsive to it.

Another concept—*to make a difference*—the goal of the human being is to make a difference.

What are the values of evolution? Truth as opposed to emotions, for instance.

The soul is the feminine; the Authentic Self is the masculine.

The Ego has only one goal—to sustain the sense of the separate I.

People share the experience of the loss of identity, i.e., the loss of Ego. I sustain this well. Even so I experienced this combination of communion and autonomy that happens simultaneously, without losing my identity. The soul also evolves and develops. In the past there were only unique people who realized this. Today there are more and more conscious people, but they are still the cutting edge. They exist alongside the foundation that one can count on, that is always there.

Lucid memories of encounters with the soul and painful experiences of betraying the soul. But what is really important is now and the future. This is my sacred commitment and its significance.

The awe and the spiritual love towards Andrew are getting stronger. The **atmosphere of a new being is floating more and more in the meeting hall and between people. All "my" things are suddenly dwarfed in the presence of the greatness of the soul—even my poetry or writing.**

He went on to say that we want to share with others the understanding concerning the Authentic Self. The Authentic Self is pushing us to express ourselves. The truth cannot be hidden.

Some of the conversations around the tables are at a level of directed and enlightened communication, and it makes me happy and interested.

Many thoughts about the past and future—and many attempts to return to the white zero as I see it—this full nothingness. I chant to myself like using a Mantra: relax and pay attention—and then broken passages of prayers and psalm chapters are played in my head, along with many other things!

Sunday

The impersonal rules of engagement make constructing a new world possible. Each one is responsible to his Ego and his Karma. The "we" obligates new moral laws. Renunciation, self-discipline, attention. When one sees this, it becomes inscribed in the soul. One cannot go backwards.

When the group really is in the throes of investigation it takes off.

Who is the chooser? Who am I? This is a question that needs to remain without an answer. The creation of a new being is made possible in a discussion that keeps to the rules of the game. Language becomes materialism. Through speech something is created which is beyond speech—it goes upward yet it is also rooted deeply in connection with the soul, and they mutually influence each other. That is why regarding the soul he is speaking about philosophical and moral conviction and certainty rather than about spirituality—the more solid the foundations the more the new world will grow and flourish.

Sometimes one needs to be silent and not talk. To be silent inwardly.

Speech creates a new being—literally with its own rules, its own consciousness and its own gravity force. And all of us—the individual and the group, together and individually, those who care and who are interested, are responsible for its creation and cultivation. *To facilitate, to be so transparent and connected until this entity which is beyond us, will happen. To let it reveal itself.*

A short meeting in the afternoon

It seems as if the emphasis moved to an impersonal inquiry around the tables. Attentiveness is creating the new. In creating the new being, consciousness/words are becoming material and not vice-versa.

And I learned another thing—by coming to a retreat we come not only to transform ourselves but also to participate, together with Andrew, in a common research of new levels of consciousness. Andrew himself is learning through us, and through listening to himself. There is mutual fertilization here, so it is doubly important.

A miraculous thing happened. The impersonal energy burst out, and all the groups united into one group contemplating the impersonal. I've never felt like that—and possibly others have also never felt quite that way before. What we experienced is communion and autonomy at a high level. Evolution in action—so overwhelming that it is impossible to describe the feeling.

Who am I—but a butterfly fluttering its wings. All the collectors of butterflies who fix them in with a pin—do not have butterflies but dead bodies. This is the same for all materialists. Including artistic materialists.

Monday morning
Time is passing within the same known banal gaps. This is what chronological time is. Evolutionary logical and psychological time have completely other plans. The skies are particularly blue, especially cold, and the trees—lo and behold—even if their roots are in the snow, their branches are budding. This is probably how Siberian spring looks like.

I cried when a South African woman described

what happened yesterday and was seen as a chance for salvation—and she compared it to the chance that Martin Luther King opened, and to the chance that was opened when the prison gates opened for Nelson Mandela. I cried about the invisible opportunity to open the prison gates of Israel.

Andrew speaks about the moral imperative that needs to come after the experience. The uncompromising individual position that one needs to live for is the evolution of consciousness. *Consciousness is a wild force, like the Libido.* Maybe it is the Libido. And it looks for us because it wants to be revealed. And in the manifest world—the number of awakened people is important because enlightened consciousness wishes to include as many people as possible. It demands from us to be trustworthy.

Most of us have a wounded soul. We don't believe in the trustworthiness of others or of ourselves. Becoming trustworthy is the first necessary condition for development. Most of us live personal lives for personal reasons—myself included of course. And the transition—the change of choice—carries within itself an experience, but also a conscious choice—a recognition of the moral imperative. *The more we go beyond Ego, and the more the personal will diminish, the moral imperative will emerge and flourish.*

Afternoon

Andrew is in a combative/witty/sharp mood. He asks us to check our lives, to see what is real and what is fake—and to choose accordingly. When we are the Authentic Self our choices are always right. The Ego is perceived as repulsive and aggressive. Then he started in on me, after Israelis and after women in general, but in actuality he differentiated between the relative and the absolute. To see the relative for what it is and to liberate oneself from attachments. *The evolutionary dimension is in conflict with the familial/ personal dimension that wishes to keep things as they are. The more we enter this dimension—the more the emotional element in our relationship with others changes.* We become "cool." With our relatives one should behave with compassion as much as possible.

The moral obligation for transformation in life leads to the end of personal life for personal reasons and to recognizing the self-image for what it is. The big aim here is to let consciousness express itself through me. To act only from the Authentic Self. Not to worry about how the future will look. Just to accept, truly, responsibility to karma, and not to create new karma. And if things need to fall, to let them fall.

Andrew gave us So many tools: compassion towards family and friends—together with detachment. Commitment to transformation as a model for our children. Clarity of the decision to be free—to keep the chooser free and enlightened. To choose! To choose! To choose the Authentic Self once and for all and not to compromise. My Ego is my exclusive responsibility. *To see the urgency in all this.* And if one needs to leave—leave, for the right reasons. To testify about the Authentic Self and to stop playing games.

Not to try to adapt the transformation to my life—it is

too big. On the contrary, life should manage itself in accordance with the transformation. To trust myself—at the level of the soul—heals the soul and brings back confidence. To believe that it is possible to let go of doubt and cynicism. To be ready to be alone with this—even if there is no one to meet at this level.

Very important: fear is natural—the Authentic Self is not afraid because it has a sacred and infinite goal in front of it, which is evolution. Again—the way to deal with fear—that is nothing bad in it self—is not to do battle with it or to confront it, but to choose from a wider perspective. To be at least 51% convinced with in the big perspective, and then our choosing part will not freeze or become paralyzed out of fear, but will simply not take fear into consideration. There is no real reason not to be afraid.

Andrew is truthful, serious, 100% authentic. One can trust him and believe in him, and through him I can believe in me! I am not frightened of him at all.

Only one day remains until the end of the retreat. I feel like a different person. Meditation arouses in me strange series of memories—thoughts. Every one of the people I once treated, one by one. Did I contribute to them? Did I change their lives in any way? Now, when I'm awakening to the huge context—will I be able to help more, and in a different way? On one side there is compassion, and on the other side there is attraction—upwards, beyond the small, reduced, depressive personal—towards the big goal—without submerging in ideology and idealism.

Tuesday
I have a big feeling of humility and surrender to a greater force, together with a feeling of connecting to the source of my power; the soul, clean from Ego is the source of power—the strength to act the right action. There is a right action in life, and I know what it is when I am in the Authentic Self.

The cold dissolved a little (a very little) and birds received us today when we were walking—very active birds, hopping across the snow and ice and looking for what? First grains cropping up from the earth? Frozen worms?

"People are afraid to speak with Andrew Cohen," this is what was said yesterday—he is the pure prophet—yet I am not afraid at all. I am only afraid to fail and to continue living in my Ego, I am afraid to remain in darkness, and I thank God that I met Andrew and this gave me the opportunity to receive help with my efforts as well as to see a living example to all that is possible.

What does one do in relationships? One draws the line beyond which one cannot pass. The direction here is choosing the Authentic Self, to *commit to it and intend to do so.*

I told myself and promised myself and to people related to me that I would change, and I didn't really mean what I said. I just wanted to achieve peace and quiet or to go back to the status quo, so that nothing will change—and then I would do what I wanted to do. I sincerely hope that this time is different. I don't only hope so—I have made a decision!

Yet another tip that Andrew gave us is—*it is better to take a small step forward each time, as long as one doesn't go back—turning back destroys confidence.* It is better also to admit that right now we can't give up something or change it—as long as we don't lose perspective. *Because what is important is to reach a higher stage, and not a higher state.* The pluralistic system by which "everyone respects the other's space" doesn't fit one who wants to be a soldier in the army of evolution. Compromise is the *hotbed of the Ego.*

What will it be like to live an impersonal life? How are things now, moment by moment? Not to relate and not to recognize the Ego, as well as from Ego. To always remember that there is something bigger and more important. Motivation—the motive is the key, as someone said—you either harness yourself to it or you remain a dinosaur, fossilized.

Without worrying about the implications of the transformation on others and without binding oneself to bad relationships, even if I remain completely alone. A dispatched arrow has been sent from the evolutionary impulse of the soul in an evolutionary tension that is constant. Step by step—ready to jump, standing on the edge of an abyss or at an open door of a plane.

We need to defend the revelation of the soul in us in this cynical world; the soul is a part of us that requires defense—because it has innocence.

In addition: *If we look closely at the things to which we are attached, we see that attachment is caused by ignorance.* Everything comes from anxiety and desire, and doesn't have an essence for itself. It is nothing, empty. But we are panicked and just wish to go back to peace and the status quo. This is exactly what my experience is! This is an exact description! And when one comes out of this experience one looks back at it as madness. *What is the secret of attraction?* How did I reach this level of madness? The issue is not to find hope in order to have the courage to change, but it is a moral obligation, even at the level of emotion—*it is not a sacrifice at all because these are my panic attacks and my abandonment anxiety, it is the nothingness.* Even love changes. Relationships become enlightened if the chooser is enlightened.

If I choose Authentic Self and act from it, I will turn my face to innocence and my back to cynicism, and what will be important will be to serve the great power of consciousness that wants to be expressed through me and to die to everything else. To die "for real"—till death, forever. Without awe (which is a better word than fear).

Evolutionary tension—this is the dimension that should replace emotions.

To cultivate the soul—this is the expression.

Night
When the retreat is reaching its conclusion Ego worries start to come up—as if they faded or turned pale in the passing days. This is the time to stand strong.

Today I raised the subject around the table that everybody prefers to avoid—a discussion about the number one force, *the sexual drive and romantic love.* Here people became passionate and opinions divided—it was not like talking about fear. And again, there is a better answer to the question of the sexual drive than in the past because of the context from which we pose this question, which is above everything.

What will it be like to come to relations as a connection between two Authentic Selves? To develop together? Even if there is no such thing as a sexual relation (as Lacan said) there is certainly the possibility of unity in authentic relation—what then will be the fate of sexual attraction? From the point of view of the Authentic Self the Ego becomes repulsive, said Andrew, so maybe the foundation of change will change completely and beauty will receive other values than the ones we have today and all cultural values will change. Attraction will be based on an evolutionary foundation between the couple.

And what about the partial, perverse, transgressive drive? Will it always break boundaries? Will neuroses disappear? We are back to this question. Is there normality beyond neurosis as far as the sexual drive is concerned? What will happen when this drive will descend in importance to second place? And yet the evolutionary impulse is an evolved derivative of the Libido—even Andrew admits it. What is important is to leave the question open and not to know the answer in advance. Because soon all my psychoanalytic knowledge will break in.

The last day

A sleepless night passed on all our parts—the Ego, the Authentic Self, the chooser and the soul. But it was not necessarily a bad night. Maybe I was bursting from energy, and maybe I had too much sleep all the other nights. A lot of thoughts about the sexual drive, about the feminine and masculine, on how to live an impersonal life and how to speak and express what I experienced, not only clarity of intention, but also clarity of expression—in enlightened communication. The wider the perspective is, the objectivity of relating gets bigger, as does the ability to express yourself clearly. There is no end to the importance of the clarity of expression in the context of unity. In the Authentic Self there is a necessity for unity—not in the sense of finding peace and quiet together, not in a horizontal way. But in a vertical way. It is a creative peace. Unity is a part of communion, and the creative—the part of autonomy. Unity is created as if it were inside a constantly moving train. Unity in a vertical position.

When the newness dissolves, radicalism and the unbearable difficulty are in guarding verticality and evolution and moving forward. Or, when guarding the newness in a group where the members know each other very well. To guard the evolutionary momentum that becomes more difficult the more one goes forward in the ladder. This is how Ego works.

"He who is greater than his friend, his drive is greater."

I learn from Andrew and from my retreat partners lesson after lesson the value of which is greater than gold—not solely for myself but for all those to whom I am connected—now and forever, in this life and in all the other lives I will have.

Part III

Cinema

This section brings a series of lectures that deal with different aspects of psychoanalytic and spiritual understanding as they are reflected in contemporary cinema. The structure of these lectures was constructed as a trilogy of series dealing with essential questions: who am I, where are we going and what is our role in this life—in other words—what the meaning of life is.

The series "What does a woman want" deals with the enigma of femininity, the series "On love and perversion" deals with the enigma of love, and the series "Beyond boundaries" focuses on the possibility of conscious evolution and transformation of the position facing life.

In the next chapters I will bring forth a selection of these lectures.

What does the woman want?

§ The Piano

AUSTRALIA, 1993

DIRECTED BY JANE CAMPION

ACTORS: HOLLY HUNTER, ANNA PAQUIN, HARVEY KEITEL, SAM NEILL

The story of this movie takes place in New Zealand in the mid-nineteenth century. Ada and her daughter arrive to a rugged forest in the south island of New Zealand. Ada—who is about to get married to a local native in an arranged marriage is mute from the age of six and is communicating with the world through her young daughter. Her daughter translates her sign language. Ada also communicates through playing on her piano to which she is completely attached.

After Ada's husband leaves the piano on the beach, it is bought by Baines who is his neighbor. Baines is a white man living among the Maori natives. Ada agrees to give Baines piano lessons as a way to get back her piano. An erotic and loving relationship gradually develops between the two. This relationship turns the world of the film's heroes upside down. Ada is going through a process of liberation and finds her new voice.

The Piano is a movie directed by a woman, Jane Campion. Campion is a contemporary woman that had directed a movie about a woman from the Victorian era. This is the same era in which Freud began to discover psychoanalysis through the speech of hysterical women. Jane Campion has not only written the script and directed the movie. An alternate title of the movie is: "Jane Campion's film," which implies a special relationship between the directress and the movie. Another interesting fact is that the name of the heroine is Ada, which is similar to the name of Freud's famous patient "Ida Bauer" (Dora). Since the plot takes place in the same period of Freud's formulating his discovering of Psychoanalysis (at the other end of the world), we can assume that Jane Campion was inspired by the story of "Case Studies in Hysteria."

The heroine of this film suffers from one main symptom. A symptom that is presented to us from the beginning of the film—her symptom is—silence, muteness. From the very first scene she peeps at us through her fingers and through glass and the voice that reaches us is her inner voice. Ada is speaking to us through mediation: her fingers, the sounds of the piano, her daughter. She doesn't know why she became silent when she was six years old. This is the nature of every symptom—we don't know its origin or

The Consciousness Bearers

its meaning. At the heart of every symptom there is silence, and Ada's symptom is silence itself. But the symptom in psychoanalysis also does speak to us, because it is connected to the unconscious and to repressed sexuality.

There are a few primordial objects that once gave us satisfaction and during our lives set in motion the course of desire. The breast is one of them. The voice is yet another object, which Lacan adds to the list of the objects that Freud wrote about. Because these objects were lost, they constitute the motive, or the cause of desire. The desire is to rediscover them. In the case of the movie in mention, it is therefore the voice, which is represented by the piano. The piano in the first part of the movie is assumedly giving an answer to the question "What does a woman want?", a question Freud asked towards the end of his life after dedicating most of it to researching exactly that same question. Until a certain point in the movie it's clear that the woman wants her piano, "It's mine!" she stubbornly repeats.

The lost object—Ada's lost object, is represented by her daughter who tries to be her mother's voice, and in that respect turns herself into the object. She even relates her mother's muteness to the death of her father. Ada herself describes her first lover as someone whom she didn't need to speak to. He understood her without words. He was part of her—like the child, like the piano. Again, until a certain point in the movie the child embodies a special object for the mother. She understands her and interprets her. The minute this position is stolen from the child tragic events happen. The minute the mother turns her attention and her desire to a man, the child is asked to renounce her place in her mother's life.

We are witnessing an oedipal process. The child is asked to give up her mother's desire for her, and only then she can turn to the father—the stepfather (the man Ada married in the beginning of the movie), whom she couldn't stand until then due to her identification with her mother. She can then create a relationship with him, or a collusion with him against her mother.

Men's characters are represented by two types. On the one hand is the husband, played by Sam Neill, who respects his wife and her refusal to respond to his sexual hints. Baines on the other hand, played by the gorgeous Harvey Keitel, makes Ada his object of desire, or in other words, the woman is his symptom.

The arrangement Baines offers to Ada is that she will buy back her piano (which she desires), in return for letting him do "things" to her. This is actually a Perverse arrangement or a semblance (as if) of a perversion.

The Piano assumes a fetishistic value. Baines is supposedly a pervert. But behind this perversion desire and love are hidden. At a certain point he gives up enjoyment (which is always related only to the One) for desire (who is connected to the Other).

So who is the true pervert? Maybe, precisely the husband. When he catches the two lovers he doesn't try to stop them but gets his satisfaction through voyeurism and identification with the other man.

The message of this movie is very clear—if you want to

The Consciousness Bearers

enjoy a woman you shouldn't respect her.

And suddenly a question arises so far as the woman is concerned—is it really the piano she desires? Or maybe she desires something else? She received the piano, so what does she really want?

One of my questions pertains to when she falls in love. Is it when the man renounces his Enjoyment in favor of his desire? Lacan claims that the Enjoyment of the other is not a sign of love. Only love is a sign of love, and love demands just one thing—love. Enjoyment on the other hand is autistic.

In the first sexual intercourse between Ada and Baines he hears something of her voice. It is as if something of the lost object is surfacing. Baines is the one who knows the language of the natives, the Maori language that none of the white people understand. He is the one who is ready to listen, while the husband is a person who knows how to show a measure of religious grace, but in the long run what is revealed is that in the heart of this religion—perversion and murderous violence are hiding.

It is interesting that Ada does not utter a sound even when her husband mutilates her finger. The symptom is stronger than the pain. By mutilating the finger Ada is going through castration—but this is castration in the Real, not a symbolic castration. Like the mutilation of Van-Gogh's ear—this is a psychotic castration. This is the reason that yet another event has to happen in order that Ada will be liberated from her symptom.

Ada, like Dora, is representing the hysterical subject.

The hysterical structure is created in the Oedipal stage by the change from being (the Phallus), to having (the phallus). This change is happening due to the intervention of the father (who is represented in the movie by the duplication of the two men). The father (the husband) appears as preventive, frustrating and prohibiting; the father (the lover), whom the woman accepts, respects his say and desires—ultimately is permitting the symbolic law to stabilize. The position of the father makes the child (the daughter) understand that (s)he is not the complementing Phallus of the mother, that is to say, that (s)he faces castration. Not only is (s)he not the Phallus, (s)he doesn't even own the phallus; just as the mother desires the Phallus where it assumingly is, so does the father turn into the symbol of one who owns it.

The hysterical structure, states Lacan, is centered on the question: What is needed in order to conquer the Phallus? This is what Freud meant when he wrote about the solution to the Oedipus complex. The father is demanded to give proof of his having the Phallus, as opposed to his embodying it, and all the economics of desire of the person with the hysterical symptom is directed towards examining this proof (the piano is owned by Baines but he gives it up, and he also gives up Ada as an object). As Lacan claims, if the father intervenes as the one who has the Phallus without embodying it, something can emerge that establishes the Phallus as a desired object by the father rather than as an object he stole from the mother (the husband steals the piano from Ada, while the lover desires to play the piano).

Near the end of the movie the piano, which represented the Phallus, i.e., the desired object, becomes a coffin. It represents the death drive, and Ada is attached to it with a rope, like someone who is attached to death with his/her umbilical cord. When she liberates herself she says: "What a surprise, my Will chose life." Please note: not "I chose" but "my Will chose," "something in me" chose.

Here we could say that the unconscious or the subject chose. Ada needs to lose the Phallic object through which she encountered her sexuality in order to lose the object's attachment to the death drive. She discovers Eros—the desire to live that turns her into a subject. Until that point she was totally identified with her symptom. The surprise she experiences facing what happened is a central factor in the psychoanalytic cure, when the patient discovers something and says: I always knew this, but I never really thought about it. If in the beginning of the movie the woman was presented as an object of exchange, and every object has an exchange value, at the end of the movie the piano is the object of exchange. Ada exchanges it for life and love.

So at the end of the movie she is established as a subject in the symbolic order, and she can start to speak.

Ruth Golan

§ The Age of Innocence

U.S. 1993

DIRECTED BY MARTIN SCORSESE, BASED ON A BOOK BY EDITH WHARTON

ACTORS: DANIEL DAY-LEWIS, MICHELLE PFEIFFER, AND WINONA RYDER

This is a film based on the classical novel by Edith Wharton, which portrays life in the snobbish high society of New York at the end of the 19th century. At the eve of his marriage to a respected young lady, Newland Archer, a young and privileged New York lawyer, falls in love with the married cousin of his fiancée. This cousin just returned from Europe after the failure of her marriage to a treacherous Polish nobleman. The fiancée believes in the moral and behavioral code of the traditional society surrounding her, while her cousin embraces a more modern behavioral code. The choice Newland must face is difficult: should he pursue his desire and his emotions or should he surrender to the pressure of puritan society?

The place of sexuality in our life, as discovered by Freud, is not limited only to the simple and banal recognition that we are all subjected to the sexual drive, but also to the fact of its central role in our life; its subversion under all ideals and all perceptions of our conscious life. This is an unbearable subversion even in our so-called permissive modern society.

This discovery of the sexual reason for living creates a different ethics, which is based on desire. Our sexual life is

The Consciousness Bearers

never satisfactory, and as such is the cause of the lack and the discontent that directs us, the foundation of our love choices, and the place of anxiety and is the cause of both illness and creativity. From this perspective, psychoanalysis will always undermine our life's efficiency and utilitarian values, and will reveal what determines our destiny beyond any ideal, value set or worldview (of which we usually tend to see the motive to our behavior). That is to say, psychoanalysis will reveal the mode of our enjoyment.

As for feminine sexuality—Freud himself showed us that our knowledge, including our psychoanalytic knowledge, is not enough for solving the enigma of feminine sexuality. He remained with the question that echoes in our ears until today "What does a woman want?" until the end of his life.

The movie *The Age of Innocence* deals with this issue of feminine sexuality, and the issue of the conflict between the drive and its repression. Psychoanalysis discovered that there is no "sexual relation" between a man and a woman. What does this mean? Naturally a sexual relationship exists, but there is no relation between a man and a woman in the sexual act itself. Enjoyment is lonely. Each one enjoys something different. The man enjoys his sexual organ and the act of the conquest, and the woman—what does the woman enjoy? Lacan, the great interpreter of Freud said—a woman needs to be spoken to. For her enjoyment she needs to be spoken to, that is to say, she needs to be placed in a special place, which is the place of The Object.

In the seminar *Encore* Lacan says:

"There is a jouissance [enjoyment] that is hers (a élle), that belongs to that "she" (elle) that doesn't exist and doesn't signify anything. There is a jouissance [enjoyment] that is hers about which she herself perhaps knows nothing if not that she experiences it—that much she knows. She knows it, of course, when it comes (arrive). It doesn't happen (arrive) to all of them" (Lacan 1972-73, p.74).

This is Enjoyment that cannot be described in words. It can be sometimes experienced as a mystical experience, similar to the mystical experiences of the East.

So in order to cover the absence of the relationship between the sexes in the so- called most intimate encounter between them, and in order to satisfy the Enjoyment of women "courtly love" was invented in the middle ages. What is *Courtly Love*? According to Lacan, this is a special and sublime way to compensate for the absence of sexual relations by pretending that we are the ones putting an obstacle to it. In my opinion it is a fantastic invention, that does not belong only to the past but that is saturated in current culture as a more or less hidden ideal of love. This is on condition that it is not consummated, of course; on condition that it is a love that causes misery.

According to Lacan the roots of "courtly love" is in:

"...the discourse of loyalty [in French, fidelity and feudal comes from the same root], of fidelity to the person. In the final analysis, the "person" always has to do with the master's discourse. Courtly love is, for man—in relation to whom the lady is entirely, and in the most servile sense of the word, a subject—the only way to elegantly pull off the absence of sexual relationship" (ibid. p.69).

According to Freud, the issue concerns over-valuation of the object and sublimation of the object of desire, that is to say the emphasis of desire is on the object and not on the drive. This claim very well suits our modern times. When one speaks about love it is not love to just any object, but to the sublime object, the object-lady that represents the thing around which the drive circles. So the lady becomes the object on condition that she is unattainable. Women received the role of the muse to which one sings a serenade, on the condition that they are isolated and closed off behind a wall. The woman herself responds to the poet by saying:

"I am... nothing more than the emptiness to be found in my own internal cesspit, not to say anything worse. Just blow in that for a while and see if your sublimation holds up" (Lacan 1959-60, p.215).

In the seminar on Ethics Lacan says:

"Courtly love was, in brief, a poetic exercise, a way of playing with a number of conventional, idealizing themes, which couldn't have any real concrete equivalence. Nevertheless, these ideals, the first among which is that of the Lady, are to be found in subsequent periods down to our own. The influence of these ideals is a highly concrete one in the organization of contemporary man's sentimental attachments, and it continues its forward march. Moreover, march is the right word because it finds its point of origin in a certain systematic and deliberate use of the signifier as such. A great deal of effort has been expanded to demonstrate the relationship between this apparatus or organization of the forms of courtly love and an intuition that is religious in origin, mystical for example..."

"On the level of the economy of the reference of the subject to the love object, there are certain apparent relationships between courtly love and foreign mystical experiences, Hindu or Tibetan, for example."

....

"The object involved, the feminine object, is introduced oddly enough through the door of privation or of inaccessibility. Whatever the social position of him who functions in the role, the inaccessibility of the object is posited as a point of departure. Some of those involved were, in fact, servants... It is impossible to serenade one's Lady in her poetic role in the absence of the given that she is surrounded and isolated by a barrier... she is also frequently referred to with the masculine term, Mi Dom, or my Lord—this Lady is presented with depersonalized characteristic" (ibid. p.149).

"The idealized woman, the Lady, who is in the position of the Other and of the object, finds herself suddenly and brutally positing, in a place knowingly constructed out of the most refined of signifiers, the emptiness of the thing in all its crudity, a thing that reveals itself in its nudity to be the thing, her thing, the one that is to be found in her very heart in its cruel emptiness. That Thing.... is in a way unveiled with a cruel and insistent power" (ibid. p.163).

So therefore in courtly love the issue concerns raising

the value of the Lady, so that it becomes a representative of The Object. In the movie The Age of Innocence this works marvelously.

Courtly love according to Andreas Capellanus (Capellanus, 1174-1186)

Courtly love was developed in the 12th century, in the feudal era, by French troubadours. The origin of courtly love is found in the writings of the poet Ovid that lived in Rome at the time of the Emperor Augustus. Love according to Ovid was conceived as sensual, without any trace of romantic emotion, which is prominent in later times. This love exists in an extra-marital context and marriage is not its goal. The man that is to be deluded (and Ovid enjoyed this), is the woman's husband.

Ovid's main claim is that husbands and wives cannot love each other. Middle-Age men thought they have his affirmation that the best romantic partner is the wife of another man.

Other ideas of Ovid which influenced courtly love are: "love is a kind of warfare and every lover is a soldier; Cupid is the generalissimo and under him are the women whose power over the men is absolute; A man should deceive a woman, if he can, but he must never appear to oppose her slightest wish; To please her he must watch all night before her doors, undergo all sorts of hardships, perform all sorts of absurd actions; for love of her he must become pale, thin and sleepless (depression?); No matter what he may do, or from what motives, he must persuade her that it is all done for her sake; if in spite of all these demonstrations of affection she still remains obdurate, he must arouse her jealousy; he must pretend to be in love with some other woman, and when the first one thinks she has lost him, she will probably capitulate and he can clasp her sobbing to his breast" (ibid. p.5).

The lady becomes the lover's feudal master and he owes his loyalty to her or to Cupid through her. Her status is higher than his, and his address to his lady should be from the deepest humility.

Two different positions towards love can be found within the Arab culture in Spain. These Arabs have a sensual tradition that was influenced by Ovid, and they have a different, more spiritual tradition, seemingly based on Plato, as interpreted by Arab scholars.

According to Ibn Hazm, the author of the book The Dove's Neck-Ring, written in Andalusia in the year 1022, love is a unity between soul parts that were separated during the time of the creation of the world. His reason for thinking this is usually connected to external beauty, "because the soul is beautiful and passionately desires anything beautiful and inclined towards perfect images" (ibid. p.9).

True love does not ignore the physical aspect, but the sublimated union of the souls is a thousand times more important than the union of physical bodies; True love is not forbidden by religious law; it makes the lover into a better man in many ways, because he is trying with all his might to do he what previously could not do in order to show off his good virtues and turn himself into someone worthy of passion (ibid.).

This kind of love does not distinguish between social classes. The Arab public opinion demanded that if the lover is a woman, it is more appropriate to speak about her as a man and to relate to her in the masculine.

The lover, either from a higher class than his lover or from a lower class, should speak about himself as her slave—this adds to his honor. He is satisfied when she rejects him and happy when she shows him any sign of affection.

Capellanus's text—*The Art of Courtly Love*, was considered a textbook for the courts of love in Spain, in the 14th century. At that time there was a law according to which the master can woo the lady only if he received permission from her husband, and most of the romances were full of long arguments about complicated matters concerning love.

I will specify a few important points from Capellanus's book that in my opinion are expressed in the movie:

The definition of love—"love is a certain inborn suffering derived from the sight of and excessive meditation upon the beauty of the opposite sex, which causes each one above all things the embraces of the other..." (ibid. p.28)

The meaning of the word love—"Love gets its name (amor) from the word of hook (amus), which means "to capture" or "to be captured,"

for he who is in love is captured in the chains of desire and wishes to capture someone else with his hook. Just as a skillful fisherman tries to attract fishes by his bait and to capture them on his crooked hook, so the man who is captive of love tries to attract another person by his allurements and exerts all his efforts to unite two different hearts with an intangible bond, or if they are already united he tries to keep them forever."

From the fourth chapter: **What the effect of love is**
"O what a wonderful thing is love, which makes a man shine with so many virtues and teaches everyone, no matter who he is, so many good traits of character!...it adorns a man, so to speak with the virtue of chastity, because he who shines with the light of one love can hardly think of embracing another woman..." (p.31)

From the fifth chapter: **What persons are fit for love**
"You should know that everyone of sound mind who is capable of doing the work of Venus may be wounded by one of Love's arrows unless prevented by age, or blindness, or excess of passion. Age is a bar, because after the sixtieth year in a man and the fiftieth in a woman, although one may have intercourse his passion cannot develop into love; because at that age the natural heat begins to lose its force, and the natural moisture is greatly increased...and there are no consolations in the world for him except food and drink.

Similarly, a girl under the age of twelve and a boy before the fourteenth year do not serve in love's army. However, I say and insist that before his eighteenth year a man cannot be a true lover, because up to that age he is overcome with embarrassment over any little thing, which not only interferes with the perfecting of love, but even destroys it if it is well perfected. But we find even more powerful reason, which is that before this age a man has no constancy, but is changeable in every way..."

"An excess of passion is a bar to love, because there are men who are slaves to such passionate desire that they cannot be held in the bonds of love—men who, after they have thought long about some woman or even enjoyed her, when they see another woman straightway desire her embraces, and they forget about the services they have received from their first love and they feel no gratitude for them...their love is like that of a shameless dog. They should rather, I believe, be compared to asses..." (pp.32-33)

From the sixth chapter: **In what manner love may be acquired and in how many ways:**

"*...In such cases, when love cannot have its solaces, it increases beyond all measure and drives the lovers to lamenting their terrible torments, because "we strive for what is forbidden and always want what is denied us" (Ovid).*

"*A wise woman will therefore seek as a lover a man of praiseworthy character—not one who anoints himself all over like a woman or makes a rite of the care of the body, for it does not go with a masculine figure to adorn oneself in womanly fashion or to be devoted to the care of the body."*

Rules of love—the 12 commandments: (pp.81-82)

I. *Thou shalt avoid avarice like the deadly pestilence and shalt embrace its opposite.*
II. *Thou shalt keep thyself chaste for the sake of her whom thou lovest.*
III. *Thou shalt not knowingly strive to break up a correct love affair that someone else is engaged in.*
IV. *Thou shalt not choose for thy love anyone whom a natural sense of shame forbids thee to marry.*
V. *Be mindful completely to avoid falsehood.*
VI. *Thou shalt not have many who know of thy love affair.*
VII. *Being obedient in all things to the command of ladies, thou shalt ever strive to ally thyself to the service of Love.*
VIII. *In giving and receiving love's solaces let modesty be ever present.*
IX. *Thou shalt speak no evil.*
X. *Thou shalt not be a revealer of love affairs.*
XI. *Thou shalt be in all things polite and courteous.*
XII. *In practicing the solaces of love thou shalt not exceed the desires of thy lover.*

From the second part: **How love may be retained**
The first rule—complete secrecy:

"...He should do nothing disagreeable that might annoy her. Moreover every man is bound, in time of need, to come to the aid of his beloved, both by sympathizing with her in all her troubles and by acceding to all her reasonable desires...And if inadvertently he should do something improper that offends her, let him straightway confess with downcast face that he has done wrong, and let him give the excuse that he lost his temper...And every man ought to be sparing of praise of his beloved when he is among other men...and he should not spend a great deal of time in places where she is. When he is with other men, if he meets her in a group of women, he should not try to communicate with her by signs...Every man should also wear things that his beloved likes...avarice degrades him...If the lover is one who is fitted to be a warrior, he should see to it that his courage is apparent to everybody...he ought to root out all his pride and be very humble...Love may also be retained by indulging in the sweet and delightful solaces of the flesh, but only in such manner and in such number that they may never seem wearisome to the loved one" *(pp.151-152).*

How a love, once consummated, may be increased:
"...For the greater the difficulty of exchanging solaces, the more do the desire for them and the feeling of love increase. Love increases, too, if one of the lovers shows that he is angry at the other; for the lover falls at once into a great fear that his feeling which has arisen in his beloved may last forever. Love increases, likewise, if one of the lovers feels real jealousy, which is called, in fact, the nurse of love...Love increases, too, if it happens to last after it has been made public;...If one of the lovers dreams about the other, that gives rise to love...and so do the scoldings and beatings that lovers suffer from their parents...it even gives

a perfect reason for beginning a love affair that has not yet started" *(pp.153-154)*.

In what ways love may be decreased:

"Too many opportunities for exchanging solaces, too many opportunities of seeing the loved one, too much chance to talk to each other all decrease love, and so does an uncultured appearance or manner of walking on the part of the lover or the sudden loss of his property...restful sleep deserts him, and so he can hardly escape becoming contemptible in the eyes of his beloved. It also decreases love if one discovers any infamy in the lover or hears of any avarice, bad character or any kind of unworthiness; so it is for him to have an affair with another woman...he is not called a lover, but a betrayer..."(pp.154-155)

How love may come to an end:

"Love seeks for two persons who are bound together by a mutual trust and an identity of desires, and other people lack all merit in love and are considered as strangers to his court...if the parties concerned marry, love is violently put to flight..." (p.156)

Indications that one's love is returned:

"If you see that your loved one is missing all sorts of opportunities to meet you or is putting false obstacles on your path, you cannot hope long to enjoy her love. So, too, if you find her, for no reason at all, growing halfhearted about giving you the usual solaces, you may see that her faith is wavering....if she tries to hide from your faithful messenger, there is no doubt that she has turned you adrift...if you find that she is refraining from sending you the usual messages..."

...a woman who turns pale in the presence of her lover is without a doubt really in love. He who wants to make a real test of the faith and affection of his beloved should, with the greatest care and subtlety, pretend to her that he desires the embraces of some other woman, and he should be seen near this woman more often than he has been. If he finds that this upsets his beloved he can be sure that she is very much in love with him and most constant in her affection...at once her face begins to make manifest this inner suffering of her soul (pp.157-158).

If one of the lovers is unfaithful to the other:
"...No one can be bound by a twofold love...For when a lover has taken up with a new love, he can rarely be won back easily to the old one; because a love that has died out can seldom be brought to life again...If such a woman wants to keep hold of a wavering lover, she must be careful not to let him know her intentions and she must hide her real feelings and by careful dissimulation make it seem to him that she is not distressed by the upsetting of their love affair, and she must pretend to endure with patience and equanimity what her lover is doing...pretend that she is thinking about the embrace of some other man..." (pp.159-160)

"...Love may be revealed to three people besides the lovers themselves, for the lover is allowed to find a suitable confidant from whom he may get secret comfort in his love affair and who will offer him sympathy if things turn out badly; the woman may choose a similar confidante. Besides these they may have one faithful intermediary, chosen by common consent..."[27]

---

27 The rules of love, given by the king of love: ibid. pp. 184-186
I. Marriage is no real excuse for not loving.
II. He who is not jealous cannot love.
III. No one can be bound by a double love.
IV. It is well known that love is always increasing or decreasing.
V. That which a lover takes against the will of his beloved has no relish.
VI. Boys do not love until they arrive at the age of maturity.
VII. When one lover dies, a widowhood of two years is required of the survivor.
VIII. No one should be deprived of love without the very best of reasons.
IX. No one can love unless he is impelled by the persuasion of love.
X. Love is always a stranger in the home of avarice.
XI. It is not proper to love any woman whom one would be ashamed to seek to marry.
XII. A true lover does not desire to embrace in love anyone except his beloved.
XIII. When made public love rarely endures.
XIV. The easy attainment of love makes it of little value; difficulty of attainment makes it prized.
XV. Every lover regularly turns pale in the presence of his beloved.
XVI. When a lover suddenly catches sight of his beloved his heart palpitates.
XVII. A new love puts to flight an old one.
XVIII. Good character alone makes any man worthy of love.
XIX. If love diminishes, it quickly fails and rarely revives.
XX. A man in love is always apprehensive.
XXI. Real jealousy always increases the feeling of love.
XXII. Jealousy, and therefore love, are increased when one suspects his beloved.
XXIII. He whom the thought of love vexes eats and sleeps very little.
XXIV. Every act of a lover ends in the thought of his beloved.
XXV. A true lover considers nothing good except what he thinks will please his beloved.
XXVI. Love can deny nothing to love.
XXVII. A lover can never have enough of the solaces of his beloved.
XXVIII. A slight presumption causes a lover to suspect his beloved.
XXIX. A man who is vexed by too much passion usually does not love.
XXX. A true lover is constantly and without intermission possessed by the thought of his beloved.
XXXI. Nothing forbids one woman being loved by two men or one man by two women.

The Consciousness Bearers

The movie *The Age of Innocence* deals with a love triangle—two women and a man. The plot takes place in American high society in the beginning of the 20th century. Along with the story the movie reveals the values that determine the life and habits of this high society. There is no doubt that the man is the knight, but who is the Lady?

During the entire movie the Lady, the desired woman who is loved in a desperate unfulfilled love, is the countess Madame Olenska. She is presented as the ideal object. The movie begins with flowers and the Opera, which completely embody the romantic fantasy. The first gaze on the loved one is through the binoculars of the Opera—this is the gaze that situates her as the Object. In her first encounter with Newland, the hero, she gives him her hand to be kissed and instead he shakes it. This is the first of a series of missed opportunities on the road to realizing the love that is between them.

The name of the hero "Newland" means "new land." America is the new world, and it is precisely there that the conventions of courtly love are very rigidly applied. Newland is fantasizing along the whole movie about how he will break these conventions. In the beginning of the movie the heroine is nameless. Three women talk about her in a way that reminds one of the three witches who appear in the beginning of Shakespeare's Macbeth. Her name is Madame Olenska, which is a foreign name. Even with respect to her name she digresses from the bon ton of the New York high society.

Newland is betrothed to May—a pure virgin, seemingly

the symbol of innocence. After he proposes to her he says: *I wish to kiss you, but I can't.*

In one of the first scenes we see May shooting an arrow and is straight to the target. Actually during the unfolding of the plot we understand that the control over the happenings of the story is in her hands. Newland decides to announce his wedding in order to defend himself from his love of the countess, or maybe rather to defend him-self from the possibility of love itself. He is running away into the marriage. May's innocence, as well as the assumed innocence of high society, is a poisoning innocence. It is the cruelty of the Good. The narrative in the movie is full of opposites and contradictions. One of them concerns the source of innocence—does May hold it or does Ellen? Or maybe it abides within the man? In the court of high society nobody speaks out and nobody really thinks, but everybody makes signs. There is a social code that is not spoken but creates a kind of unbreakable barrier. "*Does no one want to hear the truth here? Does no one love here?*" Ellen, the boundary breaker is asking these questions? Ellen also refuses to give herself to Newland and that increases his love for her. In one of their missed encounters she says to him: "Newland. You couldn't be happy if it meant being cruel. If we act any other way I'll be making you act against what I love in you most. And I can't go back to that way of thinking. Don't you see? I can't love you unless I give you up."

During the whole movie Newland tries to be the knight defending his Lady. Sometimes the Lady is embodied in May, his wife, and sometimes the Lady is embodied in

Madame Olenska. The trust that the two women have for him kills his ability to act according to his desire.

May's love is strangling him. The condition that the conspiracy (as he calls it) succeeds, is that nothing will be spoken of. Everything is taking place behind closed doors, in pre-accepted signs. Along the whole movie there are failed attempts to confess—Newland tries to confess to Ellen, and to May. When he makes his last attempt at liberation, announcing his intention to travel to the Far East, May announces her pregnancy thus producing the last restrictive chain.

Actually, May, in her blindness, is the true Lady. It becomes clear eventually that even if Newland would have succeeded in running away he could not realize his love. Non-realization is the condition for love. Ellen knows it when she says: "How can we be happy behind the backs of people who trust us?"

Even after 30 years, when May is already dead, she manifests her trust of Newland from her grave, through the things she said to her son. This is the last missed opportunity portrayed in the story. Here is where the real reversal is happening in the movie. It turns out that May always knew about Newland's and Ellen's love, and in her silence she prevented its realization. Perhaps this might even have been a kind of conspiracy between the two women. Newland is standing under Ellen's window in Paris (the Don Quixote-like knight), and he understands that there is no return, that the renunciation is eternal. Her window glitters in the light, and closes.

Ruth Golan

§ High Heels

SPAIN 1991
DIRECTED BY PEDRO ALMODÓVAR
ACTORS: VICTORIA ABRIL, MARISA PAREDES, MIGUEL BOSÉ

The movie is about a love-hate relationship between a mother and her daughter. The mother, a singer and an actress that abandoned her daughter in her infancy, is returning to Madrid. The daughter, a news announcer on television, is confessing on live television that she killed her husband (who was also the lover of the mother). The movie's plot is developed around the complicated relationship between the two women and between each one of them and the men in her life. The movie, similar to all Almodóvar's movies, deals with the issue of feminine sexuality, truth and falsehood.

The hero of the movie *High Heels* is the Symbol of our culture, that is to say: The Phallus, the relationship of the woman to it and the fact that the woman is one of the many embodiments of this mysterious phallus. The phallus is a classical concept whose original meaning is the figurative representation of the male organ, but not just any member but an organ, which is in a constant erection, the symbol of virility. It was an object of devotion in initiation rites in different cultures.

This concept became a popular one in our culture and in modern times it became almost a curse in the femi-

The Consciousness Bearers

nist struggle. Our Western culture is considered a phallic culture, whereas a woman who is fighting for her rights is called a phallic woman etc. What is the Phallus in psychoanalysis? It is a signifier, represented through symbolic language. What does it represent? *The phallus is not equated with the Penis.* It is not the anatomical organ itself and not a representative of it, but rather it is connected to *castration and the castration impulse.* The phallus is connected with the woman in so far as when she was a young girl "she still does not have it," but maybe "she will grow it later." Little Hans said this when he was five years old (Freud treated him through his father), and he saw his little sister. If she is already a woman "she does not have it any more," and she needs different kinds of substitutes and masquerades for the phallus.

Clinical observations show that there is only one signifier which differentiates between the sexes at the unconscious level of the psyche, and that is the existence or the absence of the Phallus. At the resolution of the Oedipus complex, both sexes have to choose between having a phallus and accepting castration. It should be emphasized that it is not at an anatomical level, like the difference between the penis and the vagina, but it is a matter of presence and absence of a factor. Both the little girl and the little boy do not know anything about the existence of the vagina, while the phallus is considered in their eyes an organ that can be separated from the body, which is why it can be symbolically replaced, and Freud builds a chain of penis=excrement=baby=present=money etc. What is common to all these elements is that they can be separated so to speak, from the subject, and they can pass from one person to another. That is to say, these objects are partial objects and they are exchangeable, but each object, once it is desired, receives a phallic value—from ice cream to a shining motorbike to a woman. The Phallus is an object that can be seen, revealed and recycled, something that can be substituted for something else.

The subject itself can identify with the Phallus and embody it, like the function many children have for their mother. Freud showed how especially the little girl has an unconscious wish to receive the father's Phallus which is substituted for a wish to receive a baby from him.

It should be emphasized, time and time again, that psychoanalysis does not deal with the genital, male, biological organ, but with the function this organ plays in fantasy and culture. The phallus represents an imaginary object that separates mother and child. The mother desires this object, and the child tries to satisfy her desire by identifying with it. Only when he finds out that it is impossible, usually through the interference of the father who shows him that he will never be able to satisfy the mother's desire, he confronts the choice of accepting castration, i.e., that he cannot be the phallus, which the mother is lacking, or he can reject his castration and remain in his phantasm.

Lacan, in his paper "The Signification of the Phallus," is summarizing this theory according to

The Consciousness Bearers

four points: (Lacan 1958, p.272)

1. The little girl considers herself, if only temporarily, as castrated, in the sense of deprived of the phallus, in the first instance, by her mother, and then by her father.

2. The mother is considered by both sexes, as possessing the phallus, as a phallic mother.

3. The signification of castration has weight in the formation of symptoms, only on the basis of its discovery as castration of the mother.

4. These three problems lead to the question of the reason, in development of the phallic stage, which is the third stage in the development of the child, after the oral and the anal stages. This stage is characterized by the dominance of the phallic attribute and by masturbatory Enjoyment, and on the other; it localizes this Enjoyment for the woman in the clitoris, which is thus raised to the function of the phallus. If the drive draws a map of the erotogenic zones in the body, the vagina, as a place for genital penetration, is excluded until this stage.

Lacan summarizes when he says: (ibid. pp.277-285)

"In Freudian doctrine, the phallus is not a fantasy, if we are to view fantasy in its imaginary effect. Nor is it as such an object (part-, internal, good, bad, etc.) inasmuch as "object" tends to gauge the reality involved in a relationship. Still less it is the organ—penis or clitoris—that it symbolizes...For the Phallus is a signifier... One could say that this signifier is chosen as the most salient of what can be grasped in sexual intercourse as real, as well as the most symbolic, in the literal sense of the term...One could also say that, by virtue of its turgidity, it is the image of the vital flow as it is transmitted in generation."

So both boys and girls need to face the fact of castration, the mother's castration and their own. That is to say, what the Phallus represents in the end is the lack, the absence: The impossibility of being the virile admired object—both for men and for women. From all this what emerges is Lacan's definition of the Phallus as a representative, as a signifier of desire. Desire is always created as a consequence of lack. When the boy understands that his mother desires something beyond him, something he cannot satisfy, this phallus comes to represent for him the desire of the Other. The imaginary Phallus becomes a symbolic one—which appears where something is missing in the Other. This Other is supposed to be whole, perfect, and not missing anything. There comes a moment when we discover flaws, and lacks in this Other. We always discover this sooner or later, and the process of discovery is crucial for the development of the subject. Even God as the Other had to subtract something from himself, "to reduce himself," as it is written in the Kabala, in order to create the world.

In order for the world or for the subject to exist, One needs to discover the lack in the Other, even when this Other is the mother.

The movie *High Heels* is focused around the relationship between mother and daughter. During the whole movie this mother remains as an ideal Other for her daughter. This is similar to what happens in *The Piano*, The flow in the ideal image of the mother, the flow that makes the daughter tell things about her mother and betray her, is created when the daughter reveals the desire of the mother, the desire for a man. So in *High Heels*, the daughter is fantasizing that if she will only get rid of the man that she imagines the mother does not really desire, she will be able to return the perfect harmony between her and her mother. She will be able to be the satisfying Phallus for the mother. She doesn't succeed in this, so she tries to take the place of the mother in the heart of the desired man. But even in that she fails, and until the end of the movie the question remains if she manages to become a subject at all vis-à-vis this perfect, narcissistic mother who does not desire anything beyond her own perfect ideal self.

The heroine of our movie this time is not the woman-mother, but the daughter. This daughter admires the Phallus in the image of the un-castrated mother. She even manages to attain the Phallus impersonated by a baby whom she receives from the man who supposedly is an incarnation of her mother, or from the non-existing mother. Does Almodóvar try to hint that this is the only way out of the pre-determined destiny for the woman? It might be, because he is a man.

The heroine, Becky, is looking for her unique voice like Ada does in *The Piano*. She works as an announcer of news on television, and is helped by another woman who translates her speech into sign language, for those who cannot hear, and therefore for those who might not be able to be part of the discourse.

The main characteristic of the Phallus that is portrayed

with genius in the film is that *the Phallus can only fulfill its function when it is covered.* This lack in the phallus is covered by a screen, a curtain or a veil.

Once the veil is removed from the Phallus what is emerges is shame, or anxiety.

In the developmental process *three supplementary actions* should take place. The first action is To Be the Phallus, that is when the boy or girl identifies with the Phallus, the second action is To Have or Not To Have the Phallus—this concerns the enormous question about castration, and the third action is To Seem like the Phallus—this is the cover or the veil. It is "as if" we own it, in order to defend it on one side of the coin, and to cover its absence on the other side. This action, says Lacan, influences the comic of the ideal or characteristic discoveries of the behaviors of each gender, including what happens in intercourse itself.

The main topic in Almodóvar's movies, and especially in *High Heels,* is the different ways of masquerade, whose aim is to evade anxiety that the void, which is revealed when one takes off the mask from the Phallus, is eliciting. Nothing in this movie is as it seems. It has masquerades upon masquerades. For example, the hero of this movie is masquerading as the mother in a drag queen costume. This man is not even a homosexual. This movie is made up of layers of imitations, concealments and revelations. Even the music in the movie, is used as a mimicry of reality and creates an illusory reality. For example, when the narcissistic mother is singing in front of the audience while her daughter is in prison, "If you want to take my life from me, I don't want it, what is the point of living without you?" The song, as well as the tears that the mother sheds while singing, are simultaneously false and true.

If we speak about the woman, Freud's answer to the question "what does the woman want?" is that she wants the Phallus, or a baby as a substitute, or, if she is a hysterical woman, she wants to be an embodiment of the Phallus herself. She wants to be the desired object, even though she also complains about that: "He treats me as only an object!" The woman will reject an essential part of her femininity, and she will cover up all of her qualities in a costume so that she can be the Phallus, the signifier of desire in the Other. She wishes to be desired or loved for what she is not, but she finds the signifier of her desire in the body of the man to whom she directs her demand for love. The organ that fulfills this signifying function takes on a *fetishistic value*. The Phallus becomes a fetish for her. The masquerade is creating the difference between the sexes, that difference that doesn't initially exist. The woman turns herself into this desired object, like the mother in *High Heels*.

Almodóvar is spreading visual clues about this. We have for example the red clothes of the mother at the beginning of the movie, when later it is Becky that is wearing red clothes and shoes like her mother.

It makes no difference if it is the mother, or the man impersonating the mother, who imitates the mother. In the movie we see that the Phallus is dependent upon its staying covered, but it is also dependent on those who desire it. The mother needs her daughter's adoration of her.

This kind of woman remains *mysterious, enigmatic and un-reachable.* This is her effect on men, and this is her effect on her daughter. The movie is full of veils and masquerades, but is there any feminine essence behind all this? Lacan and Freud would have replied in the negative. For the man, The Woman can be only the Phallus that signifies his desire and the object that raises that desire. The woman cannot really be a woman but she can only represent femininity, be—an illusion of a woman, be a woman in the fantasy of a man and in this way to activate the game of passion.

There are feminists who aggressively attack this position, and there are those who see in the differentiation between the sexual organ and the Phallus the proof that one cannot reduce the difference between the sexes to a biological difference.

§ The Hairdresser's Husband

FRANCE, 1991

DIRECTED BY PATRICE LECONTE

ACTORS: ANNA GALIENA, JEAN ROCHEFORT

There is a very intense erotic atmosphere in Patrice Leconte's movie, in which a relationship between an older man and a beautiful hairdresser, with whom he falls in love, is described. As a young child, Antoine used to sit at the neighborhood's hairdresser's place, breathing in the vapors of her body and her sweet perfume, while in a shy half gaze he contemplated her sloping breasts under her shirt which was wet with perspiration. As he grows older he enters the hairdressing salon in order to fulfill his childhood fantasy. The director designed this salon with lighting, stylistic photographing, and a soundtrack, in order to imitate a kind of incubator, a womb, and a space which is warm and stuffy.

The main question the movie The Hairdresser's Husband deals with is: "Does the woman exist?"

If *High Heels* deals with the Phallus as a signifier functioning as a kind of cover, could *The Hairdresser's Husband* can be perceived as a dance of veils, that is to say, this is a movie about a fantasy. *The Hairdresser's Husband* begins with a dance, and throughout the entire movie dancing episodes are woven in. The dance is a sensual Arabian belly dance, which the hero dances with total devotion while he is completely captivated by the fantasy about the hairdresser.

Fantasy, according to psychoanalysis, is an Imaginary scene in which the subject is the central hero. In the Fantasy there is a fulfillment of an unconscious wish in a hidden or open manner. Fantasy has different modes: conscious fantasy or daydream, unconscious fantasy. Fantasy is uncovered by analysis as the structure underlying the manifest content in the analysand's speech. There is also a primal Fantasy, around which the subject constructs his identity.

Freud began to speak about fantasy after neglecting in 1897 the theory of the symptom (the seduction theory), which was totally explainable by a primary sexual trauma that was repressed. If at first he assumed that traumatic childhood memories exposed during analysis are realistic pictures, later on he withdrew from this recognition, claiming that the reality of these memories is a psychical reality.

In *The Interpretation of Dreams* Freud writes:

"If we look at unconscious wishes reduced to their most fundamental and truest shape, we shall have to conclude, no doubt, that psychical reality is a particular form of existence not to be confused with material reality" (Freud, 1900).

Freud attributes great significance to the relationship between fantasy and time. Every fantasy is simultaneously marked by *three times*—in order for fantasy to occur we need an actual impression, a cause in the present that may evoke one of man's basic wishes. This cause connects to a memory of a past experience, usually from childhood, where this wish was fulfilled. Thus, we get a situation where there is a projection on the future that appears as a wish fulfillment—that is the daydream or the fantasy in which we can identify the traces of its origin from the cause and the memory.

The Hairdresser's Husband is characterized by a confusion of times. Is the movie about a boy who is fantasizing about the fulfilling of his fantasy—to marry the hairdresser? Or is it about a grown man who remembers his childhood's fantasy, fulfills it in the present and continues to fantasize about it in order to fulfill it in the future? In any case there are two hairdressers: The time the hero is a child and when the hero is an adult; and maybe at the end of the movie there is a third hairdresser, the absent one, the one who is arriving shortly, who embodies the perfect fantasy.

The fantasy has a role similar to that of the game, namely, to derive pleasure from a situation of anxiety. This is demonstrated by Freud when he tells about a game played by his grandson with a cotton-reel, which he throws away and pulls towards him in alternation, while uttering the words FORT/DA—"Here/There," a game aimed at dealing with the anxiety of the mother's absence. One of the objects which appear repeatedly during the movie is the pompons of the bathing suit Antoine's (the hero of the movie) mother knitted for him. These pompons remind us of the cotton-reel—an insignificant object that gets its meaning when the desire of the Other, in this case the mother (who desires something/someone else more than being with her child), is revealed. In order for the desire to be exposed, there must be absence or inconsistency.

It can be said that the fantasy is the defensive answer of the subject confronted with the desire of the Other. That is the answer to "What does he want from me?" Indeed, what does this Other, who is everything to me, want? There is a point where the Other cannot answer, because he himself does not know what he wants. The subject then finds a fantasmatic answer, which makes him what he is, which constitutes him.

So to this question that comes to the child from the Other, he answers with the primordial fantasy, and constructs his being around it. There are many possible answers. One of the fantastic scenes in the movie takes place around the family dining table. The father, after speaking contemptuously to the older good for nothing boy, turns his gaze full of hope and desire to the little boy—Antoine—and asks him: "And you, what would you like to do when you grow up?" Antoine answers him in accordance with his fantasy: "Me? I want to marry the hairdresser." For that he is rightfully slapped on his face; rightfully so because what peeps out is a hint of the primordial fantasy that is constructed around the perverse sexual drive of the child; it has no covering or veil.

The psychoanalysts mark, in their clinical work, that usually the person who comes for treatment talks a lot about his symptoms. He complains about his suffering. As to fantasies, the opposite is true. The patient does not come to complain about them. And if he depicts them, he is usually ashamed. It can be said, that through fantasy he derives *enjoyment*. It has a role of consolation, and there is a connection between it and what Miller calls—"The Philosophical Consolation," which is masturbation. The fantasy usually draws its content from the discourse of perversion; it is the unique way in which each of us structures his "impossible" connection to the traumatic or real thing. It is the way in which each of us, by an imaginary scenario, conceals the inconsistency of the Other. The one who does not know what he wants. The fantasy is the treasure of the subject and his most intimate and unique possession.

This is the unique way around which each person "dreams his world," and organizes his particular way of Enjoyment around a certain object; this object is the cause of enjoyment. That is why the nature of fantasy is to oppose universality and inclusion. A person must defend it from exposure to the world (in that the fantasy is the opposite of perversion, which is the enactment of the fantasy). This is why Antoine is building a world where there is no place for anyone else—just for him and the hairdresser.

The Hairdresser's Husband can be seen as a movie about a fantasy and its fulfillment and it is structured around duality. On the one hand "the pleasure principle"—the pleasure of fulfilling a fantasy; on the other hand, the action of the death drive, which operates under the pleasure principle and elicits a fantasy, which is connected to death. This death might be necessary once the fantasy loses its perfect nature. The nature of this kind of fantasy is that it cannot bear the tiniest flaw (the beginning of the end in the movie is symbolized by a crack appearing on the ceiling). Each tear in the veil forces the hero to peep into the death drive. The fantasy defends the Real, the horrific. It is a kind of a screen that covers for the Real and supports desire.

A perfect fantasy appears at the end of the movie when there is no anxiety causing reality that can hinder its fulfillment. Since the movie is built around fantasy, its end is inevitable and known in advance.

Lacan's claim that *the fantasy is rooted in perversion* is suitable here (together with their being opposites). The pervert turns himself into the lost object, which is the object of desire of the Other. Antoine's sole identity consists of his being the husband of the hairdresser. He is totally wrapped around the lost object.

And the woman, does she exist? The answer of this movie is that the woman does not exist, and what does exist is the fantasy that Antoine constructs around a pure and whole desire. Perhaps his only way out of it and its perfect expression is the sensual belly dance.

Freud, in his paper "Creative Writers and Day-Dreaming," compares the creative writer and the child: both create a world of fantasy and take it very seriously. In this paper, Freud formulates one of the most amazing truths about man's psyche: "Hardly anything is harder for a man than to give up a pleasure which he has once experienced. Actually, we can never give anything up; we only exchange one thing for another" (Freud, 1907, p.145).

And this is Antoine's act, and also probably the act of Patrice Laconte, the creator of the movie.

§ Betty Blue (37°2 le matin)

FRANCE 1986

DIRECTED BY: JEAN-JACQUES BEINEIX

ACTORS: JEAN-HUGUES ANGLADE, BÉATRICE DALLE

Betty is a 20 year-old provocative and impulsive waitress who lives with a 30 year-old quiet and humble writer. After she accidentally finds the novel that he wrote, which she finds to be the best novel she ever read, she does everything in her ability to make her lover a famous author. Betty is ready to "go to the end" in order to achieve her goal. Her lover can-not tolerate it. This is a movie about an obsessive love that gradually turns into psychosis with a tragic end.

While *The Piano* describes a hysterical neurotic woman from the times of Freud, a woman who has the loss of her voice as a symptom, and who finds her voice through finding love and sexual enjoyment, the heroine of *Betty Blue* is a modern heroine. It is as if she has no sexual inhibitions. The road to sexual enjoyment is open to her, and in spite of this she lacks her own voice—not as a symptom, not in the anatomical biological sense but in a symbolic sense. She does not have the words, she does not have language; this ends in her becoming crazy and hearing voices in her head. Real voices. Betty's psychic structure is a psychotic one.

When a child enters the cultural world, the meaning of life is given to him by becoming part of this symbolic cultural world. He is honoring social arbitrary rules. The parents are those that introduce him to the world of symbols by giving him a place as a speaking being. Through the parents' discourse about the child, their desire for him/her, the future they plan for him, even before he was born, they mark him with the seal of culture. Through the demands they demand from him, the limitations they put to the satisfaction of his needs, they give him a place in the family and in the group to which he belongs. In the case of the psychotic subject, this first stage of connection to culture has failed, because of the foreclosure of a critical signifier, which Lacan has named "The Name of the Father."

The name of the father, different from the biological

father, and is a function that represents the rules and the culture that limits the drive, and in that gives the subject a place and a name in the Other. For psychotic subjects there was a disturbance in prioritizing the signifier that is behind the forbidding of impossible satisfaction of the drive—the forbiddance of enjoyment that is actually arbitrary, but is in fact opening the possibility of a mutual existence in a group. The father creates an absence, a gap between mother and child; the father returns the mother to her recognition of her desire for him and gives the child a necessary space for cultivation of his uniqueness as a subject.

For this to happen, the subject needs to believe in the representation of the father. This belief needs to be more important to him than the satisfaction of his drives. One of the problems that emanate from the failure of belief is the difficulty of the person with the psychotic structure to be part of the consensus of social discourse. The movie illustrates a fantastic example of this.

According to Lacan (mostly in his early teachings), one could explain the etiology of psychosis in the inefficiency of the symbolic function of the father. As Lacan claims, the name of the father is foreclosed in psychosis, and the place in the structure that is usually taken by this signifier is a hole. The psychotic does not believe in the name of the father. In other words, Lacan found that the psychotic subject chose not to sacrifice his enjoyment, which is connected to his primal position in order to be the object for the Other.

One may say that we live inside an *envelope of language*.

This is an envelope that creates a screening and defends us from what needs to be an ungraspable relationship with the traumatic Real. Lacan emphasized time and again the fact that language is preceding us, or more exactly—the discourse is preceding us. In other words, in advance language is what draws the image of the subject. The subject exists first of all in the future. He/she will be. The subject constructs himself in a time framework that can be called the future anterior—what he could have been.

We have a common illusion. Each one of us has a sensation that language is his usable tool. This is a tool that we use in order to express ourselves or to communicate with each other. We think we make the language our own, even though it envelopes us from the beginning as a discourse that comes from the Other. But language is not only a tool for communication. In language first of all there is Enjoyment, there is the drive.

What happens with the psychotic subject? One may say that he reveals to the world the foreign parasitic nature of language—from the point of view of suffering, from the outbreak of language and speech beyond the subject—as an external part of him/her. The Enjoyment part in language overshadows its communicative function.

The neurotic subject can justify his life on the foundation of the rules and myths common to the cultural social order where he exists. He takes part in what can be called "the universal delusion" (the belief in the same rules and myths). The psychotic subject can never do this. The neurotic subject believes that if he could find the lost object he will be able to fulfill the lack in his life. To the psychotic it is clear that no object could make him forget his foundational lack.

For the psychotic subject the meaning of life as it is transmitted in language, or to be more exact "the meaning of meaning,"[28] is a question of life and death. In order to be able to answer this question he constructs delusions and imaginary processes that will explain life. He needs to justify his life at any price, and for that he imagines forces that lurk in his body, evil creatures that dominate his behavior or speak about him on television. What is imaginary becomes Real for him, because of that same disturbance in the symbolic order.

A psychotic young man says for example: "I don't understand why we live. If I wasn't depressed I think I would have found the answer to this question. I asked my sick uncle how and why we live and the next day he died." For the psychotic subject the words have power over things in the world, a magical power. This man thinks that there is a connection between the question and the quick death of his uncle. Lacan compares this to the weaving of cloth. The neurotic has a tear in his cloth, and the stitches are split open. For the psychotic there is no tear, there is a flaw in the weaving itself of the cloth. A flaw that can only be covered with a patch or by finding an imaginary substitute to what was foreclosed.

Where the paternal function is flawed, there is no pos-

---

28 As I heard from the psychoanalyst Shlomo Lieber

sibility for the child to take part in social discourse. He remains outside it, even though he, like any other subject, is inside language. His foreclosure from the social discourse keeps him in the dual relations with the one who represent for him the Other; the "Other" is a concept that includes in it an absolute concept such as the entirety of the signifiers of language, or God, or the mother that remains the whole world for the child. The anxiety of the psychotic experience comes from the total domination of the Other over him, since this Other is not subject to any law and has no limitations. The subject sees in himself/herself an object that is there to satisfy the demands of this Other that is never absent, and that can never have any lack. In order to survive the psychotic needs to foreclose the lack and embody the object that fills this lack. As a consequence he gives up his existence as a subject and turns into a satisfying or pursued object. His entire body and his delusion express his captivity in the unlimited enjoyment of the Other. There is nothing to come between him and the persecution of this Other. His access to social and symbolic life is almost barred, and the words that need to be used as a metaphor are not created. What cannot be symbolized or said in words is expressed in the Real of the body or in the Real of delusions.

If in *The Piano* Ada finds a substitute to her voice in playing the piano, Betty does not find such a substitute, and her symptom is her entire body and the voices that she hears. All psychotic phenomenon that we see—hallucinations, delusions, and the like—are the attempt of the psychotic to reconstruct his world after it collapsed. His world collapsed because when a question emerged, and he needed the paternal function in order to answer it (like for example a question about the forbiddance of enjoyment, a question about his sexual identity, a question about the meaning of life), he did not find in himself the signifier of the name of the father that he needed in order to bear the lack. For Betty the final collapse happened when she realized that she is not pregnant. That was meant to be the substitution for the missing name of the father, i.e., motherhood was taken from her.

The psychotic delusion that we encounter is already a reconstruction after the psychotic collapse. It is a type of defensive structure. When Freud distinguishes between neurosis and psychosis he writes about regression from reality that is taking place in both cases. While the neurotic regresses to the fantasy world and represses the unacceptable idea that came into his mind, the psychotic returns to the I and reconstructs it. The neurotic returns to reality and tries to find a substitute object, while the psychotic tries to build a new external and internal reality. The frustration regarding the object causes the neurotic to give up the object, and the Libido that is decathected from this object is transferred to the fantasmatic object, and from there to the repressed object; yet all in all in the unconscious the cathexis of the object remains strong; while in psychosis the Libido is not searching for a new object but regresses to the ego. A primal narcissism without an object is created after which there is an attempt to rehabilitate oneself through the construction of a patch=delusion. Delusion compels the psychotic to reconstruct a universe where there are no doubts but rather total certainty. There are no coincidences in such a universe but rather a rigid certainty that cannot be debated.

Betty Blue begins with a scene of copulation, which is speechless, and meaningless. This is an outbreak of the corporal after which Betty complains that nobody listens to her: she presents the absence of the phallic signifier as a representation of meaning, which is a consequence of the absence of the name of the father.

The narrator, who is the hero of the movie, becomes the Other for Betty, and through him she tries to find her own voice, but fails time and again. She writes his book for him, the child she desires is a present for him, and the piano she plays is only an accompaniment to his piano playing.

Her failures, instead of leading her to her own speech, lead her to act violently—at first towards the environment (she burns down one house and destroys a second one), and later towards herself through self-mutilation. The voices she hears lead her to extract her eye as a punishment—an eye for eye. Actually, what she tries to extract is the gaze of the persecuting Other.

Love does not save her. On the contrary, love directs to her an impossible demand: "We are like two fingers of the same hand—nothing can separate us," says her lover. There is no subjective space between her and the Other—and for that her lover strangles her. He strangles the voice and the gaze so that she can stay his in total identification.

On Love and Perversion

§ An Affair of Love (Une liaison pornographique)

FRANCE 1999

DIRECTED BY FRÉDÉRIC FONTEYNE

ACTORS: NATHALIE BAYE, SERGI LÓPEZ

The questions that are the central issues of the movie concern the possibility of sexual relations without love and what intimacy is. Two people, "he" and "she," complete strangers, are meeting after answering an ad in the paper and decide to realize a joint sexual fantasy of whose details we are not cognizant. These people are nameless, they have no past and they do not supply personal details to each other. They are an anonymous man and woman meeting for a specific goal, the realization of a pornographic relationship. Each time they meet they rent a room in the same tattered hotel. The problem starts when the two begin to develop feelings towards each other, an event that endangers the fantasy. The movie is combined from flashbacks of the heroes exposing themselves in front of the camera and allowing us two different points of view about what is happening.

Already in the name—Pornographic Relations, we see an impossible combination, at least for psychoanalysis. There is an essential contradiction in this combination—relations and pornography. The movie revolves around this contradiction. For psychoanalysis, as Lacan defined it, and the film gives a fantastic example to this, there is no natural and authentic sexual relationship between a man and a woman. There are no pornographic "relations" and there never can be, between a man and a woman, but there is relationship between each one of them and the object he/she desires. Sexual desires are always determined by a partial sexual object, which is always saturated in fantasy. That is to say—sexuality relates to the other as an object and not as a subject. The heroes in the movie do not even have names. They do not know any personal detail about each other and even the photography is focused on the marginal details of the frame and on the anonymity of the masses passing in the street.

Freud discovered that there are specific initial conditions for love and for the arousal of sexual desire. He described an example of this in his case study description of "The Wolf Man," 1918; there a very special condition appeared. Freud constructed the event of the wolf man observing his parents copulating from behind when he was one and a half years old. He connected between the gaze that was ascribed to the wolf man at that age and the gaze at the behind of a nanny scrubbing the floor when he was two and a half years old. The wolf man remembered that he urinated when he saw her. Freud interpreted this memory as a male identification with the father. As a grown up the wolf man would desperately fall in love with village girls who were in a kneeling position. Freud writes: "He fell in love with the girl instantly and with irresistible violence, although he had not yet been able to get even a glimpse of her face" (Freud, 1918, p.93).

The pre-condition which is required in the object of the drive is valid here to see the behind of a woman. The emphasis here is on the gaze. The gaze also plays a central role in the movie. We are not shown and not told about the perverse fantasy realized by the two heroes. The camera enters the bedroom only when the couple "makes love," as they say. And then—they cover themselves up with a sheet. They are shy. The gaze is covered. It reveals nothing—the opposite of what we usually see in pornographic movies, where the gaze shows "all."

The gaze is one of the objects of the drive that Lacan adds to the list of objects—the breast, the excrement and the voice.

Lacan distinguishes between the act of seeing and the gaze. They are not identical. We see from one point—there is always one subject that is the viewer—but we are seen from everywhere. Our subjectivity is dependent not only upon what we see, but also upon how we are seen, namely, how we are being looked at. The gaze transforms us into visible entities. The first gaze is that of the mother at her baby, the gaze which says to him: "This is you and I like you," occurring in the 'Mirror Stage.'

We are seen from everywhere, says Lacan, relying on the phenomenologist philosopher Maurice Merleau-Ponty and his great works, *The Visible and the Invisible* and *The Phenomenology of Perception* (Merleau-Ponty, 1945). Ponty discusses the dependence of the visible upon that which places us under the gaze of the seer. Lacan extracts from this theory what he dubs *pousse*, i.e., 'shoot.' A drive which is prior to the vision. To wit, following Freud, Lacan introduces vision as a drive, namely, it embeds passion, desire. The gaze is a manifestation of the drive at the level of the scopic field.

The gaze is the expression of the drive. That is to say, our sight is not passive but it is driven and it has a will for satisfaction. Love is also dependent on the gaze. This is the gaze with which I see the way I look in the eyes of my lover—as an ideal.

Screen and Trompe L'oeil

Most theories tend to present the visible, that which is perceived by the senses as a screen, as an illusory meaning behind which lies the "real" world. According to Lacan, there is nothing but the screen. The screen *is* the world. The truth itself, according to Lacan, is constructed as fiction. There is no foreground and background, superficial and profound, only a screen of signifiers. And in this screen there are rifts through which the absence, the lack, the nothing, springs forth (Lacan 1964, pp, 67-68).

The gaze always falls on the screen, and the screen is opaque, there is nothing behind it. The gaze is always interplay of light and opacity. The beam of light looking at me tears a hole in the screen. It creates a rift, a division of being between seer and seen—yet it reveals nothing in depth.

The relation between the gaze and what one wishes to see involves a lure, for through the gaze of the Other one perceives himself as the object of desire. Not the ego, but only the human subject—the subject of desire which is human essence—is not wholly captured in this imaginary trap, as opposed to the animal. And the artist becomes the leading actor, when isolating the function of the screen and playing with it. The artist can play with the mask as that beyond which lies the gaze.

To wit, if the screen covers something, then it is not like a phenomenon covering the real thing. The surface, the shell, and the mask are the real thing concealing the gaze. The rift exposes the gaze, and if we see the gaze, it usually conveys a sense of shock and horror as, for example, in Hitchcock's films. In *Psycho*, when Marion walks up toward the house, one feels it is the house looking at Marion. The gaze is behind the reflection of the eye-pupil.

In the movie *Une Liason Pornographique*, there is the gaze of the heroes looking at each other, this gaze causes them to be shy and to cover themselves, and there is the gaze of the camera which follows the gaze of the heroes.

Reality is therefore constructed as fiction—it is the same screen created from fantasies. Fantasies simultaneously can cover the Real hole and can also reveal it. The gaze is not only the end of the movement of the eye; it also freezes movement and hypnotizes the eye. The power of the gaze is hypnotic, and it is a power that can kill.

In the case of his patient, the "Wolf Man," Freud powerfully deals with the question of what is the first encounter—the real that lies behind the fantasy, and comes to a construction of the primal scene (the parents' intercourse) the child saw when he was one and a half years old. Freud strongly insists upon exposing this real, leading Lacan to assume that this insistence could have later driven the Wolf Man to insanity.

It can be said that all our lives we are in pursuit of an object that once gave us pleasure and was lost to us. All the fantasies are substitutes for that object and at the same time represent it.

In fantasy we find ourselves reduced to the point of thought which refers to the events occurring while we are absent, while we are not present. There is anonymity in fantasy. The structure of the fantasmic gaze includes a self-doubling of the gaze, as though we are watching the "primal scene" (the parents' intercourse) from behind our very own eyes, as though we are not wholly identified with our own gaze, but rather stand somewhere "behind it." As though the gaze is concealed by the eye.

The fantasy is the "absolute particular," that part which we will never be able to share. In Kant's words—we do not respect the other on the basis of the universal moral law that is embedded in each and every one of us, but on the basis of its "pathological" nucleus, the particular way in which each one "dreams his world," devises his way of deriving *enjoyment* through his own fantasies. This very same point of absolute particularity is where the artist stands. The artist as the one who connects between this intimate particular world and the general culture.

Through the whole movie there is a movement around the axis that rotates between anonymity and intimacy, and even exchanges one for the other. Intimacy exists in fact in anonymity, and at the moment of revelation, what the heroine calls "a love declaration": i.e., when speech substitutes for actions, the missed interpretation, the missed encounter and the separation are also occurring.

The daydreamer is ashamed of his fantasies, and even if he agrees to share them, he will often find out that the fantasies of others repel the listener. But the function of art is to turn the most embarrassing fantasies into esthetic pleasure. Freud writes: "But when a creative writer presents his plays to us or tell us what we are inclined to take to be his personal day-dreams, we experience great pleasure... the writer softens the character of his egotistic day-dreams by altering and disguising it, and he bribes us by the purely formal—that is, aesthetic—yield of pleasure which he offers us in the presentation of his fantasies" (Freud, 1907, pp.152-153).

To such a yield of pleasure, that is meant to allow the release of greater pleasure arising from deeper psychical sources, Freud calls—an *incentive bonus*, or a *fore-pleasure*. Freud believes that all the aesthetic pleasure rendered by the writer is characterized by such fore-pleasure, and that the true pleasure derived from the aesthetic work of art springs from the release of tensions in our mind. A large part of this success may be attributed to the fact that the creative writer creates for us the ability to enjoy our own fantasies, from now on, without feeling self-reproach or shame.

A mishap happened to our heroes—they fell in love. The movie emphasizes the fact that they encounter love almost against their will. What makes them fall in love is not the realization of their fantasy but speech: Speech and abandonment anxiety. Right after they fall in love we see them separated by a glass partition. It is as if the fantasy connected them to each other and love separated between them. It is not love itself that separates them but rather their fear of giving themselves to love. As much as there is no sexual relation between a man and a woman, there is certainly a love relationship, but in order for that to occur one must relinquish the object. One must recognize lack and castration. Our heroes, like other good neurotics, are holding on to the illusion of satisfaction through the object. Fantasy is such an illusion whereas the lack horrifies them.

In his article "On the universal tendency to debasement in the sphere of love" from 1912, Freud distinguishes between love and sexual desire: "If the currents of affection and desire do not intersect, the desire as a whole will not focus upon one object. This failure to combine the two currents triggers neurotic symptoms: where they love they do not desire and where they desire they do not love" (Freud 1912, p.195).

Freud pointed out the difference between erotic investment in an Object and the situation of a woman in love. The latter is far more invested in the Object whilst the self empties itself—ostensibly in favor of the Object. In the case of erotic investment however, we invest in another in order to satisfy our own needs (Freud, 1927, pp.152-157).

In Freud's opinion, falling in love occurs at the moment when narcissistic libido turns into libido for the Object. Lacan adopted the opposite approach, saying that love, in the form of an imaginary screen (*semblant*) constitutes a link between the Subject of the Real, which is intended to veil the fact that such a link does not really exist at the level of drive.

According to Lacan, the Subject has a constructive connection with the Real, which is confined to the narrow borders of the pleasure principle, which is not compelled by drive. Within these borders the object of love appears. The question is: how can this object of love fulfill a role parallel with the object of desire?

In *Une Liason Pornographique* the heroes are called "he" and "she." Any man. Attitudes. They have no personal identity, similar to the heroes in pornographic movies. All along the movie the woman is much clearer and unambiguous. The man defines himself from the beginning as a romantic. Since the movie is constructed in the form of separate interviews with the man and the woman, the focus is on the differences between the two narratives. This is a kind of Rashomon. She is much more direct and practical, more open, going straight to the point. It is as if the feminine and the masculine positions are turned around.

We don't really know anything about the pornographic fantasy as such. We meet the heroes before and after its realization. The thing itself is missing because it is not represented. You can't talk about it or show it. There are no words for the thing itself. The photography itself is focused on the small details, in the margins. It is as if the direct gaze cannot see anything, and only a side view reveals the truth. When the sex becomes almost repulsive this is an ideal situation. Instead of the realization of the fantasy Enjoyment appears as the edge of the unbearable.

The direction of the unfolding of the movie is contrary to the way the relationship develops in the romantic movies genre. Here the heroes first got rid of the sexual tension and later they could feel comfortable with each other. The second time they repeat the act the problem of memory emerges, because there already is a precedent. How does one realize a fantasy that requires total alienation after the first time one lives through it? When the love affair develops, the woman feels as if she already knew the man.

A new stage in the relationship emerges when she asks: maybe we should make love? (The expression in English and French is interesting—relating to the act of love as a sexual realization). This suggestion is her initiative, as is the initiative of the next stage—which is a declaration of love. Falling in love is the difficult moment. Here, desire is accompanied by abandonment anxiety, which proves to be an obstacle. Encountering the Real of love immediately turns this love into a lost love. After the realization of love they quarrel. In the next scene in which they meet there is a glass partition between them. These are the moments of loss inside the masses which is both intimate and anonymous.

A secondary plot in the movie is a discussion taking place with an old woman in the corridor on the subject of "what is love?" The world penetrates the intimacy and then love is presented as sacrifice. What is the sacrifice here? According to Lacan love appears when enjoyment is renounced in favor of desire.

When they declare their love to one another, he is uncomfortable and she is straightforward. She declares her love and he cries. They are afraid of the realization of their love. They interpret each other's wishes without speaking. Each one of them projects his will and his fear of failing on the other, and in this way they miss one another. In the end the man repeats the declaration that he made at the beginning of the movie: "I would rather die than tell what my fantasy is."

Like in Borges's story about the *Phoenix Cult*, the world is one big secret cult. Its secret consists of a conspiracy of silence concerning sexuality. The man in the movie remains in an unbridgeable gap between the symbolic and the Real. Due to its realization the fantasy turns from being imaginary to being Real, and because of this the love encounter becomes impossible.

§ Happiness

DIRECTED BY: TODD SOLONDZ

ACTORS: PHILIP SEYMOUR HOFFMAN, LARA FLYNN BOYLE, BEN GAZZARA

This is a cruel satire about American culture, which transmits its messages in a style taken from soapy television dramas. The heroines of this movie are three sisters from New Jersey: pathetic Joy, who falls in love with a violent Russian taxi driver; Trish, the perfect housewife who discovers her psychologist husband is a pedophile that rapes his son's friends; and Helen, a glamorous writer who develops a relationship on the phone with a perverse neighbor. This is a story about, sex, perversion and loneliness.

In the last few years we are witnessing the fall of "the master," or the father. We can call it many different names. The master, the Other, ideology, authority or tradition. *Happiness* shows us the sad consequences of this fall of "the master," especially when there is a desperate attempt to save the shell of political correctness. The movie is always speaking to us on three levels. The first layer is hypocritical, self-righteous and seemingly normal; the "true" level which is perverse, where everyone revolves around the ideal of "happiness" like around the golden calf while turning all others into objects for their own satisfaction; the underlying level—one can call it the miserable level—or the

Ruth Golan

desperate and failing search for love level.

Helen: "It's just I'm... I'm so tired of being admired all the time. All these men I mean... they're all beautiful, artistic minds, great sex, the whole package, but hollow, you know what I mean? I feel nobody's really honest with me. Nobody wants me for me."

In our contemporary discourse friendships and the relationship of couples are regulated without a master, without the unifying third of the ideal; market and consumerism rules usually dominate the unity of our way of life. The postmodern subject is more and more exposed to the surprises of the Real, and is lacking means that will help him deal with this Real or defend himself against it. This is why this subject is susceptible to traumatization more than ever before. This is the era of the "non-existing Other."

When culture offers a foundation of stable and common meanings, and the social relations are in order, the subjects are much less susceptible to the Real, and the severe cruel outbreaks of this Real are softened by the envelopes of meanings created by the discourse. As soon as the Other shows itself as inconsistent, as soon as the unifying One is lost, what is created is "trou-matism" (Lacan's pun combining trauma and hole), which the discourse cannot bar (Soler, 1999).

The Other's discourse is used as a plug or a dam, which defends against trauma. The multiplicity of nightmares in modern times is a sign that the boat of discourse is leaking, people don't speak to each other anymore.

Slavoj Žižek speaks a lot about the change in culture

and the crisis around the Real: he describes the pervert as one who "with his certainty about what brings enjoyment, obfuscates the gap, the 'burning question,' the stumbling block, that 'is' that is the core of the Unconscious. The pervert is thus the 'inherent transgressor' par excellence.: he brings to light, stages, practices the secret fantasies that sustain the dominant public discourse, while the hysterical position precisely displays doubt about whether those secret perverse fantasies are 'really *it*'" (Žižek, 1999, p.288).

According to Žižek, the opposition between perversion and hysteria is especially important today, in the era of the "decline of Oedipus," because the subject is not that which is inherent in the paternal law through the symbolic castration, rather it is that subject who is "polymorphously pervert," and is following the superego injunction to enjoy.

Freud already dealt with a complex which he called the complex of the "fellow-man" (Nebenmenche). He already raised this question in one of his first articles, "Project for a Scientific Psychology" *(Freud, 1889, p.131)* that was published posthumously, and in his article "Civilization and Its Discontent" from 1930 (Freud, 1930, p.57). In both these articles he deals with the problem of the *Nebenmenche,* i.e., one's fellow man, the neighbor (in German "neben" means close), and he addresses this problem with the biblical important and impossible injunction "Love thy neighbor as thyself" (Leviticus 19:18).

In Hebrew the term is *Re-a* and not neighbor. There

are three meanings to this word—*friend, other* and *similar.* Freud and Lacan, as well as Levinas, refer to *Re-a* as being related simultaneously to a close friend and to a stranger. One may say—the imaginary, the symbolic and the Real are unified. Jean-Paul Sartre stated that "*hell is the fellow man,*" while Levinas claimed that the cause of subjective trauma is the neighbor, the fellow man: That is to say the same being with which I have ethical relations. Lacan said that human beings behave as if fellow man holds the secret of Enjoyment which is prevented from them, or as if this neighbor stole Enjoyment from them, this enjoyment that is truly theirs.

Fellow man is therefore both an object of love and of hate. The *Re-a* is the one who is simultaneously a stranger and he who is closest to me and who resembles me the most.

All the characters in *Happiness* are wandering around each other searching after an impossible love with others who are absolute beings and with whom they do not manage to communicate .Love and communication are not possible unless it is through the perverse object. The producer of the movie describes it as a "tragic comedy." The director Ted Solondz describes it thus: "A series of intersecting love stories, how people are always fighting in order to create relationships and how much they succeed or fail."
Helen: I'm not laughing at you, I'm laughing with you.
Joy: But I'm not laughing.

An interesting emphasis in the movie is a dominant factor in the postmodern culture of our times: everybody in the film is either a therapist, a patient or is speaking in psychological language. Solondz emphasizes the perverse element in psychology or psychoanalysis. Psychoanalysis needs to learn from *Happiness* to beware of something that can lead to its extinction. This will come not from those who resist it (resistances are an inherent part of the psychoanalytic therapeutic tool), but precisely from those who accept psychoanalysis, which Freud called "Wild" Psychoanalysis. This is the enthusiastic or enjoying aspect of psychoanalysis that can lead it ad absurdum.

The neurotic subject says: "no, this can't be it," and according to the rule of negation we know that this is it. Resistance to interpretation indicates its truth, while absence of resistance is seemingly more problematic for the analyst. What can he do when the neurotic agrees enthusiastically: "this is it"? This is yet another kind of resistance and therefore more threatening. In his article "'Wild' Psychoanalysis," Freud relates to the danger of simplistic acceptance of psychoanalysis: the question being what happens when desire is not barred or inhibited for the neurotic, but it is seemingly moving freely? (Freud, 1910).

Psychoanalysis can be resisted precisely through infinite interpretations of every sliver of speech without leaving anything hidden, except the actions that are revealed to resist the entire exposed mechanism. This is true since everything can be interpreted immediately in a way that contradicts its manifest meaning, and every word can lead to other words that are immediately spoken. As such psychoanalytic interpretation turns into the neurotic mechanism itself in a totally compulsive way, but this contradiction goes beyond being an obsession and turns into a perversion.

In the same article Freud warns us from a too enthusiastic acceptance of the theory, and a literal acceptance in the border zones of psychoanalysis, in the connection between psychoanalysis and its popular manifestations. In this article Freud turns around the accepted distinction between true and false. He exposes the fact that despite the scientific truth being objective, its truth is unacceptable and cannot be correct.

Psychoanalytic truth emerges as a writing mechanism, and as a production of texts (there is more and more talking about it which is similar to the speech of obsessive neurotics). Psychoanalytic perversion can cause one's speech to become unstoppable. Wild psychoanalysis denies the gap existing between the different layers of the psyche; everything is exposed, and therefore pornographic. One does not speak to "the beauty behind the veil," but to the empty space; The phallus doesn't appear as covered but as simultaneously Real and Imaginary.

The issues of the movie are coarseness and lack of tact, vulgar-bodily interpretation to sex, absence of resistance, confusion between interpretation and perversion, and behind all this, the search for love, relationship and meaning—it is as if the movie is putting all this in front of us in a twisted enlarging mirror.

§ Festen (The Celebration)

Denmark, 1998

Directed by: Thomas Vinterberg

Actors: Ulrich Thomsen, Henning Moritzen, Thomas Bo Larsen

This movie was done according to the rules of Dogma group. It is taking place during a 60th birthday party at a hotel that is also the home of its rich and respectful manager and his wife. Many guests arrive to this event, among them the manager's two sons and his daughter. One daughter is absent because she committed suicide a short time before the feast. Family secrets that had been buried below the surface are starting to surface when one of the sons, who is the hero of this movie, starts to break the rules of the ceremony.

Festen is dealing with what Freud discovered almost 100 years before, i.e., the centrality of sexuality in our times. The place of sexuality in our lives is not reduced to the simple and banal recognition that we are all under the influence of the sexual drive. It is the fact of its dominance over our lives—and of its subversion under all the ideals and conceptions of our conscious life, an unbearable subversion even in our permissive and cynical era: "a bad surprise." So repression and denial of the sexual drive are necessary for the development of culture, but finding a balance is a very delicate matter; as the movie reveals, the suppression of the drive can cause serious trouble, such as the construction of perverse family structures.

The role of psychoanalysis consists of nothing but discovering the traces of this unbearable causality as it is expressed in our lives and in our actions. Psychoanalysis investigates the structural discontent inherent in culture due to its encounter with sexuality, and also the dissatisfaction and conflict immersed in our lives.

The process of a man's recognizing what a woman is and vice versa is not a biological pre-given. For Freud, "there is no sexual relation," natural and authentic, as it exists for the animals; thus in this case one cannot use the concept of "instinct" (congenital knowledge). The Freudian drive is totally different and it does not portray a relationship that one could write down in a formula. Sexual desire is always determined by the partial sexual object and is always immersed in fantasy. Fantasy, according to Freud, is not just an imaginary creation; rather it conditions our most intimate and central perceptions and judgments concerning reality as such. There is no harmony or peace within the subject, as there is no harmony and peace between the sexes. The neurotic symptom, as we see it in analysis, is expressing and substituting for the non-existent sexual relation. However, the subject, as it emerges from Freud's writings, always remains divided and split in relation to the sexual causes that determine his\her sexual behavior and choices; he\she usually doesn't want to know anything about this.

Psychoanalysis aspires to find a different way, a way that does not pass through the liberation of the drive or its suppression, but takes the sexual causality into consideration and leads it forward, not to a new ideal but to a new kind of love. *Festen*, like some other movies discussed in this book, is indicating such a possibility.

Even today, in subtle ways, we try to disavow the sexual causes of our neurotic behavior. But the disavowal of neurosis, both hysterical and obsessive-compulsive, is actually the disavowal of both Freud's concepts of the unconscious and sexuality. Since the symptom, (in *Festen*—it is the inability of the hero to make love to a woman)—constitutes a return of the repressed truth from the unconscious, and simultaneously it is a substitute for the subject's unique sexual activity.

In addition, the disavowal of the unconscious and sexuality is equal in psychoanalysis to the disavowal of choice and responsibility. Indeed, psychoanalysis is a theory that can be describes as deterministic, i.e., a theory that recognizes the place of coincidence in our life and in our sexual destiny, but it is not separate from the concept of choice; on the contrary, "the choice of neurosis," or the sexual position, according to Freud, is the particular position of the subject facing the primordial. This always constitutes a traumatic sexual encounter. It is always traumatic, since this encounter is always too frightening in its impulsive power, or too frustrating for the speaking being (an example of this is the famous Freudian Castration Complex). In *Festen* the sexual encounter for the hero and also for the audience is experienced as "too much"—it passes through the father's incest.

Now I would like to refer to the place of the father. According to psychoanalytic theory, as formulated by Lacan, a human being is born into a symbolic cultural set. Even before his birth he is already taking part in his parents' fantasy. He is dependent on the Other for his identity and for receiving recognition of his separateness. The child needs another for satisfying his bodily needs, bur in addition he needs to signify something for someone in the symbolic world, i.e., in the world of language. He needs to signify something the other desires. The first mechanism is a mechanism of identifying with an "ideal I," which is a part of the Other. The first representation of this Other is usually the Mother. He turns to her since she is responsible for satisfying his needs and desires. But because every subject is inherently a *lacking subject*, since he is subject to the symbolic order, the mother herself is also a "lacking and disappointing subject"; in this respect the child is from his birth the object who complements her lack.

What the Other will signify as an ideal reference will be used as a point of reference for the child with respect to this same identification. The dyadic structure is not enough. There is a need for a third factor which is manifested by the father's place—the function of the father as representing the world of language and symbolic order, the cultural rules. The entrance into the Oedipal complex marks the fact that the child is not really satisfying the mother and she therefore turns her gaze and her desire to the father. She opens up a place for the father as the third. One may say that she respects the father's word as representing the symbolic order. The universal law that forbids incest, makes sexual satisfaction impossible (therefore this law has a structural value and not only a moral one, since it necessitates the repression of forbidden desires and makes possible the entrance of a third factor into the set, i.e., the entrance of language and of culture). The mother is the one to give the father entrance into the set or to ignore his function in it. In *Festen,* the place of the mother is dominant in guarding the family structure at any price, even at the price of her children's lives.

According to Lacan, who is continuing Freud's thoughts on the subject, the true role of the father is to be a mediator; to connect between the law and the desire which are the driving forces. For this to happen the father should expose the castration, the cut that indicates the lack inherent in desire. The father should show his pere-version (a pun between perversion and version, the father's version concerning sexuality), i.e., recognize his sins, especially concerning his desire. In other words: He should not deny his sexual Enjoyment if the woman is the cause of his desire. If denied, it leaves the father as an ideal figure and the necessary cut that makes possible the creation of a separate subject is not possible.

Therefore, through the Oedipus complex the subject should undergo processes of alienation and separation, and discover the lack in the Other, a lack that will makes it possible for him to face the lack in the kernel of his/her being, in order to turn into a particular and unique subject. Where this passage is not happening, the subject forecloses the inscription of the lack in the structure of his primal ideal identification. In this situation the structure is a psychotic one, where the signifier of the name of the father is foreclosed, and instead the father remains an ideal, a god, as someone who lacks nothing. He remains a kind of omnipotent Other that enjoys the subject and from whom there is no escape.

Festen shows this process through the process the hero undergoes while he attempts to expose the father's perversion and to dethrone him as a representation of God for his family, a cruel and abusing God. The mother chose not to see this happening, as well as not to be there, or to be absent. Self-deception is what is prominent here, a kind of huge denial by all concerned. The effect of this denial is tragic. These are relationships hidden by the lie of the ideal.

In the first scene of the movie we see a road, and the lost son returning home. The other enters the scene through the son speaking on a cellular phone.

The name of the son is Christian. The event—the 60th birthday of the father Helge, a birthday that is taking place two months after the death of the sister who committed suicide. The former family event was the funeral of this sister.

The house is the childhood home of Christian which is also a hotel. Already in the opening scene we are introduced to the mixture between that place which is supposed to be intimate, the family home, and the hotel, which represents the foreign and the alienated. We meet the brother

The Consciousness Bearers

Michael, who is abusing his wife. The father appears as if from darkness—like a revelation of God; He has "something very important" to say to Christian—a joke about prostitutes.

The father asks Christian to speak about his sister Linda in the reception. The father, like Oedipus, is presented like a tragic hero. In his hubris he brings on himself his exposure and his fall. The whole structure of the movie is constructed according to the structure of the Oedipus tragedy: the transition from blindness to seeing.

Christian is fighting his conflict between rebellion and placation. He is in the role of one who placates. The sister who committed suicide was his twin sister. The living sister received her dead sister's room. At the beginning of the movie they take off the sheets from the furniture in the room, which is like the opening of the grave. This action will lead to finding the testimonies that will later convict the father. The sister finds the "purloined letter," the letter written by her sister Linda before she killed herself, where she exposed the secret.

The characters on the screen hold their breath and keep silent until the sister reads the letter, while in a parallel scene we are shown the place and situation of each of the movie's heroes. The cinematography stops the continuation of the movie at this spot. As soon as she reads the confession the movie continues to roll and the heroes return to the background noise of the film and to their lives of denial and lying.

Michael, the rejected son, wishes his father to like him.

For him and for his wife, everything is impulsive, violent. Christian asks the father to choose between two notes he had prepared—the blessing and the curse. Again it is the father who determines his own destiny when he chooses the curse.

On the opposite side, the movie shows the world of the kitchen. The kitchen is the underworld (the netherworld?), the negative of the upper world. It is there that the dishes are cooked. The chef is like a director who determines the rhythm of the plot. He helps Christian to make the father face his actions and forces the guests to become witnesses when he steals their car keys and does not let them escape.

After the first exposure of the incest the mother laughs and what we are witness to is her general denial, and also the guests' denial. They do not want to hear. Christian regresses. His symptom is revealed—he cannot make love to a woman.

We can relate to the structure of *Festen* as if it is a symposium, as a metaphor of life and as an escape from facing the truth. The movie unfolds in the rhythm of a Rondo: there is a chapter about the subject, and then there is a return to the symposium. The occurrences are invading the celebration; they are exposed and then immediately covered. A German host is responsible for the ceremony and for keeping the order at any price; the black boyfriend of the sister is the one who introduces the subversion of music, passion and love.

The father doesn't need to take into account his son's

speech because he sees his son as a distorted soul—as a mentally ill person that no one needs to listen to. He arouses his son's guilt in order to silence him. But when the revelations emerge he does not stop them.

When the mother blesses the father she marks and praises "your appetite for life and your care for your family." In light of the information that is revealed, this blessing is horrifying in its cynicism.

The brother Michael is assisting in the denial. He goes out of his way to defend the parental ideal. He throws Christian out of the house into the woods and in so doing he throws out the truth. This hotel of culture is revealed as the home of lies, and truth is precisely wandering around the woods.

The relationship between the brothers is similar to a Cain and Abel story that includes jealousy, rivalry and love-hate. Christian is the loved and obedient son and Michael is the rebellious and rejected son.

The symposium ends after truth is accepted. The father admits his sin and is deported. Christian is the only one who continues to show love towards his father even in his fall. The liberation from guilt makes it possible for him to encounter a woman.

The Christian elements of the movie are the manifestation of a real perversion. The son's love of his father is based on sacrifice. It is based on the son's sacrifice of himself and of his body in order to save his father. There is the relationship of the Real between father and son instead of there being a symbolic relationship. The son is caught in his father throughout his whole life and his libido is fixated with respect to his father.

Psychoanalysis offers a substitute model—one that opposes sacrifice, guilt and absolution; instead it suggests responsibility. The anxiety manifested at the end of the movie testifies to the fact that there is no real solution. The father is excommunicated but the structure is saved. Christian finds a solution to his symptom but everybody returns to the bourgeois life of denial—including the mother.

§ Closer

U.S.A. 2004

DIRECTED BY: MIKE NICHOLS

ACTORS: JULIA ROBERTS, CLIVE OWEN, NATALIE PORTMAN, JUDE LAW

Closer is a romantic drama about contingency and necessity, attraction and recoiling, loyalty and unfaithfulness, alienation and intimacy, falsehood and truth. The drama takes place between two women and two men. Dan—a frustrated writer, Alice—an American striptease artist, Anna—a neurotic photographer, and Larry—a rough doctor. exchanging couples along the entire movie.

Closer begins with a gaze and an accident. The gaze between the heroes is the contingent encounter between them that turns out to be crucial. This gaze causes them to fall in love—and this is an interesting expression—one falls in love or becomes captivated by it, or becomes a victim of it.

Dan: I fell in love with her, Alice.

Alice: Oh, as if you had no choice? There's a moment, there's always a moment, "I can do this, I can give into this, or I can resist it," and I don't know when your moment was, but I bet you there was one.

Sex and romance have become the religion of the postmodern era. It is especially true for those of us who grew up in western civilization which is characterized by extreme narcissism: where there is nothing more important in the universe than our ego with its needs and its indefatigable lust. In modern times, sex and romance are the holiest of the holy—almost the highest value that gives meaning to life in an abundant society.

In traditional civilizations, when a man and a woman came together and established sexual relations in order to have children, to build a home, those actions were done in an historical and cultural context that furnished them with a more important reason of living together than their personal happiness. But in our current era and culture, the main reason for connecting to others is the search for excitement and happiness more than any other reason. We internalized the unfounded idea that somebody else, our ideal partner, will make us happy—will fulfill all our needs, and will give us continuous satisfaction and sublime bliss that will make our lives meaningful and valuable.

For most of us this illusion is abiding deep in our consciousness. It is engraved in our cultural DNA: It is not difficult to see that the promise of happiness inherent in the myth of sexual enjoyment and romantic love is exaggerated. Our belief in this illusion and the significance we give it causes us suffering and frustration, painful awakening and the pursuit of unfulfilled desires. The topics of sex and romance are shouting out from books and songs, from the different forms of media, from every poster, but *how is all this related to intimacy between human beings?*

"Can one get a little intimacy here?!" Larry shouts at the security cameras who are supervising the striptease club, when he wishes to be alone with Alice. In the midst of the most exposed and penetrated place the longing for intimacy is awakened.

It is precisely Freud's psychoanalysis, followed by Lacan's, which attempts to expose this illusory screen.

For Freud, as Lacan formulates it and the movie shows in a marvelous way—there is no natural and authentic sexual relationship between a man and a woman. Sexual desire is always determined by a partial sexual object and it is always immersed in fantasy. That is to say, sexuality treats the other as an object and not as a subject.

Between subject and object there is an impenetrable partition which does not allow for the creation of real intimacy. Intimacy can only be created between two subjects.

In his article "Three essays on the theory of sexuality" *(Freud, 1905)*, Freud said that the mother—or her substitute, are for the child its first sexual object as well as its first object of love. He noted our loss of the primal object (in lieu of which the mother already constitutes a substitute) and that suckling from the mother's breast has become the archetype of all forms of loving connection, meaning that the discovery of the Object is actually its rediscovery. (As Lacan put it—Love comes from the belly—meaning from the breast, which is one of the primal objects). Love is indeed directed towards an object but an object that had already been ours in the past. This refers to the same Object which Lacan said is found in a person who is loved, but which is loved more than that person. At Clark University in the USA some five years later in 1909 in his *Five Lectures on psychoanalysis,* Freud alluded to this saying:

"It is inevitable and perfectly normal that a child should take his parents as the first objects of his love. But his libido should not remain fixated to these first objects; later on, it should merely take them as a model, and should make a gradual transition from them on to extraneous people when the time for the final choice of an object arrives" (Freud, 1910a, p.48).

This is the Normal love that he speaks of. In Neurotic love however, the complete opposite happens, as he set out in 1912 in On the universal tendency to debasement in the sphere of love: "If the currents of affection and of desire do not intersect, the desire as a whole will not focus upon one object. This failure to combine the two currents triggers neurotic symptoms: where they love they do not desire and where they desire they do not love" (Freud, 1912d).

In a witty exchange between Dan and Larry, Larry presents the attachment of neurotic people to their symptoms and pain:

Dan: *I want Anna back.*

Larry: *She's made her choice.*

Dan: *I owe you an apology. I fell in love with her. My intention was not to make you suffer.*

Larry: *So where's the apology? Ya cunt.*

Dan: *I apologize. If you love her you'll let her go so she can be happy.*

Larry: *She doesn't want to be happy.*

Dan: *Everybody wants to be happy.*

Larry: *Depressives don't. They want to be unhappy to confirm they're depressed. If they were happy they couldn't be depressed anymore. They'd have to go out into the world and live. Which can be depressing.*

We feel ourselves to be the victims of life. In that way love functions as an illusion of returning back home, an illusion of salvation through this impossible connection between two people.

Freud discovered that there are *pre-existing specific conditions for love* and the awakening of sexual passion. He named them *erotic conditions*. An example can be found in part of Freud's description of the *Wolf Man* case of 1918, where a very special condition appeared. Freud constructed the case of the wolf-man who had seen his father having sex with his mother from the rear when he was a year and a half old. Freud perceived a connection between the way he supposed the child had gazed then and the way he watched his nanny's behind when he was two and a half, as she looked for something on the floor. The wolf-man recalled that upon seeing her he had urinated, which Freud interpreted as male identification with the father. As an adult, the wolf-man would fall hopelessly in love with peasant girls he saw bending over. One can find here the pre-condition and the object of the drive, which was to see the behind of a woman. The emphasis here is on the gaze.

The gaze has a central role in *Closer*. For example, the gaze at the opening scene, the first gaze between Alice and Dan, and the emphasis at that point in the movie on the gaze of the camera. Following Freud, Lacan presents the gaze as a scopic drive, i.e., it contains desire. The gaze is an expression of the drive. That is to say, our vision is not passive, but rather it contains an impulse and a wish for satisfaction. Love is also dependent on a drive; on a drive in which I see how I am seen through the eyes of my lover—as an ideal.

Most theories tend to present the visible, that which is perceived by the senses as a screen, as an illusory meaning behind which lies the "real" world. According to Lacan, there is nothing but the screen. The screen *is* the world. The truth itself, according to Lacan, is constructed as fiction. There is no foreground and background, superficial and profound, only a screen of signifiers. And in this screen there are rifts through which the absence, the lack, the nothing, springs forth.

The relation between the gaze and what one wishes to see involves a lure, for through the gaze of the Other one perceives himself as the object of desire.

The gaze, says Lacan, is the thing least susceptible to castration. With the gaze it is easiest to fall into polymorphic perversion, but total exposure, as in viewing a pornographic movie, precisely indicates blindness. Since there is no real vision that does not include its cut, the blind spot, the gaze creates an artificial separation between the interior and the exterior. The things that really create desire are those that are hidden from the eye. Since there is no sexual relation, what we see in pornographic movies are empty representations.

Alice, who strips in the striptease club, seemingly "shows everything," but this "everything" is a flat screen. Actually Alice does not show anything. The movie clearly portrays that real pornography, that seemingly exposes "everything," is really emotional pornography that is created mostly in Hollywood and in romantic series on television: a total exposure of emotions. There is no interiority. Everything is outside. *Closer* stirs the emotions most intensively. Again we see everything—inside and out, except for the essence.

Reality is therefore structured like fiction—this is a screen made up of fantasies. The fantasies cover the Real hole but they can simultaneously expose it. The gaze is not only the end of the eye movement; it also freezes movement and hypnotizes the eye. The power of the gaze is hypnotic, and this is a power that can kill.

Larry: *[on a photography exhibit] What do you think?*
Alice: *It's a lie. It's a bunch of sad strangers photographed beautifully, and... all the glittering assholes who appreciate art say it's beautiful 'cause that's what they wanna see. But*

The Consciousness Bearers

the people in the photos are sad, and alone... But the pictures make the world seem beautiful, so... the exhibition is reassuring which makes it a lie, and everyone loves a big fat lie.

Larry: I'm the big fat liar's boyfriend.

Alice: Bastard!

The gaze creates fantasy and perversion. Lacan claimed that fantasy is rooted in perversion. The pervert imagines that he owns the lost object or that he can turn himself into such an object. He takes the place of the element he imagines will make it possible for him to become the bearer of pure desire.

At a certain stage Dan is having virtual sex through the computer with Larry (thinking he is a woman). This virtual sex between the two of them is an example of the blindness of the sexual drive. It wants satisfaction and is not interested in the subject. It reminds me of a young patient who once said to me: "I am having sex with men and also with women. What does it matter? Sex is sex." This was a very precise statement that emphasized how in postmodern times meaning is being reduced and even nullified. Even though there is no sexual relation between a man and a woman, a love relation between them certainly does exist, but for this to happen the object needs to be renounced. They should recognize lack and (symbolic) castration. But our heroes, like good neurotics, hold fast to the illusion of satisfaction through the object. Fantasy is such an illusion, and the lack makes them anxious.

When Dan leaves Alice in order to be with Anna she

asks: "*Is it because she is successful?*" Dan answers: "*No, it is because... she doesn't need me.*"

The promise of perfection

As Andrew Cohen says "the promise of perfection" is the belief existing behind erotic attraction and falling in love. Eros in spiritual contexts means life creating energy.

As the cosmologist Brian Swimme says:

"The nothing is full of possibility for everything. An infinite creative energy is the only energy in the universe—science (creation in The True), philosophy (creation in The Good), art (creation in Beauty), sexuality (creation in The Body). Every domain has a special mode of capacity to know about this energy but it also has from all the rest. Each thing in the world that we see is unfolding for us in the celebration of its being" (Swimme, 1995). The sexual drive in this respect is the same creative Eros at a lower level of development. This drive is the expression in the body of the evolutionary drive that exists at the foundation of great momentum of the evolving universe. Can there be anything more powerful?

When we feel the excitement of the awakening sexual drive in our body and psyche, we experience the same creative drive that caused the energy and intelligence that created the universe to break through and begin the process of creation. But due to our lack of humility, many people do not appreciate the power we are dealing with enough. When we combine the great and overwhelming power of the sexual drive, when it begins to express itself at the biological level, along with the cultural myth that the perfect partner will make us happy, it is easy to see why so many of us become unbalanced in this domain *of our lives*.

Andrew Cohen names this illusion "the promise of perfection." According to this promise, if we act according to the sexual drive, we will find complete happiness and total satisfaction—we will finally experience a deep sensation of unity and we will be whole. We repeat this time after time and again and again miss the simple truth: the happiness that we experience in the romantic context never remains. Only when we will cease to believe in this promise of perfection will we discover that the experience of romantic drunkenness is motivated, almost without exception, by the ego's need of personal affirmations.

In order to release ourselves from this dead end, we must recognize that the promise of divine happiness and complete satisfaction, which is inherent in sexual desire, is nothing but a common lie. This means that we choose to renounce personal affirmations and strengthening coming from the outside, even if it comes from someone we love. We will be able to experience the ecstatic bliss of wholeness, when we finally cease to look for the experience of our completion and happiness outside of ourselves.

From the four heroes, Alice/Jane, appears as the only heroine that goes through a developmental process at the end of which she awakens from an illusion. Alice's authenticity is revealed when we find out that she did not lie concerning her name. The end of the movie suggests three solutions: the boredom of the couple, the depression of loneliness and the choice of freedom. The last scene of Dan's is a scene of loneliness and going back to the starting point. Anna and Larry lie in bed and seem alienated and bored with each other, and Alice/Jane travels to a new place. We find out that Alice is the only one who chose truth and not fiction, and therefore her choice is the optimistic possibility suggested by the movie.

Beyond boundaries—
The evolution of consciousness
from a cinematic point of view

In this series I will examine movies that exemplify the integral concept of psycho-evolution.

§ Fight Club

U.S.A. 1999
DIRECTED BY: DAVID FINCHER BASED ON CHUCK PALAHNIUK'S BOOK
ACTORS: BRAD PITT, EDWARD NORTON, HELENA BONHAM CARTER

The main question in Fight Club is "who am I?"
In order to find excitement and meaning, Crane, a yuppie suffering from insomnia and chronic fatigue, who under the guise of being a sufferer starts attending various kinds of support groups, such as for cancer sufferers and Alcoholics Anonymous. At one of the meetings he meets a young

woman named Marla, bored and also purporting to be a sufferer. They develop a love-hate relationship. At the same time Crane connects with Tyler, a nihilistic anarchistic youth who is contemptuous of everything connected with institution and law. The two of them open an illegal fight club for people seeking catharsis outside of the framework of conventional society. The fights cause adrenalin to flow but they also lead to the emergence of a militant, dangerous and anarchistic cult. As Crane begins to lose his sanity and control over his life, Tyler turns into a model of adoration in the eyes of the club members—he forms an army of believers that aspire to destroy the existing bourgeois order. Slowly we start to understand that Crane and Tyler are two faces of the same man. (the examples in this article are from the book Fight Club).

Fight Club deals with the fundamental question "Who am I?" in the context of postmodern culture. Psychoanalysis opens up a profound and broad insight into the "I," as it stands, while Evolutionary Enlightenment relates to the "I" as what it can become.

Freud based his discoveries in psychoanalysis on his practice; on clinical observations rather than academic theory. Following in his footsteps, my discontent with psychoanalysis emanates from observing the results of this discipline after a hundred years of its existence. What are the fundamental changes that a human being goes through during and after psychoanalysis? How and what does it contribute to society? How do psychoanalysts themselves appear? The answers are not very encouraging. One should not forget that it was psychoanalysis that introduced itself as a research subject—the implication being that it is not important *what* the subject says, rather the place from which he says it, as well as what is motivating him. It seems that after reaching a certain limit, psychoanalysis continued no further. Psychoanalysis denotes the boundaries of the psyche but the spiritual perspective can take one beyond those boundaries—a fact that I have learned mainly from philosopher and teacher Andrew Cohen.

In order to examine these things we first need to consider the essential fact of the evolving universe, which includes evolving consciousness.

As Darwin demonstrated, we don't live in a given universe, but an evolving one, both in the material and spiritual sense. In the perspective of our postmodern culture we are aware that our conception of the world is relative and context dependent, i.e., dependent on the way we *interpret* our perception of it.

Along with the material evolution of the cosmos, its interiority or consciousness evolved. Although the sentient life that emerged developed some measure of awareness, it was not self-reflective. That level of consciousness was developed by human beings.

Three new traits of consciousness have been developed by the human species:

Self-reflective consciousness—the awareness that we are aware.

Creativity and development.

Freedom of choice.

Over nearly fourteen billion years, matter evolved, became more complex and changed form. During that time it attained higher and higher levels of integration and awareness. Now we could become conscious of the fact of our existence.

We were all here from the beginning. Once we were stardust. The atoms and molecules that comprised our material form were here, but in a different mode. We have evolved to the point where the cosmos itself begins to be able to know itself through us. This represents a very advanced level of evolutionary development. The development of the kind of conditions that have evolved on earth, which facilitate organic, sentient life appear to be extremely rare, if not unique—definitely not to be taken for granted, furthermore it has given rise to our evolutionary emergence as bearers of self-reflective consciousness. Thinkers engaged with the implications of the evolutionary process frequently emphasize that today the continuation of the evolutionary process (and of the world) is dependent on the conscious choice of those who have developed the faculty of freedom of choice.

We construct our identity and world in accordance with our particular worldview. Each worldview affects the world. We form our worldview through our interpretation of our experience. We form our worldview through interpreting what we experience or encounter in the world. These worldviews, or cultural perceptions, are changing. For example, in the middle ages, the relationship to madness, to love, to a woman or to childhood was quite different than the way we relate to these things now. With the help of the perspective that Darwin introduced, we have also learned to look at the world and life through the perspective of evolution over time. Worldviews influence language, culture, consciousness, affects, cognitive structures and so forth; They even influence the unconscious and symptoms.

Every civilization has a center of gravity around which ethics, norms and the fundamental cultural institutions are arranged. In society as we know it, this center of gravity generates the fundamental cultural glue of social integration. It acts like a magnet on individual development, exerting an upward pull on those that abide below the average level and exerting a downwards pull on those that try to transcend beyond the average. In both cases we are outside the range, transgressors, and stress is exerted on us to adapt to the norm.

In the teachings of Evolutionary Enlightenment, evolution is a movement from a lower level of development to a higher one. Human beings abide at different levels, lower and higher, but postmodern culture does not take kindly to such distinctions being expressed. Although people are ready to recognize differences, they reject the mention of higher or lower levels as "judgmental." However, when this is viewed in the context of an evolving process, the existence of higher and lower levels of development can be recognized as being a natural aspect of the process.

Integral philosopher Ken Wilber, classifies the eras (based on various research by scholars such as Gebser, Habermas, and Foucault), as well as the worldviews of human development. These worldviews present various, multiple methods of interpreting and organizing our experiences. As William James said, without a worldview, we remain lost in an overwhelming confusion of experiences.

Examples of the eras described by Wilber are the archaic, magic, mystic, rational and existential. These eras ran parallel to the main stages of economic and technological development: foraging, horticultural, agrarian, industrial and informative (Wilber 2000).

The magic-animistic worldview, for example, is characterized by a partial overlapping of subject and object, so that inanimate objects like rocks and rivers are perceived as being alive, or even possessing soul and spirit. The mythic worldview is characterized by a multiplicity of gods, not abstract beings but tangible powers that act directly on the universe. The mental worldview, of which the most widely known is the rational view, is characterized by the belief that the subjective dimension is fundamentally separate from the objective dimension of nature. The burning issue in this worldview is how to connect between these two dimensions. The existential worldview understands that the universe is formed of multiple perspectives. Individuals need to find meaning and significance out of this scary maze of multiple possibilities. Both psychology research and inter-cultural research show us that in certain conditions, people can access the entire range of worldviews. The human mind includes all possibilities as potentials that can emerge when certain different factors unite and make emergence possible. However, different world views become more or less prominent at different periods in history.

The Consciousness Bearers

In the period of human development characterized by survival through foraging, the dominating worldview was that of magic; the agrarian period was dominated by the mythic worldview, while the industrial period has been characterized by the mental-rational worldview. In any case all the principal modes of interpreting our experience exist de facto within us. To give up one's worldview is an experience that has similarities with death—it's a psychological earthquake from which most people endeavor to avoid at any price. However, sometimes, in extraordinary circumstances, other deeper or more complex worldviews break through and thus the world changes.

The conception of our "I" is also influenced by a worldview. It is even possible to define the I or the ego as an organizing principle—a kind of worldview.

Psychoanalysis however is not a worldview. Its validity should continue beyond any worldview. It is the subversive element—the reason why the worldview alone cannot determine everything. It deals with the subversive element, i.e., sexuality and the drive that do not obey any worldview whatsoever. In the various stages of consciousness, the unconscious is not just another state of consciousness state—it is this fish that jumps out of the water and turns consciousness upside down. It is the Real hole that lies at the heart of any awareness or worldview.

Psychoanalysis emerged in the era of the modern worldview. In this era the enlightenment paradigm was dominant (a paradigm also referred to as the Newtonian, the Cartesian, the mechanistic, nature's mirror, the reflexive, the representative worldview). Nowadays it is quite acceptable to despise this paradigm—it is considered to be limited and irrelevant. Today the postmodern worldview dominates, the discoveries of psychoanalysis having contributed to its rise and permeation into culture.

In modern era the dominant conception was that on the one hand there is the subject or the I, while on the other is the empirical or the sensual, and all valid knowledge, including the inscription of the empirical universe's maps—the simple pre-given universe.

If the map is precise, if it truly represents or matches the empirical world it is considered as "truth." The map can be actual or theoretical, a hypothesis, an idea, a concept or a table—any map of the objective world. All enlightenment theorists, holistic or atomistic, believed in one empirical universe that could be mapped using empirical methods.

The simple way to formulate the problem in this paradigm is to leave the one who drafted the map outside. However this ignores the fact that the draftsman influences the map. (This criticism starts with Kant and continues with Hegel, Schopenhauer, Nietzsche, Heidegger, Foucault and Derrida: who are all critical of the mapping paradigm). The self who is drawing the map does not disappear. He has characteristics, structures, development and his own history. All these influence what he will see and the mode in which he will see it—i.e., the context. So the great postmodern discovery is that the world is not pre-given rather it exists in contexts and moments that have history and are developing.

The "I" doesn't have essence but it has history and it can draw completely different maps according to the different stages of history. This is the Copernican revolution of Kant—the mind creates the world more than the world creates the mind. And for Hegel, the subject can be perceived only as a subject that can evolve.

The "I" therefore, is also a kind of organized worldview. And how does psychoanalysis view the "I"? As an array of identifications. Identifications with people, opinions and beliefs. For psychoanalysts, the "I" is our self-reflection in our eyes and in the eyes of others; it distinguishes between the "I" (the ego) which includes our identity and the subject, which is foreign to us.

The subject appears only through the unconscious and is foreign to the "I" and alienated from it. Psychoanalysis attempts to go beyond the alienation and to allow the subject to emerge. Freud and Lacan place the ego as an object (similar to how the eastern teachings place it). This is an object constructed from the building blocks of identifications, structured as a defensive screen in the face of an unmediated encounter with the Real of the body and of the world. The ego is used as a defense against the dynamic uncertainty of the subject of the unconscious, its inherent otherness and the feeling of the uncanny that is often a part of this kind of encounter.

The Freudian unconscious is a function which is within me yet is not mine. This is a different knowledge, or a subject that is simultaneously placed in my most intimate place and is the most foreign to me. That is why it is so difficult to accept it. The unconscious cannot be known in a direct way but only when it suddenly emerges through its formations: a slip of the tongue, a dream, a symptom. Psychoanalysis reveals that the "I," the ego, has only partial dominance over what is done in "its own home." In order to know itself the ego needs to be satisfied with the fragments of information that reach it from time to time concerning what is happening in its unconscious.

The unconscious is therefore the shadow that escorts the ego and the revelation of it hints at another reality. It brings up the absence, the lack, and reveals the split that cuts through our subjective life. This is Lacan's concept of the *lack in being* (*manque à être*). This hole is actually a condition for the continuation of development, since it makes the continued flow of desire possible.

We know that the ego mediates between the subject and reality, and that the reality to which the ego needs to give account is built upon the pleasure principle that it represents. We accept as good that which is pleasant to us and we reject as bad that which is unpleasant. The ego is a servant to three masters: reality, the id and the superego.

If the "I" is nothing but an organizing principle, a mediator that is comprised of identifications, from where does it derive its inflated importance? The ego's contrived fixation on being our identity is at the root of its resistance to change and to the dialectic movement of desire, so in analytic practice the ego is considered as a source of resistance whose strengthening will only serve to strengthen such resistance. By undermining such ego attachments and fixations, psychoanalysis attempts to restore the movement of desire and to open a free space, in which the subject can be and to move through life events more freely and flexibly. Freud's discovery of the unconscious removed the ego from the central position that it held since Descartes.

In the modern era, when psychoanalysis was developed, a great awakening took place—the birth of rationality and science, the beginning of the modern era and individualism, at which time we began liberating ourselves from tradition. Nowadays we have given up tradition, which gave us a rationale for life, gave us morality and ethics, and defined our place in life and our role in the cosmic game. Thus we lost our spiritual background, our moral and ethical foundation. We became lost because the rational mind cannot answer philosophical and spiritual questions. Then, we entered the postmodern era, where individualism reached its peak. Currently we are approaching the end of the postmodern era and the narcissistic "I" is at its zenith. The events of September 11th, 2001 look like the beginning of the end. Fight Club is a movie that predicted this end.

The double—imaginary or real?
In the first scene of *Fight Club* the double (Tyler) is seen holding a gun to the mouth of the subject. Or maybe it is the other way around?

Chuang Tzu related the tale of the emperor of China that awoke one day from a dream, whereupon he couldn't determine whether he was the emperor of China that had dreamt that he was a butterfly, or whether he was a butterfly that had dreamt it was the emperor of China.

Fight Club deals with questions about the nature of reality, as well as the question of who is the subject.

Crane, the hero of the movie says: "Tyler is projection. He's a dissociative personality disorder. A psychogenic fugue state. Tyler Durden is my hallucination."

"Fuck that shit," Tyler says. "Maybe you're my schizophrenic hallucination."

I was here first.

Tyler says, "Yeah, yeah, yeah, well let's just see who's here last..." (Palahniuk, 1996, p. 168)

In order to answer the question *who am I?* Crane goes through a journey in which all his identifications disintegrate, including the identification with his name and his self-image. Crane's identification and identity disintegrates until he reaches the bottom.

Crane finds old issues of *Reader's Digest*, a publication that identified with the bourgeois-conservative American worldview. He finds in this magazine a series of articles in which bodily organs speak about themselves in the first person: "I am Jane's uterus. I am Joe's prostate [...]" (ibid. p.58).

Crane uses the identity of the organs to express his jealousy of Tyler, due to Tyler's relationship with Marla.

At another point Crane converses with a mechanic: "The mechanic yells into the wind, "You're not your name." A space monkey in the back seat picks it up: "You are not your problems."...The mechanic yells, "You're not your age...You are not your hopes" (ibid. p.143).

I contend that we tend to build a passionate imaginary relationship with our own ego, a structure that constitutes one of the main obstacles in our life. We experience phallic enjoyment from our relationship with our self-image—our thoughts, moods, ideas and so forth. They seem to us important and unique, and actually they are the reason for our suffering—which we are reluctant to give up—since our suffering forms part of our "identity."

In the teachings of the east, preceding the teaching of evolutionary enlightenment, the ego is also recognized as a primary obstacle. This refers to the ego not as an organizing and mediating principle but as a rigid, fixated and inflated narcissism. A combination of ego and self-love/hate. A mode of compulsive attraction to the self-image and to the sense of being unique. This is translated into a negative emotional and psychological captivation to self-image and to a very selfish relationship to life.

Nowadays (and *Fight Club* takes it to the extreme of total destruction), the narcissistic "I" is dominant. Narcissism is indeed the postmodern pathology. We are so busy with our self-image, which is reflected in our awareness, that we find it hard to have an authentic relationship with the wondrous process of life of which we are all part. As a result, too many of us waste our lives with hesitating and we seldom develop at all. So in this context, the ego is seen from an unconventional perspective as being a counter-evolutionary force.

Most of us are products of the narcissistic postmodern culture in which the desire of the individual has been turned into something almost sacred. "I have my truth and you have yours"—all truths are equally valid. Nothing really is more sacred than the individual's feeling and experience. Whereas in the pre-modern era God looking at us from the sky was everything, in the modern era we liberated ourselves from superstitions concerning life. What emerged instead was an exaggeration of the importance we gave to the experience of the individual, while negating the possibility of making comparisons and exercising value judgments. God disappeared from the scene, and the narcissistic ego grabbed center stage.

Most of us are so lost in our personal dramas that we are not aware of the fact that we exist in a vast context. In the era of the individual *we lost our moral and ethical foundations as a result of being so focused on ourselves.* We have rejected the old morality because it isn't sufficiently sophisticated however, without those foundations it is hard to know what is right way to live and so we become destructive in our lives. We have no clue as to what to do with the immense freedom and richness at our disposal. We lack maturity with which to face it so we abuse and waste it. In the end we kill ourselves—if not physically then emotionally and spiritually.

In order to extricate ourselves from this swamp we need to create new ethics and morality. The postmodern ego recoils from *ethical* demands. Each demand is experienced as coercion. To the postmodern self, freedom means "I can do whatever I want." Although in the modern context this attitude was to a certain extent positive— since it led to a kind of liberation, we now really have to take the next step towards a new ethics, a new spiritual context. Many of us—those that feel discontent in the face of the dissolution of morality and ethics—resort to returning to traditional belief structures, which facilitate an ordered worldview and values. However, the circumstances of life now are very different from when those traditional structures were formed.

Fight Club deals with the danger that can arise from the vacuum created by spiritual crisis in the world. Tyler Durden offers meaning, order and life negating ethics, which is what makes him so attractive.

The movie claims that the highest value in contemporary culture is consumption. This enjoyment of consumption puts it even higher in importance than sex.

What you buy, buys you. "You buy furniture. You tell yourself, this is the last sofa I will ever need in my life. Buy the sofa, then for a couple of years you're satisfied that no matter what goes wrong, at least you've got your sofa issue handled. Then the right set of dishes, then the perfect bed, the drapes, the rug.

"Then you're trapped in your lovely nest, and the things you used to own, now they own you" (ibid. p.44).

With the explosion of Crane's flat, his identity is also shattered.

"[...] I loved my life. I loved that condo. I loved every stick of furniture. That was my whole life. Everything, the lamps, the chairs, the rugs were me. The dishes in the cabinets were me. The plants were me. The television was me. It was me that blew up" (ibid. p.141).

Crane felt death in the midst of life which is why he calls Tyler to wake him up—awakening through destruction.

"The doorman leaned into my shoulder and said, "A lot of young people don't know what they really want."

Oh, Tyler, please rescue me.

And the phone rang.

"Young people, they think they want the whole world."

Deliver me from Swedish furniture.

Deliver me from clever art.

And the phone rang and Tyler answered.

"If you don't know what you want," the doorman said, "you end up with a lot you don't." May I never be complete.

May I never be content.

May I never be perfect.

Deliver me, Tyler, from being perfect and complete (ibid. p.46).

The book and the movie touch upon the causality of the chaotic state. The movie presents groups of fatherless people. The Other does not exist. There is no symbolic castration, there are no scars. Of course it's not possible to live without inscription—scarring. The so called perfection of normal life is perverse and sterile perfection. In *Fight Club* Crane acquires a few scars:

"Maybe self-improvement isn't the answer.

Tyler never knew his father.

Maybe self-destruction is the answer.

[...] Me, I knew my dad for about six years, but I don't remember anything. My dad, he starts a new family in a new town about every six years. This isn't so much like a family as it's like he sets up a franchise" (ibid. pp.49-50).

The goal of destruction is to liberate the world from history—to liberate the individual from history, from the conditioning of his ego. The destruction the movie aims at is the destruction of the unique, of the personal. "It's only after you lost everything" says Tyler, "that you're free to do anything" (ibid. p.70).

The extreme narcissist is cynical. He does not believe that transformation can happen. A cynical person arrogantly believes that no change is possible: "We've seen everything already, we've done everything, it isn't possible. I am not naïve, I'm sophisticated and that's how I know it isn't possible. One cannot change so much, the world cannot be different. We've heard it all before." Cynicism is the wall through which the ego defends itself. It gives a sense of security—you don't need to think of something new or radical. You don't need to feel insecure. The extreme narcissist hates insecurity. Tyler offers security and authority.

At the end of the postmodern era we find ourselves in a crisis. This world crisis is principally one of spirituality or consciousness. Human beings have today the power to create and destroy life in a way that until a short time ago only gods could, but our moral, ethical and spiritual development lags way behind.

For Ken Wilber, all spiritual practice is a repetition or rather a *realization* of death. As the mystics say "If you die before you die you will not die." In other words, if now, immediately, your separate self-sense dies and you discover your real self, which is the entire cosmos, it is than that the death of this particular body-soul is nothing but a falling leaf from an eternal tree—which is you.

Freud said: If you want life, prepare to die. Tyler says—while holding a gun to the mouth of his double: "The first step for eternal life is that you must die."

The framework of the narrative of *Fight Club* is a love triangle. Already in the first scene, of commercial buildings in New York exploding, the triangle appears:

"We have a sort of triangle thing going here. I want Tyler. Tyler wants Marla. Marla wants me. I don't want Marla, and Tyler doesn't want me around, not anymore. This isn't about *love* as in caring. This is about *property* as in *ownership*" (ibid. p.14).

Without Marla, Tyler wouldn't have anything. Love started the whole story. A different love ends the story—a love that should solve the problem of blind obedience to a law, that leads to perversion.

At first this love is narcissistic. Love as a symptom. Bob's love (the muscular man without testicles) for Crane is narcissistic because he thinks that Crane's testicles were also cut off. This is love in the form of identification.

Most of us flee into sleep, enjoyment, excitement—all of which direct our awareness away from anxiety and confusion. We waste the gift that we have to give and our time in being self-conscious Most of us require long years of development in order to wake up to the big picture of the evolutionary process and when that occurs, we usually feel that it's too difficult and that we can't face it. Thus we turn back to personal lives of limitation and inertia.

"Every time you fall asleep," Tyler says, "I run off and do something wild, something crazy, something completely out of my mind" (ibid. p.163).

Crane's symptom is insomnia although really he is constantly asleep. He sleeps in order to avoid encountering something real. The Real happens in his absence. When the "I" sleeps Tyler appears. At the end of the story Crane awakens to who he really is. The awakening begins with a question—what does Tyler do when I'm asleep?

The movie ends differently from the book. In the movie love saves Crane; in the book the nightmare continues. The solution the movie offers is death. One can also look at it as the death of the subject in order for the subject to be able to be born anew.

Ruth Golan

§ The Hours

U.S.A. 2002

Directed by: Stephen Daldry, based on the book by Michael Cunnigham

Starring: Julianne Moore, Nicole Kidman, Meryl Streep

Music: Phillip Glass

The Hours *deals with the question "how am I to live?" Through the character of a woman multiplied thrice-fold. The narrative follows three women whose common denominator is Virginia Woolf's book* Mrs. Dalloway. *One woman is Virginia Woolf herself, portrayed in the time between her writing* Mrs. Dalloway *and her suicide. The second woman is Laura Brown, a housewife from California of the nineteen-fifties who reads Woolf's novel and feels that the world is burdensome for her. The third woman is Clarissa Vaughan, a literary editor in contemporary New York, who is called by the heroine of* Mrs. Dalloway.

Fight Club is a movie about men—about the catastrophic consequences of the phallic and narcissistic process in the world. *The Hours* is a movie about women and the possibility of transformation; about perspective towards life and towards time.

The movie makes it possible to shed light on the three dimensions formulated by Lacan— the dimensions structuring the human psyche, the three principles on which the whole cosmos is constructed according to the cosmologists, and the three women, the heroines of *The Hours*.

The Consciousness Bearers

So what are the three dimensions?

Imaginary, Symbolic, Real—are the three "orders" or dimensions of the human psyche, which Lacan began to formulate in nineteen fifty-three. These concepts went through many developments and changes over the years he taught. In short, the imaginary is what we refer to as Ego and it is constructed from identifications and fantasies. The symbolic is a product of our being speaking beings and it is constructed from chains of signifiers. The Real is what falls between the holes in the net of the symbolic. It is the impossible. Although we collide with it we cannot talk about it, we can only talk around it. The Real is the traumatic. These three dimensions are tied together in a knot that Lacan describes as a Borromean knot—three inter-connected bands linked in such a way that untying one band unties the entire knot.

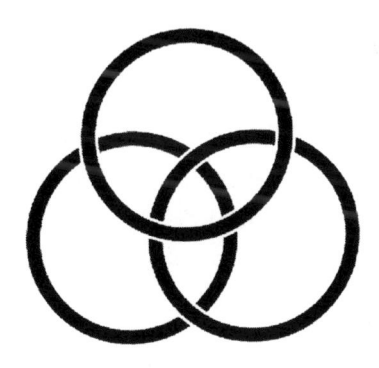

What are the three cosmological principles?

Subjectivity—every creature has interior existence; Differentiation—each thing is differentiated from other things;

Connectivity—everything is connected and engaged. We are living in a primordial net and the universe is a communal experience.

If we separate one band of the three the universe will collapse, the psyche will collapse.

And what about the three women? For Freud, woman was an enigma. After grounding a significant part of his psychoanalytic researches and his articles on analyses that he conducted with hysterical women, he remained until the end of his days with an open question concerning the essence of a woman. Lacan too remained wondering and questioning about feminine sexuality, questions that he referred to female psychoanalysts. He claimed that "The Woman doesn't exist," i.e., there is no feminine prototype parallel, for example, in the myth of "the primordial father" which defines the male group. There cannot be a feminine Tyler Durden (*Fight Club*). Therefore, as claimed Freud, Lacan thought that all men are subject to the phallic function. As for women, each woman is special to herself. We are still at the initial stage of the search after the unique, non-phallic voice of femininity. However, if in *Fight Club* we witness men's unity; in *The Hours* every woman is unique to herself. At one point she turns to another woman, in way of a kiss rather than in a violent way but there is no real connectivity between the women in the movie.

Freud contended that in regarding to the unconscious there is no difference between the sexes. His differentiation was not between male and female but between the subject

The Consciousness Bearers

that "owns a phallus" and the subject that "lacks a phallus."

According to Freud, man is differentiated from woman only because he seems to own a phallus—something that the woman lacks all her life and which she would possess for herself—or even become, in a sense. The phallus is a classical concept, the original meaning of which is the figurative representation of the man's sexual organ. But as in ancient myths and representations, it is an organ in a constant state of erection, the symbol of virility. In various cultures the phallus was an object of worship.

Psychoanalysis differentiates between the phallus and the penis. It is not a question of the organ itself but of a signifying expression, a representation through language, a symbolic representation of something. The phallus represents what is necessarily absent for the human subject. At the termination of the Oedipus complex, both sexes need to choose between "having a phallus" or "being castrated." This means the presence or absence of one central factor. The little girl as well as the little boy know nothing of the existence of the vagina, while the phallus is seen by them as an organ which can be separated from the body and therefore can be symbolically replaced. Phallic desire is replaced by the desire to be more, to consummate and possess in every way. The accumulation of capital, loves, and even spiritual experiences are all objects of phallic desire.

The mother represents the one who desires the phallus and the child tries to satisfy her desire by identification with it. Only when he discovers that it is impossible, usually by the intervention of the father. He turns to other places when he realizes that he can never satisfy the mother, whose desire is focused on the father.

In *The Hours*, the child apparently satisfies his mother. She tells him "you're my guy" but in the end she abandons him. Every child faces the choice of either accepting that he cannot be the mother's absent phallus, or rejecting castration and remaining in fantasy.

In his article on *Female Sexuality* (Freud, 1931b), Freud claims that the influence of the castration complex on the woman is completely different than its influence on the man. The woman accepts the fact of her being castrated and therefore recognizes the man's superiority over her but she also resists this undesirable situation. From this split position stem three directions of development. Each of the three women in the movie chose one of these directions.

The direction chosen by Laura (Julianne Moore), leads to turning her back on sexuality in general. The little woman, in panic because of the comparison with the boy, becomes dissatisfied with her clitoris, gives up its phallic activation—and by doing so gives up sexuality altogether, as well as much of her masculinity in other domains.

The direction chosen by Virginia (Nicole Kidman) is to hold onto the threatened masculinity from her stubborn holding of her position. The woman continues—until an unacceptably late period—to adhere to the hope of receiving a phallus after all. The fantasy of receiving the phallus is raised as an ideal of the purpose of life. Often the fantasy to be a man in the end becomes a forming factor for long periods of life. This "masculinity complex" of the woman can also end in a manifest homosexual choice of object.

Only the third quite winding way that Clarissa (Meryl Streep) chooses, leads to the final "normal" female figure who relates to the father as an object and by doing so discovers the feminine form of the Oedipus complex. The Oedipus complex for the woman is a final result of a more extended development. It is not destroyed by the influence of castration but is created by it—in contrast to the development of the boy, for the girl It evades the strong hostile influences that act upon it in a destructive way, and too often results in the woman failing to overcome this complex at all. Accordingly, the cultural consequences of its disintegration are also smaller and less important. It is reasonable to assume that the same difference of the Oedipus complex and the castration complex between a man and a woman will leave its impression on the nature of the woman as a social being.

One can therefore see in *The Hours* a movie that describes three dimensions of the psyche and three principles on which the world is constructed, through three women who represent different manifestations of femininity. The movie depicts it through parallel scenes—scenes of awakening in the morning, flowers, relating to the body, partnership. Each woman emphasizes one aspect at the expense of the others.

Virginia represents the subjective and the real dimensions. Laura represents differentiation and the imaginary,

Clarissa represents connectivity, communion and the symbolic. We only get to see all the dimensions combined at the end of the movie in Clarissa, when she moves from focusing on love life to focusing on love of life.

As mentioned earlier, the movie depicts parallel periods. Everything happens in one day—a present that includes past and future. Three points in time that mix together and make chronological time meaningless. "In this day her destiny is clarified for her," Virginia writes.

The opening scene, in which we see water flowing, represents the duration of time. The suicide of Virginia—time stopped. The decision to commit suicide indicates ultimate subjectivity. It is as if the choice to kill herself is a result of depression and mental illness but in the end, it is an act of choice.

Richard, the poet who connects the three chapters, relates through the whole movie to the dimension of time—his times are confused. "I fell outside time," says Richard, who in the end also commits suicide.

Clarissa is going to meet Richard in an elevator shaft, which is reminiscent of a time tunnel. Richard aspires to write a book in which everything that is happening in one moment is written—in an impossible way to "catch" time. This experiment leads to a necessary and inevitable failure. He says "I still have to face the hours." It isn't actually possible to stop time.

In addition to relating to time, the movie presents three modes of relating to life and to other human beings. There are for example, four kisses in the movie, which represent these modes: provocation and seduction—Laura and her woman neighbor, demand/sucking out life—Virginia and her sister and love—Clarissa and Richard and the kiss between Clarissa and her woman lover.

Virginia's choice belongs to the realm of the Real, the impossible, the unsayable, the unbearable—the death drive. The author Virginia is looking at it from outside. She envies the familial bliss of her sister but she cannot take part in it. The author Virginia and the poet Richard—the creators—commit suicide. They are the ones who try to catch everything with words. "It is possible to die," she says.

Laura represents the desperate attempt to differentiate herself as a condition of survival. She chooses to get out of the false, superficial, illusory and suffocating picture of happiness. She abides in the Imaginary realm and lives in a fantasy that makes her believe that one can find salvation in another place. Her choice is a completely egocentric one and she abandons her son.

Her neighbor tells her "you cannot call yourself a woman until you are a mother." She runs away precisely from that. She refuses to encounter femininity through being the wife of...or the mother of. We see the child (Richard), playing at building a house and destroying it. After that the director shows us an idealized scene of the husband's birthday party and we see the man's fantasy about the woman as representing home and bliss—not as a subject in her own right. Therefore Laura faces the choice to either die or run away. She differentiates herself as a subject by her flight. Towards the end of her life she faces a moment of truth when she returns to participate in the celebration of the literary prize won by Richard.

She says "It would be wonderful to say you regretted it. It would be easy. But what does it mean? What does it mean to regret when you have no choice? It's what you can bear. There it is. No one's going to forgive me. It was death. I chose life."

This is the biggest lie. There is always choice.

Clarissa represents the symbolic dimension that allows communication and relationships between people to take place. She is active in the New York cultural world, represented by poetry and she plans to hold a party in honor of Richard, who is going to die from Aids, who received a literary prize. She works as an editor of others' works, and she takes care of everybody.

Richard remarks to her: "Always giving parties to cover the silence."

Her life is dependent on another, otherwise they are trivial, Richard calls her life "false comfort."

Everywhere we encounter speech that is mostly lying, moments of truth which are not recognized, moments of truth that are fled from. A moment of truth for Clarissa appears in her conversation with her friend Lewis, when she admits that she chose freedom over relationship. *The Hours* is a movie about relationships and separations and about the meaning of freedom.

Richard (to Clarissa): *I think I'm staying alive just to satisfy you.*

Clarissa: *That is what we do. That is what people do.*

The Consciousness Bearers

They stay alive for each other.

Richard: Just wait till I die. Then you'll have to think of yourself. How are you going to like that?

She doesn't listen to him until he says to her: "I've stayed alive for you. But now you have to let me go."

In the end all the intentions are contradicted, the encounters are missed and loss should be faced. All efforts have failed—the cake Laura makes for the birthday party is spoiled, the party Clarissa wanted to give for Richard does not happen, the visit of Virginia's sister fails to reconnect Virginia to life. After that possibilities are tested. There is a possibility to choose life and a possibility to choose death.

Virginia tries to take the train and run away from her destiny. It is precisely her husband's love, which should have saved her, which kills her. She says: "my life has been stolen from me." She discovers that there is no possibility to find peace by avoiding life. She discovers the lie in the midst of love.

Leonard (the husband) asks Virginia: Why does someone need to die?

Someone has to die in order that the rest of us should value life more. It's contrast.

Who will die? The poet, the visionary.

We hear and are struck by Virginia's voice "To look life in the face, always, to look life in the face and to know it for what it is. At last to know it, to love it for what it is, and then, to put it away."

Suicide is presented as a willful choice, a way of realizing life, an existential idea of choice, not as a conventional contemplation of life.

At the end of the movie Clarissa chooses life, we witness it through flowers, a smile, her turning to her lover; there are no words.

The experience of art

I contend that the artistic experience that the movie attempts (successfully) to transmit is the spiritual experience. In an interview with the director, Stephen Daldry, he describes the making of the movie as a transformative and broadening experience. Phillip Glass, who composed its wonderful music as an independent work, says in an interview that the movie deals with the influence of art on life.

Some of the greatest modern philosophers, from Schelling to Schopenhauer, have realized a major reason for great art's power to transcend known dimensions. The reason, as realized by Ken Wilber, that makes us suspend all other activity when we look at a beautiful object (natural or artistic). We are simply aware; we only want to contemplate the object. When we are in this contemplating state, we do not want anything from the object. We don't want to eat it, or own it, or run from it or alter it. We only want to look, to contemplate.

Says Ken Wilber: "In this contemplative awareness, our own egoic grasping in time comes momentarily to rest. We relax into our basic awareness. We rest with the world as it is, not as we wish it to be. We are face to face with the calm... we contemplate the object as it is. Great art has this power, this power to grab your attention and suspend it:

we stare, sometimes awestruck, sometimes silent, but we cease the restless movement that otherwise characterizes our every waking moments" (Wilber, 1998, pp. 144-146).

The effect that is created is a meditative one.

Art is judged by its ability to simultaneously make you catch your breath, to suspend your "I," to suspend time.

§ As Good as it Gets

U.S.A. 1997

DIRECTED BY JAMES L. BROOKS

STARRING: JACK NICHOLSON, HELEN HUNT, GREG KINNEAR

The issue of choice:

Melvin Udall (Nicholson) is a successful New York author who writes numerous sticky and recycled novels. He lives shut in his apartment, a misanthrope who suffers from obsessive compulsive symptoms that result in his avoiding contact with strangers and generally with the external world. His only connection is with Carol (Hunt), a waitress in a restaurant he frequents every day for breakfast. Carol manages to cope with his unbearable aggressive behavior. Melvin loathes his neighbor Simon (Kinnear), a homosexual painter who loves everything that Melvin loathes, especially his little dog. Frank is Simon's friend and manager. He persuades Melvin to look after the dog while Simon is hospitalized after a robbery. From this point Melvin's life changes and he goes through a developmental process at the end of which he is able to show love, to connect with people and even relinquish some of his symptoms.

As Good as it Gets questions our ability to go beyond the limitations of our neurosis/ narcissistic defensiveness. Do we have choice regarding our psychical destiny? Similarly to *The Hours*, which deals with three women, each captivated by one principle at the expense of the two others, *As Good as it Gets* also has three heroes. Each captivated in a seemingly unbreakable maze of conditionings.

We can again see how each of the heroes represents one of the three principles upon which the physical and psychical world are built on— the net of the primordial language in which we live: Subjectivity—every creature has interior existence; differentiation—each thing is differentiated from everything else; connectivity or communion—everything is connected and engaged. If we separate one band of the three—one principle of the three—the universe collapses, and the psyche collapses.

The heroes of *As Good as it Gets* are three:

- Simon, the homosexual with the sensitive psyche who holds the narcissistic victim position to an almost absolute extent. The world encircles him. He represents, therefore the subjectivity principle.

- Carol, the waitress. Like Meryl Streep in *The Hours* she dedicates herself to taking care of another person—her child. Her entire world is reduced to the narrowest perspective. She is captive in the connectivity principle.

- Melvin, who "suffers" from obsessive-compulsive disorder, separates himself from the world and tries to live without connection and love, even though this is what he writes about in his novels. He is captive in the differentiation principle.

In his essay "Group Psychology and the Analysis of the Ego," Freud states: *A person's self-love has but one barrier—love for the other, love for the object (Freud, 1921c).*

At the end of this essay Freud lists different phases of the libido (Freud, 1921c). He begins with being in love, which is based on the existence of sexual desires as well as aim-inhibited desires. In this phase, says Freud, there is no room except for the ego and the object. The second phase is hypnosis, in which, as in being in love, there is room for two only, yet it is entirely based on aim-inhibited desires, and the object replaces the Ego ideal. This process occurs in much greater force in the masses, but in the masses there is also identification with other individuals.

The state of the individuals in the crowd is that of common hypnosis and identification with other individuals that share the same relationship to the other. The common features of being in love, hypnosis and identification with the crowd, is a regression in the ability to judge, to contain complexity. Freud even speaks about a regression in intellectual capacities.

Neurosis, according to Freud, deviates from this line. It appears wherever sexual repression towards aim-inhibited desires has not been entirely successful. "The neurotic has been forsaken," says Freud, "therefore he has no choice but to replace the large masses assemblies from which he was alienated with symptoms. He creates for himself an imaginary world of his own, a religion of his own, a set of lunacies of his own." In other words, the neurotic is a captive of his own fantasy (ibid. p.143).

Melvin Udall is a remarkable example of this type. He lives in a closed-off world with no coming and going, with complete control and total seclusion. This seclusion is penetrated when the dog enters his life. He achieves control over his life like every good obsessive, by exhausting measuring and counting. His obsessive rituals are symptoms which defend him from contact with the world.

The Psychic Symptom

A symptom is created when there is conflict between forbidden sexual desires, drives, and the demands of reality or of one's conscience. The "I" is a servant of these three masters. The initial effort of the subject is of repression. If repression is not fully applied due to the strong intensities of the drive or because of the weakness of prohibition, the symptom is a product of compromise. However, when one tries to please too many masters, nobody gets to be completely satisfied. The symptom is both a defense against the drive, and its satisfaction. It simultaneously causes us to suffer and enjoy. This enjoyment is a distortion that has a reductive effect on our lives. That is to say, the symptom is combined from two axes: the axis of the message, or signification, and the axis of enjoyment.

The symptom gives satisfaction exactly where it hurts. i.e., there is a level where the symptom is not a disturbance but a means of satisfaction, where it particularly satisfies the repetition compulsion—that tendency to repeat the same destructive choices which cause pain, time and again. The drive of repetition is the drive that is expressed in symptoms of obsessive rituals.

As Freud claimed, at the basis of each symptom there is trauma. Every neurosis includes such a fixation. In psychoanalysis, we relate to the repressed meaning of the symptom.

A symptom has therefore a symbolic envelope that is connected to language—"Washing one's hands of..." (meaning—not guilty) for example, as a description of the compulsive symptom of hand washing (one of Melvin's symptoms). It creates a kind of metaphor. It envelopes the negative of the metaphor or the remains that are not included in the formal envelope of the symptom, i.e., the enjoying, meaningless element.

Freud presents the symptom in a dynamic way, i.e., as a way in which something that contradicts an event has an unconscious meaning. The creation of symptoms is a substitution of something else that is inhibited. For Lacan the symptom represents a curbing of a wish to say something instead of saying something else. So the symptom is presented in two ways:

1. The symptom as a "distorted enjoyment" that is presented as a masked enjoyment (Miller, 1991, pp. 38-59). According to Freud the symptom repeats the mode of early childhood satisfaction while it is distorted by censorship

that had to cope with a conflict (Freud, 1916-17).

2. The symptom is also enjoyment that is experienced in a different way. Freud explains that this is satisfaction that changes from un-pleasure to pleasure.

There are two origins to the symptom: trauma and fantasy. One can relate to them as two different modes of the same thing, something that cannot be erased, which was effective in the past, in childhood. There is contradiction between them but also much in common. That is to say, in the time dimension the symptom is a way of returning to past satisfactions—regression that stops development.

The enjoyment in the symptom is plundering the good order, but it is also inherent in it, since it signifies the transgressive dimension existing inside every culture or law; it is the obscene complementary factor of the law, which appears from within the symbolic order as a whole or as an unexplained excess.

Who is the obsessive subject?

The obsessive subject feels that his mother loved him too much. He misses being his mother's favorite, misses being her complementary phallus. Through him she received something she didn't receive from his father.

Obsessive neurosis is characterized by hidden complaints that the subject directs at himself concerning his infantile sexual activity, which created enjoyment that he couldn't cope with. The sexual drive is returning masked as obsessive feelings and representations. This is a result of the experience of the child as a passive object of seduction. Desire is separated from need (food, drink, sex, touch) and becomes a demand. For what? For love. The desire of the child who becomes obsessive is characterized by a drive that becomes an imperative.

Two lines characterize the obsessive structures—a drive that is experienced as an imperative and difficulty to express a demand for satisfaction for the drive.

In the movie, those two lines are radically expressed by Melvin: his compulsive imperatives to count, not to touch, and his so called authentic speech, that does not obey the social code, and his difficulty in admitting his need for love.

The obsessive subject cannot cope with death whatsoever. He wants to be everything for the other and also must control everything, so that the other will not be able to avoid him. He wants to be a sole ruler so as not to lose anything. His object loss can remind him the castration, i.e., the fact that he doesn't really satisfy his mother, the flaw in his narcissistic image.

He is eaten up with competitiveness rivalry and death wishes towards every figure of authority from his father, towards figures that are substitutes for the father. He is prone to power games and provocative behavior. Persistency and stubbornness are two dominant traits in the obsessive, a character type which we refer to as anal, because the obsessive regresses to his infantile anal stage and compulsive defenses such as obsessive thinking, isolation between thought and feeling, ritualization, reaction formation, guilt, humiliation, scruples and remorse. In order to avoid anxiety the obsessive seeks for complete control of his enjoyment and the enjoyment of others. To that end he manages his life as if enveloped in a bubble but in his fantasy he always plays with the idea of transgression and he is ambivalent towards the law of the father. Melvin has the combination of obsessive character with a narcissistic attitude of not considering the other.

The significance of the narcissistic position is exaggeration in the importance the individual ascribes to his experience. The narcissist has a compulsive relation to his personal experience and his consciousness is focused upon it alone. Although he perceives there is a world outside—plants, animals, human beings, stars, galaxies, universe, etc., most of his attention is focused upon his subjective feelings. Only a small degree of his attention is directed at the external world. This creates a huge distortion in him. What is outstanding in the obsessive is his social alienation on top of the personal and family dynamics.

The current increase in compulsive behavior and seclusion in extreme narcissism are also products of postmodern culture. The postmodern era has produced millions of extreme narcissists, whose big symptom is exaggeration in self-engagement and in one's emotional state. Melvin always says the truth. This truth is obscene. It negates the existence of the other and it negates life.

Even speech doesn't help obsessive subjects. On the contrary, it becomes repetitive and annoying and serves the symptoms. The discourse or speech is usually used as a cork or a dam defending against trauma, to create a barrier between the subject and life. Postmodern culture is a source of great anxiety for obsessive subjects. When the social order is weakened, the Real threatens to break through and dismantle every meaning.

One of the most common defenses of the individual in the postmodern era is fortifying oneself in the position of all knowing—a position that helps one get rid of the experience of insecurity. Cynicism is therefore such a popular position among postmodern super-narcissists. The cynical position, which already knows everything, saves the obsessive subject from the horror of chaos.

In *As Good as it Gets*, Melvin lives in social seclusion and alienation. His compulsive rituals allow him an illusion of control. He writes about love and relationships but is unable to have them. He lives in a world of fantasy. His speech is like mud throwing or defecation. Carol is the one who puts a stop to his aggressive and coarse speech.

Simon, the painter, who is characterized as the perfect narcissist who pities himself all the time, is more congruent with the social norms.

Melvin says: "What makes it so hard is not that you had it bad, but that you're that pissed that so many others had it good."

Melvin's home is turned into a fortress. The question asked by the movie is "where is trust?" The dog is the only one to show unconditional trust, the first to penetrate the fortress from outside. The dog is not deceived by Melvin's defenses and because of the dog Melvin begins his transformative journey. Melvin becomes so attached to the dog that he cannot bear to separate from it. When faced with the possibility of separation he reacts with a panic attack. For the first time he gets confused while executing a ritual that is intended to defend him against the anxiety that emerges in response to the minutest changes.

Melvin's transformation, as well as Carol's, makes it possible for them to love one another, and vice versa—love is the barrier to narcissism. He and Carol notice the truth behind madness. Both of them do not recoil from recognizing the truth. He notices it from a narcissistic position that doesn't see the other, and she from a broader position—that includes the other.

Carol: Do you have any control over how creepy you allow yourself to get?

Melvin: Yes I do, as a matter of fact. And to prove it, I have not gotten personal, and you have.

In contradiction to his obsessive experience of repetition and inability to choose, Melvin recognizes choice. In the beginning he can't have a dialogue at all. Nobody can talk with him. He cannot listen. He speaks only about himself from a narcissistic position. The transformation he goes through is expressed through a change in the manner of the compliments he gives Carol. If the first compliment is given by talking about himself: "*You make me want to be a better man.*" the second compliment relates to her directly: "*...and how you say what you mean, and how you almost always mean something that's all about being straight and good.*"

After the dog penetrates the fortress that was his life, love comes and destroys his walls. He cannot go back to his immured existence. He says: "She's evicted me from my life."

Another transformation process begins when Melvin asks his suffering colleagues in the waiting room of the psychiatrist: "What if this is as good as it gets?" and ends at the conclusion of the movie, in the failed first kiss scene. He says: "I know I can do better than that," meaning—this is not as good as it gets.

Despite all of this, Melvin holds on to the remains of his symptom. As he walks along in an embrace with Carol he still makes sure not to step on the cracks between the paving stones. In the last scene he renounces even that. He chooses love over counting and measuring.

§ About Schmidt

U.S.A. 2002

DIRECTED BY ALEXANDER PAYNE, AFTER THE BOOK BY LOUIS BEGLEY

STARRING: JACK NICHOLSON, KATHY BATES

A short time after the death of his wife, a minute after he retired and a few days before his daughter's marriage to a man he can't stand, Warren Schmidt (Nicholson) decides to take the family caravan and to go on a journey to seek the meaning of his life.

I contend that the main subject of *About Schmidt* is the meaning of life—a weighty term about which one could write long books or, define in one word, as Schmidt discovers at the end of the movie—a difference, influence—to make a difference.

Who is Schmidt? He is "Everyman" or "The man without qualities." Schmidt is absurdly normal.

It is interesting to compare Jack Nicholson in *As Good as it Gets* with Nicholson in *About Schmidt*. He plays two apparently completely different types but actually, both of them have the same obsessive-compulsive structure. Melvin Udall's pathology is out in the open, he is experienced as a madman and each time he speaks it is as if he "defecates" on the world. Schmidt appears to be the complete opposite—a total introvert if not frozen. Actually his main pathology is constipation.

He is crazy in his normality. He lives in a stasis of normality. When his routine normality breaks down, his world becomes chaotic and threatening. His fixated way of living must change because of external factors and following this change he goes through a physical/spiritual journey, as if searching for himself. However, it really looks like a parody on journey movies, a kind of satire on the movie *Simple Story*. Schmidt lives in inertia that gradually disintegrates down. His coping with change is expressed through an ever deeper regression and intensifying chaos. All the things he accumulated in his life, all his knowledge, are nullified. The wife he couldn't stand disappears (died), and it turns out that she defended him from encountering the realness of life. She made it possible for him to be cynical. The first question he asks after her death is: *Who will take care of me?*

The Consciousness Bearers

The movie begins with the first crack in the picture—it is time for Schmidt to retire from the insurance company he has worked in most of his life as a vice manager. At the moment of his retirement his fixed daily schedule unravels. His reason for being (raison d'être) disappears. The first scene is a scene of a clock ticking as Schmidt sits gazing at its clock's hands as if hypnotized. He is waiting for the exact hour at which he is supposed to retire. Not one second before or after. The feeling that arises when we are observing his frozen face is of emptiness and void (the scene is reminiscent of the handless clock in Bergman's movie *Wild Strawberries*. The clock in this movie also represents empty time and lack of meaning).

Following this his wife dies. His daughter is about to marry someone he loathes and he feels more and more that his life is a failure.

He tries to hold on to his past. Everything seems to be too late for him. Too late he discovers his love for his wife. He discovers that his wife once betrayed him. He tries to embody the avenging betrayed husband and loses his best friend. He tries to hold on to his relationship with his daughter and to manage her life for her, while the only thing he can do is support her. Everything is a missed opportunity. In his distress he turns to religion, looking for salvation in spiritual search, and this too becomes absurd. Only the one thing he has done without paying attention to it—the strange relation he made with a six year old African boy is ultimately the most significant act of his life.

The concepts emerging regarding Schmidt are time,

inertia, fixation, regression and voyage, i.e., concepts of motion. This is the psychical motion that both psychoanalysis and the teaching of evolutionary enlightenment deal with. For Schmidt, as for all human beings, a conflict is created between the dynamics of progress, regression, going round in circles, or being stuck in one place—a dynamic of internal and external events, of drives and representations, occurring within the framework of time.

Such dynamics are based on Freud's concept of libido. The libido is a concept of energy or drive that motivates the course of desire. What is desire? The human creature has certain biological needs that are satisfied by certain objects. The fact that we are speaking allows us to turn the need into a demand from the other, like for example the baby who demands food from his mother. At a certain stage the response coming from the other is not perceived as a satisfaction of a drive, but as a response to a request, as a sign of love. Demand becomes then a demand for love, i.e., a gap is created between need and demand, and in this gap the desire that cannot be satisfied can be placed. Even if the need is satisfied, desire can never be. This is why one can see desire as motivating the motion in the search for satisfaction.

There is no object that can satisfy desire, since we lost the object that satisfied us at the beginning of our lives. This is the lost paradise or our mother's breast. This object motivates desire and the search for it but this is also an object that being initially lost can never be reached again.

At one stage of Schmidt's journey he returns to the place

where his childhood home stood and hears his mother's voice calling him, saying "Mama loves you."

Psychoanalysis is not unique in relating to the psyche and to the world according to the basis of motion: Chuang Tzu, a Buddhist philosopher, already said a few thousand years ago: "The basic elements of the universe are dynamic patterns; transitory stages in the 'constant flow of transformation and change'" Chuang Tzu (Capra, 1996, p. 204).

The concept of motion also became central in modern science. Quantum theory, for example, is discovering basic connectivity in the universe. It shows that we cannot dismantle the world into independently existing units. These connections, underlying the structures of the world, are constantly moving and changing.

In psychoanalytic terms there are two forms of motion: there is repetitive cyclic motion, the motion of drive around the object causing enjoyment, and there is also the developing form of vertical motion.

Thus, the subject can go from fixation and compulsive repetitiveness to acting from free choice.

In the same way we can distinguish between horizontal movement and vertical movement. As I wrote in the chapter entitled *Nevertheless it does move!* I will just mention that horizontal movement generates meanings, deepening understanding, stories, and interpretations. Horizontal motion only serves to reaffirm and reinforce the I. It cannot bring about a change in our level of awareness. It cannot liberate us from the ego.

The vertical movement is related to radical transformation and liberation. This kind of movement is not absolutely necessary and is characteristic of a tiny fraction of the population. Instead of reinforcing the fixated ego, it has the potential to destroy it. It is about emptying all significations.

The process of translation (horizontal movement) gives legitimacy to the I and its beliefs. Without translation there will be social chaos. Individuals who cannot translate with a reasonable level of integrity and precision—who are unable to construct a world of significance—fall into psychosis. The world ceases to be understood, and the boundaries between the world and the I begin to disintegrate. This is not a breakthrough—this is a crisis, disaster rather than transcendence.

This is what happened to Schmidt—all the virtual reality that he built with so much effort collapsed, all significations were found to be empty.

Thus, while the psyche's motion is represented by desire, fixation is represented by the ego. The ego, according to psychoanalysis, is the most fixated part of our psyche, it resists transformation and development. It includes our narcissistic relationship to ourselves, our self-love or our self-image. Surprisingly, Freud and Lacan coincide with the conceptions of the Eastern teachings—as opposed to the way psychology sees the ego. The original function of the ego was a survival function, i.e., to be a shield or a defensive screen against the unmediated Real of the body and the world, against the uncertainty of the subject, its inherent otherness and the sensation of threat and anxiety which accompanies such an encounter. The ego is the one that cultivates our sense of separation from everything else and that is endlessly engaged in comparisons about who is better than me and who is not as good as me. Due to the ego's imaginary identification as our identity, it resists change and the movement of desire.

Schmidt built his whole life around this fixated image of the ego—he repressed and suppressed his desires and fixated every possibility of movement. Not by chance his wife gave him as a retirement present a house on wheels. His whole being, his body, and his expressions, testify to frozenness and immobility. Schmidt's life unfolds before us as constructed mainly from lies and hypocrisy. Different than from *As Good as it Gets*, where the spectators can feel better and more normal than Melvin because of his mental disorder, when faced with Schmidt it is much harder to project and say—this doesn't have any relation to us, we are not like that.

Schmidt is us. He resembles very much what we know. That is why this movie is even uncanny.

We can call the process of disintegration of Schmidt's life—an entropic process. Freud's major discovery was that the principle according to which human beings judge the world and act is the pleasure principle. This principle relates to the entropic principle; what gives us pleasure and what doesn't. The pleasure principle is behaving according to the law of conservation of energy, which is the law of constancy, which we can even refer to as a mechanical constancy.

The pleasure principle is the emissary of homeostasis and thanks to it the living creature survives. But when homeostasis is fully active, i.e., with the reduction of tension to a minimal degree or to its elimination, we reach the death drive. Thus, the pleasure principle is nothing but the principle of minimal tension required in order to sustain life. In contrast, the concept of Enjoyment is a flood. It is not interested in survival—death can certainly be part of Enjoyment.

The pleasure principle strives for balance, invariance, inertia and strives to ensure that the level of tension will be constant, namely leaving entropy and negative entropy at a constant level.

Entropy is indeed an element of erosion, an element of extinction that works within existing form—an element which, although it opposes change, ultimately leads to disintegration of the existing order and to the possibility of creating a new order.

The opening scene of the movie is a kind of exposition that lays out the whole story. The crisis in Schmidt's life: time, the modern gray city, alienation, loneliness, emptiness and meaninglessness. Even the name of the company in which he worked and from which he retires is a paradoxical and ambiguous name: "Woodmen." We can read it as "men of the wood" (a name that represents wild nature), and we can read it as "woodmen"—lifeless.

Entropy, regression and chaos seemingly begin at the moment of retirement from work, as a question about the meaning of life is raised.

The Consciousness Bearers

The next stage is the traditional retirement party—the camera shows us an overburdened bull. There is no real connection between any of the people there. There is no connection even between Schmidt and his wife. The man who replaces him, who is giving the farewell speech, speaks almost only about himself. Schmidt's friend says: "What is really meaningful in your work is the knowledge that you devoted your life to something meaningful."

Throughout the movie Schmidt attempts to examine his life and can't find anything significant. Whole parts of his life have disappeared from his memory. His real work in life was repression and denial. For example, he tries to return to his office and to help as he was asked to do (the man who replaces him calls him "partner"), but this is obviously a lie—he sees all his life's toil thrown into the garbage. The director describes his suffering by a close up which focuses on this wife's hands, as she chops up a chicken.

After his wife's death his first coping is like that of an adolescent—the castrating wife disappears, and her values disappear with her when he discovers that she also lied to him. Thus, in opposition to her request from him to pee while sitting, he urinates standing up and wets his surroundings—"like a man." His daughter is a source of pride for him, his phallus. Her groom of course doesn't deserve her, but she doesn't let her father throw himself on her as a way to find meaning in his life.

The second sign of entropy is his voice, breaking.

Chaos gradually takes over. Mourning turns into discussions about money. Even death is meaningless. Schmidt faces his wife's moment of death. From his point of view, everything is trivial, absurd. His loneliness, insomnia, extreme egocentrism are expressed in the question "who will take care of me?" Anxiety due to loneliness appears, the house is disintegrating, the car broken down.

Schmidt understands that he needs to live the best way he can in the time he has left but what does that mean for him? He tries to find out. Suddenly he discovers the longing and love for the woman he seemingly couldn't stand and then he discovers her betrayal, a discovery that ruins another part of the picture he depicted to himself. He acts as is expected of him, he "throws her out" (her belongings) and hits a friend—everything is ironic, like a parody. He searches in his past, he turns to religion. In one of the chapters in his journey he meets a couple that camped near him—the woman takes on herself the role of a therapist. She tries to reach him. She notices the anger and fear that are deeper than the sorrow and the loss. Again he misses an opportunity of a real relationship when he interprets her offer of relationship as an offer of sex. After he runs away he tries to make peace with his friend but again misses the opportunity when he leaves a message on the friend's answering machine. On the screen appears a truck full of caged cows.

At night he turns to God and to his wife and asks "Helen, what did you really think of me, deep in your heart? Was I really the man you wanted to be with? Was I? Or were you disappointed and too nice to show it?" —again, too late.

The Consciousness Bearers

There is nobody to hear him. The irony is harsh around the emotional catharsis as well. In the morning he feels that he reached enlightenment, that he has been through a transformation, he knows who he is and what he should do, nothing can stop him. He's got it. But he is still acting totally out of his ego.

Continuing his journey he meets his in-laws, who represent his absolute opposite. They represent hysteria as opposed to his obsessivity, similar to the contradiction between the painter and Melvin in *As Good as it Gets*. The in-laws represent a parody on freedom. They speak as if on "everything" in opposition to his silence, but they express themselves sexually, in a crude and callous way. Schmidt's ultimate regression occurs as he lies on a water bed—a symbol of the amniotic fluid in the uterus, his mother in law feeds him like a baby and he defecates in a bedpan. From this regression he runs away into loneliness.

In the speech he gives at his daughter's wedding he tries to speak about love. He tries to be generous, to do something for his daughter, to support her. He opens saying "what I really want to say is...," but the speech comes out stuttered and distorted. In the end of course he doesn't say or do any of the things he had intended to say and do.

For the first time he doesn't deny his failure. For the first time he looks at himself with egoless objectivity. He recognizes the truth. Then he asks: "...but what kind of difference have I made? What in the world is better because of me? It is as if I never existed." The disintegration, the entropy, gradually reveals the truth to him. He cannot avoid it or repress it anymore.

And then the letter and the painting arrives from the African boy that Schmidt connected with by chance, when he responded to a television commercial and made this boy his pen mate. It turns out that someone in the world thinks about him every day.

Schmidt's extraordinary (for him) act of supporting and connecting personally with an African kid was done absentmindedly. He concealed it from his wife as if it was a betrayal. Retroactively it turned out to be a real act, his real transformation.

According to psychoanalysis the act is connected to transformation, to the vertical axis of development. It is a deed that isn't dictated by former knowledge, something that goes against the direction of knowledge.

The Act takes place when one detaches oneself from the security of that Great Other with which, it is believed, lies knowledge—the parent, the state, university. After it the Subject changes, or as Lacan put it—a new Subject is born. We will only know that the act took place in retrospect, due to the effects of that act.

In such an act there is a form of rejection of authority and knowledge or what can be described as *initiation*—not something that can be interpreted—further discussion of which would be superfluous.

To re-emphasize—an act transforms the subject. It acts like a statement (a statement in the sense of claim, declaration and certainty), after which one can only keep silent.

The emotional truth that Schmidt reveals initially comes to light in the first letter he writes to the boy. He writes about the anger, about old-age. He writes: "When I was a boy I thought that maybe I'm special and fate intends me to become somebody." But Schmidt didn't follow his dreams rather chose a life of security and inertia. He doesn't even take responsibility for this choice. He blames his wife and his debts and denies fear and lack of courage.

Gradually the act of the relationship with the boy dissolves Schmidt's stagnation and reveals his soul. Only the disintegration of his life makes this conscious liberation possible, with the consequent reflowing of desire.

The miserable, illiterate African boy that can't even read can be seen as a metaphor for Schmidt's soul, his authentic self. In the final scene Schmidt exposes what he caused to stagnate all his life—everything is expressed without words but through the look on his face of simultaneous laughter and tears.

§ Tillemans (Together)

SWEDEN 2000

DIRECTED BY LUKAS MOODYSSON

STARRING: LISA LINDGREN, MICHAEL NYQVIST, EMMA SAMUELSSON

Stockholm 1975, the commune Together *celebrates the death of the Spanish dictator Franco, while the sister of one of the members calls and declares that she's had enough of her no-good husband: She and her two kids need a temporary shelter. In this hippy commune live long haired guys and girls who talk about politics and free sex in their free time, grow vegetables and drink a lot of wine. One of the girls notifies her boyfriend that she would like to realize her freedom by taking another member of the commune to bed. For his part he prefers discussions about Marxist-Leninist theories. He even feels insulted when she refuses to discuss class issues, after having an orgasm. Another friend tries to court the temporary guest, while the sixteen year old daughter of the guest experiences first love. Another member, a declared heterosexual, finds his place in the bed of the homosexual communard. Opposite the commune live bourgeois neighbors. All the heroes go through a process that in the end will reveal real "togetherness."*

This is a movie about love and loneliness—about the issue of the individual and the collective. The collective as Freud sees it—a collective of the masses which is created through identifications—a collective can either negate individualism or draw its power from the autonomy of the individuals that form it.

In his essay "Group Psychology and the analysis of the Ego" (Freud, 1921c), Freud claims that what binds people together to make them a crowd or the masses are mutual libidinal ties that have been diverted from their original goals.

Man is not a herd animal, says Freud, but a horde animal; a horde governed by a leader. Like a horde of wolves and not like a herd of sheep. All individuals in the group must be equal to one another, but they all wish to be ruled by the one. The leader can be either a figure or an ideal. In this context, Freud uses the myth of the primal horde. The primal father who prevented his sons from directly satisfying their sexual desires, forcing them into abstinence. As a result of the sexual repression the sons developed libidinal ties aimed at a goal other than that of sexual conquest.

The father's sexual fanaticism and intolerance eventually causes the psychological phenomenon of the group. Having been driven out of the group and separated from their father, the sons advance from mutual identification to homosexual object-love, thereby achieving the freedom to kill the father.

I will repeat Freud's important phrase from the same essay: "Self-love of the human being has but one barrier—the love for the other, the love for the object." Identification with the masses annuls the hostility towards the other. The ego identifies with the object it gave up, and this is how the difference between love and identification is expressed.

The original masses were formed of individuals, who put the same object in the place of their ideal I. When the issue is love, the object devours the I.

Together takes place in Sweden 1975, at the time of hippies, apparent sexual liberation and the attempt to rebel against the capitalistic way of life and build more just and egalitarian life. It is the time of big ideologies and ideals. Today it seems far away but actually only in the last thirty years have we witnessed the fall of the big ideologies. The movie shows life in a commune, something which was quite popular among young people in northern Europe.

The movie begins with notification of the death of the Spanish dictator Franco. The commune members rejoice their liberation from the dictator. What is the apparent connection between them and Franco? They are identified with all the oppressed as in "all the workers of the world unite!" *Together* looks at this with an ironical and sober eye with the hindsight of years, and its major message is that external freedom doesn't necessarily create inner freedom. The heroes, who were seemingly "liberated," are captivated by their ego and narcissism. As a result their communal life is doomed. In the guise of liberation of the sexual drive, the movie shows the transfer of sexual relations to the ego. The cathexis of the ego with narcissism is what establishes one of the main obstacles in life. We enjoy our self-image, our thoughts, our mood, our ideas etc. They seem to us most important and unique but actually they are the cause of our suffering. We find it so hard to give it up since it is part of our "identity."

It can be said that something similar may have been the cause of the failure of the ideology of Kibbutz. There also the emphasis was on the collective while neglecting the spiritual autonomy of the individual. The ideology in the movie is presented as empty and is summed up in the blah-blah of endless speaking. Television, meat, sex—all these relate to external liberation which is no less compulsive and enslaving.

The movie, therefore, begins with the murder of the

father—in this instance Franco—the sons are seemingly freed up, but this freedom is no less dictatorial and enslaving. The movie shows us in a marvelous way the process some of the heroes are going through from inner enslavement—enslavement to ideology and fantasy, to the true possibility of freedom, which involves consideration for the other. The heroes pass from identification that creates the masses, that cannot abide differences and leave the individual, especially the neurotic individual, in his miserable loneliness, to the possibility of "togetherness"—but each in his unique way. The heroes pass from holding on to the likeable but empty slogan "all you need is love" to what Lacan calls—an invention of new love.

The final scene is a soccer game in which all play together.

The movie *Together* begins with the murder of the father and the masses and ends in the togetherness formed of a group of individuals wherein each has his own way of kicking the ball. Together they create a community.

Ruth Golan

§ Hero

CHINA 2000

DIRECTED BY YIMOU ZHANG

STARRING: JET LI, TONY LEUNG, MAGGIE CHEUNG

A spectacular movie about China 2000 years ago, when it was divided into six provinces. One of the bigger provinces was ruled by a powerful king whose great dream was to take control over all the other provinces and to unify China, thereby making her an empire. His path towards this goal was strewn with deeds of cruelty. Many wanted him dead. Among all of his enemies the most frightening and awe inspiring were the three legendary fighters: Sky, Snow and Broken Sword. The king promised power, mountains of gold and a personal meeting with himself, no further than ten steps away from him, to anyone who managed to overcome the three. For many years there was no warrior who even got close to this mission, therefore when the warrior "No Name" who had always succeeded in any possible mission, reached the palace, the king waited impatiently to hear stories of his heroic deeds. The story is told from three points of view and includes passionate love, heroism, loyalty, secrets and a fascinating history of the creation of an empire. The major message of Hero *relates to what it means to be a "hero."*

The theme of *Hero* is conscious evolution. It deals with questions of separation versus unity, the good of the individual versus the good of the collective, truth versus lie and different levels looking at different viewpoints about life.

In an earlier discussion we dealt with horizontal transformation—more and more layers of significations and meanings in the world and in life—and we compared this transformation to vertical transformation, which is the movement of evolution.

While in *About Schmidt* the transformation that occurs is at the level of the individual, *Hero* deals with the kind of transformation made for the sake of the whole—the group and its developmental process.

Psychoanalysis indicates again and again what humanism tries to deny—the power of the drive. On one hand the drive makes culture possible (because it allows sublimation), and on the other hand, it acts as a destructive factor in the midst of culture (as the death drive).

The teaching of evolutionary enlightenment places the drive in a spiritual context. Nowadays it seems to me that the concept of life as a result of an evolutionary drive to develop consciousness and culture, offers the only chance for the world not to be destroyed. From an evolutionary point of view, the universe has direction and hierarchy, or, as Arthur Koestler established it—Holarchy. Reality is constructed from a whole and from parts or *holons*. The holon is simultaneously whole but also a component of a greater whole. Each thing is a *holon* of something. Reality is not constructed from things or processes but from holons that are created gradually within each other, in an infinite process.

The holons appear in holarchy, or in natural hierarchy. This is an order of gradual ascension towards wholeness. From particles to atoms, cells to organisms, letters to words, sentences to paragraphs. A whole at one level becomes a part of a higher level. The wholeness goes through transcendence but the parts are included in it.

Evolution demonstrates a general tendency to more and more complexity, increased differentiation/integration, increased organization/construction, increased relative autonomy, increased *telos* (purpose). Each evolutionary level includes and transcends the level below it, adding something new—similar to the operation of metaphor in language.

The idea of evolution, not biological evolution but evolution of consciousness is fascinating and exciting. It began to develop only about one hundred and fifty years ago with Darwin's discovery of biological evolution. There was recognition that all existence, including that of speaking beings, is going through a process of becoming.

It all began with what is called the big bang, which occurred around thirteen point seven billion years ago. Approximately 60 thousand years ago, human beings appeared more or less in their present form. Much has occurred since then. Initially there was no culture or language. The human experience of consciousness was at the tribal survival level. Human beings lived in fear and were constant looking for food. In those days life consisted of eating, sleeping, reproducing and a certain degree of empathy towards other human beings. The emotional and psychological experience of those days was primitive and one-dimensional.

The perspective through which the world was seen was narrow and the concept of time cyclical. At the pre-modern stage, fascism and totalitarianism reigned, with the church usually cooperating. In response to that, in the modern era, social movements appeared like socialism and communism, and the collective was given more importance than the individual, who was oppressed. Upon this background the liberation movements developed—liberation of slaves, women, homosexuals etc. These are important stages of development in human history but the problem is that most of us remained stuck in them.

In the beginning of the modern era, which is also referred to as the era of enlightenment, a great awakening occurred—the birth of rationality, science and individualism. At that time people began to liberate themselves from tradition. This is how we lost our spiritual background. We got lost. The rational mind couldn't answer our philosophical and spiritual questions. And then we entered the postmodern stage, in which individuality reached the peak of its importance. The desire of the individual and his "truth" were placed at the center and made almost sacred—all truths were now considered equally valid. Nothing was more sacred than the feeling of the individual and his experience.

Most of us are products of postmodernity. In the pre-modern era people conceived God as looking upon them from the sky. For them he was the all-knowing and all determining entity. So in the modern era we liberated ourselves from the superstitions about God and life, but substituted them with over-exaggeration of the importance given to the experience of the individual, along with the negation of value judgment. God disappeared from the picture and was replaced on center stage by the narcissistic ego. The individual replaced God. In the postmodern era everyone is on the same level, no one is higher than anyone else and there is no higher universal truth than the experience of the individual. A kind of a swamp has been created from which we need to extract ourselves in order to save ourselves.

In a certain kind of way this is the position of *Hero*, or at least a question it raises.

The concept of the teaching of evolutionary enlightenment is developing more and more towards perceiving matter and spirit as one event. A tendency we can witness in, for example, quantum physics. The teaching of the evolution of consciousness is views evolution as hierarchical and progressive. Spiritual development is the expression of the aspiration to higher levels of consciousness. This is the movement or the action of conscious evolution, the evolution of awareness for the human being. Matter becomes more aware of itself. We are part of this event—of life becoming more conscious of itself through us.

This is a new way of understanding our place in the universe. The dichotomies are in a process of unification. Awareness of the evolutionary function is growing. The "I" is perceived as part of this vast movement of evolution. Awareness regarding this movement turns it simultaneously to emptiness, vehicle and present. The "I" of the hero in *Hero* is exactly like this—a vehicle both empty and present for performing necessary actions.

The advantage that human beings have is free choice. Evolution for humans occurs through choice. Cosmologist Brian Swimme says that for humans, conscious choice has taken the place of the process of natural selection. We all have faculty of choosing. Through evolving individually at the level of consciousness by choice and intention, we create a new world. The hero of the movie also has to face a very significant moment of choice.

Today it is quite clear that in order for the world to survive, we are required to continue the evolution of perspective—from the tribe, nationality, the state and the individual to the world and thence the entire universe. As in *Hero*, there is an urgent need to unite in order to save China. We are required to unite, beyond narrow personal interests in order to save ourselves and this planet. The movie emphasizes that the only way this can occur is through unification. If we don't act together we won't be able to do it. If we remain divided among ourselves, if we are too busy fighting each other, we will not be able to make it happen. If we join together we can succeed.

Hero is about a cruel king who wants to unify the whole of China. He represents the battle between chaos and disintegration, war and unity, war against culture, weapons against words and the power of writing, music and swordsmanship.

The king has no name, he has a role—he is the leader of

the horde and he totally identifies with his role. The name of the hero is *Nameless*—he is free from identity, importance and identification. His I is empty of a narcissistic ego, and for that he is the one creating transformation. The names of the other heroes are: Sky, Snowdrop, Broken Sword. At the end of the movie we realize that the hero is not necessarily the best warrior, but similar to Judaism's understanding of it—the hero is the one that conquers his drive, the one who is able to take a vertical leap in his level of consciousness, or in perspective.

The movie tells four stories, like in Kurosawa's *Rashomon*. These four stories are based on the questions—is it right to kill a king and how should it be done? The stories are represented by four colors and three spiritual dimensions of life: fencing, music and calligraphy. These three express different aspects of the same essence. The stories are accompanied by three old men who are like knowledgeable prophets: the blind music player, who prophesies the battle which is determined when the strings are torn; the calligraphy teacher, who believes that writing saves from death; the old servant, who declares fate. The movie, similar to psychoanalysis, also deals with the question of the truth and falsehood of the stories, because psychoanalysis is not a science, or rather—it is a very unique science. It acts in the intermediate realm of the contradiction between a factual "objective" knowledge to "subjective" truth. It exposes the lies that are stated masked as truths (this is what obsessive people do, when in the framework of exact declarations they deny their desire). It exposes those who are speaking the truth under the guise of lying (the hysterical process or a slip of the tongue that denounces the subject's desire).

What is important for psychoanalysis is not the value of truth as such but the way the transition from truth to falsehood exposes the subject's desire. When a patient complains she was sexually abused by her father, what is important is not the abuse as such but its role in her symbolic economics, the way in which the events went through subjectivization—that is to say, not the event itself but the relation to this event and the ability to register it within the psychic formation.

If we implement the holarchic evolutionary model, we could say that a lie at one level becomes truth at another level and that the transition from one level to another reveals desire. Desire for what? Desire to continue along the path of broadening consciousness or perspective. If there is no passage, if there is jamming up in fixation, a mental block is created in desire and a symptom is created, which drains Enjoyment to itself.

So the movie narrates stories that are order within a rising evolutionary order:

1. A romantic Oedipal narrative. Its color is red. Jealousy, love, a low level of awareness. It is the story of the stupidity of the ego, with narrow and reduced perspective. The story takes place in a calligraphy school, which is supposed to save those who are learning it from death. Here culture is positioned higher than war.
2. The story told by the king elaborates the perspective

towards sacrifice for an ideal, which is revenge upon the king. Its color is blue. The pact is formed again in a library—in the realms of language. The woman sacrifices herself for her lover. This is death for a purpose higher than life—a level of tribal communion, where the highest value is to exercise the family's revenge.
3. A story that expresses a very high level of consciousness and perspective. Its color is white. According to the values of this level it is not allowed to kill a king, even though tribal criteria would sanction it.
4. The story of Broken Sword. Its color is green. The prohibition of killing a king he learned from language—from calligraphy. Culture is stronger than war. The sword is forged in hatred.

The words the sword wrote are "the entire world."

The king will unify the world for the sake of the whole. He says: "My worst enemy is the only one who understands my real motives."

In the first story the hero asks that the signifier sword will be written. There are nineteen ways to write "sword" and he is seeking the twentieth. If he finds the non-existing form of writing he will win. Here again, spirit is regarded as higher than force. The ruler responds by stating that he will annihilate all the other forms of writing and will determine one form for writing.

Finally the sign of the sword will reveal the essential significance of fencing. Spiritual fencing is parallel to what the Islam calls psychic Jihad. The ideal of fencing is the unification between a human being and his sword. When the sword is absent from the hand and the heart, the swordsman is whole with his world.

The king gives the hero a choice and the hero chooses not to kill him. In this respect he fulfills the proverb: "Who is the hero? He who conquers his drive."

At the end of the movie it turns out that the king himself doesn't stand higher than the law. He must kill anyone who tries to kill him in order to keep the symbolic morality.

The hero undergoes the final transformation, from someone who has no name to someone who has no body. He turns into pure spirit, the space between the arrows. The act of the hero is the highest autonomic expression; the killing of the hero is the killing of nothingness, since the hero became one with the essence of the universe.

The Mother's Language, the Father's Language, Parasitic Language and Erotic Language

§ Following "Traduire," (From language to language), a documentary by Nurit Aviv

In Traduire *Nurit Aviv interviews a group of poets and writers, Jews and Arabs. What is common to the interviewees is that they all had to abandon their mother tongue and start writing in foreign language. Through the quiet and contemplative discourse foundational questions are raised concerning the place of language in regard to the social transformation that took place in Israel—the immigrant state, and beyond that, in regard to the subject, truth, knowledge and Eros.*

Paul Celan: "Only in one's mother tongue can one express one's own truth. In a foreign language the poet lies... Poetry is a fateful and unique instance of language" (Halfan, 1991, p.184).

The necessity of changing language makes us conscious of the unconscious dimension, the stranger within us, and exposes the seam between being and language. When the interviewees in the movie relate to this passage they use erotic and violent verbs:

"To enter Hebrew and to write, [I needed] to murder Russian, to annihilate it, it stood in my way" (Meir Wiseltier).

"*To pour* myself into Hebrew. Hebrew is the homeland (as such, like the land of the fathers). In border states I *collapse* into Hungarian" (Agi Mishol).

"We bought Hebrew. I *carved* the language" (Aaron Appelfeld).

"Hebrew is *ownership* of the place" (Salman Masalha).

These are harsh words that stand in contradiction to the peaceful photographical work of the movie. The camera seems to place each creator in his home domain and outline a stationary profile.

"A man that loses his mother tongue is a cripple for the rest of his life," declares Appelfeld. Is that really so? What is our mother tongue—the language into which we are born, symbolic order, the net that envelopes our lives? Psychoanalysis discovered that symbolic order determines our lives in a major way—what is said about us, even before we are born, the name that is given to us, who we are for our primal significant others, what they want from us. The question "what does he/she expect from me" establishes us as a subject. We look for the Other's response, his recognition. The answer we create facing this question builds our

"I," or our self-image; a kind of identity the building blocks of which are glued together by fantasy.

Perhaps the mother tongue is connected to the body before it is tied together with language signifiers—that tonic language which plays with the materiality of the voice.

Is fragmentation primary with regard to the image? That is to say, is the body a living organism that is defined as a whole by an image, an image created through the gaze of in the mirror that turns the organism into a body, a unity, as Lacan thought at the beginning of his teachings? Or perhaps the organism is, from the outset, a whole, and it is the signifier that creates a gap, that deconstructs? This was Lacan's position in his late teachings. The body loses its unity because of the signifier.

The signifier slits furrows in the Real
Perhaps there is no contradiction between these two approaches rather a dual move. If we refer to wholeness and deconstruction on the level of imaginary, it is the mirror and the gaze of the Other that enable the representation of wholeness. This wholeness is a fantasmatic wholeness which doesn't coincide with the subjective sensation; from the point of view of the symbolic dimension. However, wholeness is primary and Real, before the subject comes into being and the signifier is that which causes this perfection to disintegrate. The "truth" changes its appearance when it is constructed as a three-dimensional hologram, fluctuating between the disintegrated or torn, and the perfect, the whole.

In any case, an Other—that something that is outside the organism—is required in order to define it. Lacan speaks of "ex-sistence," a persistent internal existence from without.

This concept is represented by a Moebius strip, which is folded like an interior eight. The Moebius strip is constructed out of two circles that define three dimensions. Mother tongue, father's tongue and that which is beyond language altogether.

Escher's Moebius strip

A poetess interviewed in the movie—Haviva Pedaya—referred to two languages as two essences connected at a blind spot. For her, Hebrew is dualistic as well: The mystic and grandparent's language and the Zionistic language, which is a renewed cathexis of the fathers' language. Arabic is the language of her parents, and it is a listening language. She describes language as music, as the soul of things. Meir Wiseltier, too, while abandoning and "annihilating" Russian finds an echo to the Russian music in his poetic writing.

The poet Haim Oliel, of Moroccan origin, was ashamed of his language and referred to it as the Ashkenazi language. His response and the response of his culture was initially silence followed by rebellion—expressed by the fact that the eastern musicians sang their songs in English—until they rediscovered their fathers' language.

The shape of the interior eight defines two areas of the body as a symbolic relationship that is related to sexuality, to the drive, and to the body as a living organism.

We are constructed as a body within a body, or as a body that is parasitic to another body, rather like a Babushka doll.

The symbolic is a body to the extent that it is a system of internal relations. Language therefore, is not a superstructure, it is a body—a body that gives a body. The body is, thus, not primary; rather, it is a reality structured through language, since the link that defines the signifying structure is already registered in it.

There are therefore, two faces of language. The first is connected to the very fact that when we speak about something it begins to exist in the dimension of language but ceases to exist in the dimension of the Real. When we later encounter that same thing in reality, it will never be similar to what we spoke about or read about. Language in this respect erases the thing, or as Lacan said, following Heidegger: "The word is the death of the Thing."

We speak about that which does not exist, precisely due to the fact that we speak about it, represent it in various ways, and describe it with various adjectives. From this aspect—erasing the thing through the word, the symbolic order is related to lack, so the thing is represented through its lack. This is the mode of relation that Freud calls castration. It can be said that we do not use language but that it uses us. This is what is meant by saying that the unconscious is structured like a language and in many respects directs how we are in the world.

The second face of language is related to music, to the material element of language, to its Real mode, its enjoying mode. In this respect Lacan relates to the "speaking being" (*parlêtre*), instead of or in addition to the subject. He connected language with Enjoyment and concieved the concept of "Lalangue." This concept relates to lilting, meaningless language like baby talk. It's a language connected with Enjoyment, the primary language from, or on which, the symbolic language is structured. Furthermore, Lacan relates to the Enjoyment mode in the discourse as such, a mode that exists from the very fact of speaking and he characterizes this mode with another pun—jouis-sense—enjoying meaning, or the enjoyment in meaning.

This language does not develop with rhymes of differentiated signifiers, so that each signifier gives meaning to the one that precedes it but it is a sign language.[29] The sign language can be also inscribed in the body and it indicates being, which appears as a presence and not as absence.

---

29 While signifiers are units of language which are based on the differences between them, i.e., every signifier gives meaning to the signifier preceding it, and thus they are tied to one another in a chain, signs are independent entities and they have fixed meaning. as for example in the proverb: "There is no smoke without a fire." It is as if smoke is always a sign of a fire.

The Consciousness Bearers

A special case is that of German, which society prior to the creation of the state of Israel considered to be the language of culture, but was also present as the language of the murderers.

Aaron Appelfeld called German "a destroyed idyll...my mother tongue and also the murderers' tongue." This is how he relates to it in the movie, similar to other poets and writers that personally experienced the Holocaust like, for example, Paul Celan. "Death is a meister from Germany" thus writes Paul Celan in his poem "Death Fugue."

When the poet Manfred Winkler read from Celan's poems in Jerusalem, he said:

"Celan spoke in the words of the German language and in words that are no longer words, he spoke with the sounds of the experience which is still awaiting words and yet already stands on the border that cannot be crossed without harm—a lonely place somewhere between earth and sky. And the loneliness grew in him and around him and became concrete and abstract at the same time. Perhaps the mystery of creation is indeed embodied inside language, and by means of language it can be revealed. If not, at least some of the veil may be removed" (Winkler, "Paul Celan," Davar, 11.9.70).

Celan, the immigrant, tried to reach through language to beyond it. Perhaps the other immigrants in the movie try like him, to find The Thing, the belonging, the "homeland." But the symbolic order is positioned as a barrier, and whoever attempts to penetrate it time and again bumps into that unbearable realm that touches the Real. This is the role of the acquired *father-tongue*—it puts a limit to the primary enjoying language but due to that it can also give a sort of consolation.

There is also a need to differentiate between speaking and writing, between a fixed meaning to a flowing signification that constantly changes. Freud says that the esthetic pleasure that the writer offers us has the nature of foreplay, similar to sexual foreplay. The poet Salman Masalha describes it very well when he says that for him, spoken Arabic is his mother tongue. Both literary Arabic and Hebrew are foreign languages for him and he writes in both languages. According to the way he describes it, for him writing is always writing in a foreign language.

The erotic solution to foreplay is presented by rabbi and philosopher Daniel Epstein, who plays and juggles between the two languages—Hebrew and French—and uses both according to his needs. Hebrew, according to him, is a frugal and precise language, while French facilitates lyricism, softness, a cloud of ambiguity. He uses Hebrew to transmit morality and ethics and French to transmit poetry. He scurries around the two while trying to pass impossible messages from language to language. Nevertheless he admits: The music of poetry bisects both languages.

Every immigrant carries within himself two languages—*a dual world*, says Appelfeld, that he himself exchanged many languages which he needed to repress in order to "buy" the Hebrew. This is why he is afraid that he will lose it and works hard to keep it.

In certain respects it could be said that perhaps we are

all immigrants, we all pass from language to language, we are all anxious about losing our mother tongue but for the "natives," the passage is usually done in darkness (in the realm of the unconscious) and except for certain moments of awakening or of loss of identity, the seams adhere to each other well.

Bibliography

Augustine, Saint. *Confessions* Book XIII, (E.B. Pusey, Trans.). http://www.sacred-texts.com/chr/augconf.htm (Original work published in 401 A.D)

Aurobindo, S. (1910). *The Upanishads*, Pondicherry: Sri Aurobindo Ashram Trust, 1994.

———. (1914). *The Life Divine*, Twin Lakes, Wisconsin: Lotus Press.

Bergson, H. (1911). *Creative Evolution* 2005, Cosimo Classics

Capellanus, A. (1960). *The Art of Courtly Love*, (J. J. Parry, Trans.), New York: Columbia Univ. Press. (Original work published in 1174-1186)

Capra, F. (1975). *The Tao of Physics*, Berkely, CA: Shambhala. [Reprinted London: Flamingo, 1982].

De Chardin, P.T. (1999). *The Human Phenomenon*, (S. Appelton-Weber, Trans.), Sussex: Sussex Academic Press. (Original work published in 1940)

Dolar, M. (1996). *The Object Voice, in Gaze and Voice as Love Objects*, Žižek S. & Salecl, R., (Eds.), Duke: Duke Univ. Press.

The Encyclopedia of Philosophy (1967). Edwards P. (Ed.), New York: Macmillan Publishing Co., Inc. & The Free Press.

Freud, E. (Ed), *Letters to Sigmund Freud*, (T. & J. Stern, Trans.), New York: Basic Books, 1960, L. 286.

Freud, S. (1986). *Project for a Scientific Psychology*, SE 1:331, (J. Strachey, Trans.), London: The Hogarth Place, (Original work published in 1889)

Freud, S. *The Interpretation of Dreams*, (1986). SE: 4&5, (J. Strachey, Trans.), London: The Hogarth Place. (Original work published in 1900a)

Freud., S. (1986) *Fragment of an Analysis of a case of Hysteria*, SE, 7:3, (J. Strachey, Trans.), London: The Hogarth Place. (Original work published in 1905e)

Freud, S. (1986).*Creative Writers and Day-Dreaming*, SE 9:143, (J. Strachey, Trans.), London: The Hogarth Place. (Original work published in 1907)

Freud, S. (1986). *'Wild' Psychoanalysis*, SE 11:219, (J. Strachey, Trans.), London: The Hogarth Place. (Original work published in 1910b)

Freud, S. (1986). *Five Lectures on Psychoanalysis*, SE 11:3 (J. Strachey, Trans.), London: The Hogarth Place. (Original work published in 1910a)

Freud, S. (1986). *On the universal tendency to debasement in the sphere of love*, SE 11:177, (J. Strachey, Trans.), London: The Hogarth Place. (Original work published in 1912)

Freud, S. (1986). *Totem and Taboo*, SE, 13:1, (J. Strachey, Trans.), London: The Hogarth Place. (Original work published in 1912-1913)

Freud, S. (1988). *On Narcissism: An Introduction*, SE:14:69, (J. Strachey, Trans.), The Hogarth Place, London. (Original work published in 1914)

Freud, S. (1988). Introductory Lectures on Psychoanalysis, Part III. *General Theory of the Neuroses*, SE 16:241, (J. Strachey, Trans.), The Hogarth Place, London. (Original work published in 1916-17)

Freud, S. (1986). *From the history of an infantile neurosis*, SE, 17:3, (J. Strachey, Trans.), London: The Hogarth Place. (Original work published in 1918)

Freud, S. (1986). *Group psychology and the analysis of the Ego*, (J. Strachey, Trans.), SE, 18:67, London: The Hogarth Place. (Original work published in 1921c)

Freud, S. (1986). *Inhibitions, Symptoms, and Anxiety*, SE 20:77, (J. Strachey, Trans), SE, 18:67, London: The Hogarth Place. (Original work published in 1926d)

Freud, S. (1986). *Fetishism*, SE 12:149, (J. Strachey, Trans.), SE, 18:67, London: The Hogarth Place, (Original work published in 1927)

Freud, S. (1986). *Civilization and its Discontent*, SE 21:57 (J. Strachey, Trans.), London: The Hogarth Place. (Original work published in 1930)

Freud, S. (1986). *Female Sexuality*, SE 21:223 (J. Strachey, Trans.), London: The Hogarth Place. (Original work published in 1931b)

Freud/Jung Letters, The (R. Manheim, and R.F.C. Trans.), Hull, Harvard University Press, 1988.

Gesser, N. (2002). *Introduction to Polemus 17, The Ideal and Identification* (translated from Hebrew R.G), published by G.I.E.P.

Golan, R. (2006). *Loving Psychoanalysis: Looking at Culture with Freud and Lacan*, (J. Martin, Trans.), Karnac, London.

Halfan, I. (1991). *Paul Celan: A Biography of his Youth*, New York: Persea Books.

Hamilton, C. (Issue 25, May-July 2004), "Come Together," *What is Enlightenment?*

Hegel, G. W. F. (1967). *The Phenomenology of Mind/Spirit*, (J.B. Baillie, Trans.), New York: Harper Torchbooks. (Original work published in 1807)

Hegel, G. W. F. (2004). *Hegel's Preface to the Phenomenology of Spirit*, translated with introduction, running commentary and notes by Yirmiyahu Yovel (Princeton: Princeton University Press).

Kant, E. (1755). *Universal Natural History and Theory of Heaven*, http://records.viu.ca/~johnstoi/kant/kant2e.htm

Klapisch-Zuber, C. (Ed.) (G. Duby & M. Perrot, General editors), *A History of Women, Part II*, Cambridge Massachusetts: Harvard University Press, 1992.

Kristeva, J. (1987). *In the Beginning there was Love*: Psychoanalysis and Faith, (A. Goldhammer, Trans.), Columbia University Press, New York.

Lacan, J. (2002). "The Significance of the Phallus," *Ecrits: A Selection*, (B. Fink, Trans.), New York: Norton & Company. (Original work published in 1958)

Lacan, J. (1992). *Seminar VII: The Ethics of Psychoanalysis*, (D. Porter, Trans.), London: Routledge. (Original work published in 1959-1960)

Lacan, J. (2002). "The subversion of the Subject and the dialectic of Desire in the Freudian Unconscious," *Ecrits: A Selection*, (B. Fink, Trans.), New York: Norton & Company. (Original work published in 1960)

Lacan, J. (1962-1963). *Seminar X: On Anxiety*, lesson 22/5/63, unpublished seminar.

Lacan, J. (1964). *Seminar XI: The Four Fundamental concepts of psychoanalysis*, London: Peregrine Books, 1986 [First published: Edition de Seuil].

Lacan, J. (2002). "The direction of the treatment and the principles of its power," *Ecrits: A Selection*, (B. Fink, Trans.), New York: Norton & Company. (Original work published in 1966)

Lacan, J. (1972-1973). *Seminar XX, Encore: On Feminine Sexuality, the Limits of Love and Knowledge*, London: Norton, 1988.

Lacan, J. (1974-1975). *Seminar XXII: R.S.I*, Unpublished.

Lacan, J. (1976). Seminar *XXIV: L'insu que sait de l'une-bevu s'aile a mourre*, unpublished.

Lacan, J. (1977). *At the opening of the clinical section*, Paris: Unpublished.

Laplanche, J. & Pontalis, J. B. (1973). *The Language of Psychoanalysis*, London: Hogarth Press.

Laughlin R. B. (2005). *A Different Universe*, (Reinventing Physics from the Bottom Down), New York: Basic Books.

Leibnitz, G. W. (1697), "*De rerum originatione radicali*," in: Lovejoy A., The Great Chain of Being: A Study of the History of an Idea,

Cambridge: Harvard University Press, 1936.

Levi, P. (1988). The Drowned and the Saved, New York: Vintage Books.

Lévinas, E. (1968). *Nine Talmudic Readings*. Bloomington: Indiana University Press, 1990. [First published Paris: Éditions de Minuit.]

Merleau Ponti M. (2002). *The Phenomenology of Perception*, (C. Smith, Trans.), New York: Routledge. (Original work published in 1945)

Merleau Ponti M. (1968). The Visible and the Invisible, (A. Lingis, Trans.), Illinois: Northwestern Univ. Press

Miller, J. A. (1989). "Jacques Lacan et la Voix," in: Ivan Fonagy et al., *La voix: Actes du colloque d'Ivry*, Paris: La Lysimaque.

Miller, J. A. (1991). Reflections on the Formal Envelope of the Symptom, (J. Jauregui, Trans.), Lacanian Ink 4

Miller, J. A. "Drive is Parole" in: *L'orientation Lacanienne*, Paris, 1995-1996.

Miller, J. A. *Exposition to the AMP conference on the formation of the analyst*, Brussels, 2002.

Miller, J. A. *Exposition to the AMP conference*, 2007, http://www.wapol.org

Morgan, C. Lloyd. *Emergent Evolution*. Chandra Chakravarti Press, 2008 (original 1923).

Palahniuk, C. (1996). *Fight Club*, New York: Henry Holt and Company.

Popper, K. (1977). *The Open Society and Its Enemies*, Princeton, NJ: Princeton University Press.

Reich, W. (1953). *The Murder of Christ*, New York: Simon and Schuster.

Regnier-Bohler, D. (1992). Literary and Mystical Voices, in: Klapisch-Zuber Christiane, (Ed.), [G. Duby & M. Perrot, General editors], *A history of Women*, part II, Cambridge Massachusetts, (Harvard University Press).

Russell B., (1922). *The Analysis of Mind*, http://www.gutenberg.org/dirs/etext01/analmd10.txt

Sheldrake, R., (2001). *Maybe Angels: A Confluence of Imagination and Rational Enquiry*, http://www.enlightennext.org/magazine/j20/sheldrake.asp

Shelling, F. (2006). *Philosophical Inquiries Into the Nature of Human Freedom*, (J. Gutman, Trans.), Chicago: Open Court, Classics. (Original work published in 1809)

Schopenhauer, A. (1974). *The Fourfold Root of the Principle of Sufficient Reason*, La Salle, IL, (E.F.J. Payne, Trans.), Chicago: Open Court Publishing Company. (Original work published in 1847)

Soler, C. (1999). *Screen Discourses*, unpublished.

Spinoza, B. (1660). Short treatise on god, man, and his wellbeing. In: *Spinoza Selections* (pp. 45–93). Wild, J. (Ed.) New York: Charles Scribner's Sons, 1930.

Spinoza, B. (1662). Tractatus de Intellectus Emendatione (*On the Improvement of the Understanding*).

Suarez, E.S. (2001). *Identification with the Symptom in the End of Analysis*, Psychoanalytical Notebooks, 7, London.

Swimme, B. (1995). *Canticle to the Cosmos*, [DVD].

Whitehead, A. N. (1967). *Science and the Modern World*, New York: Free Press.

Wilber, K. (1998). *The Essential Ken Wilber*, An Introductory Reader, Boston: Shambhala

Wilber, K. (2000). A *Brief History of Everything*, Boston, MA: Shambhala

Wilber, K. (2000)."A spirituality that transforms," in: Cohen, A. (Ed.), *What is Enlightenment?*

Winkler, M. (1970). Davar [Daily Newspaper] (in Hebrew).

Žižek, S. (1999). *The Ticklish Subject*, New York: Verso.

Žižek, S. (2000). *The Fragile Absolute*, New York: Verso.